Fred and Ginger

About the author

Hannah Hyam earns her living as a freelance copy-editor and (occasional) proofreader, specialising in academic, educational and literary texts. *Fred and Ginger*, her first published book, is purely a labour of love, inspired by a passionate appreciation of Astaire and Rogers and an abiding affection for their films.

Fred and Ginger

The Astaire–Rogers Partnership 1934–1938

Hannah Hyam

Pen Press Publishers Ltd

First published in Great Britain by
Pen Press Publishers Ltd
25 Eastern Place
Brighton
BN2 1GJ

ISBN13: 978-1-905621-96-5

Printed and bound in the UK

A catalogue record of this book is available from
the British Library

Cover design by Jacqueline Abromeit

In loving memory of
my mother
who first introduced me to
Fred and Ginger

CONTENTS

LIST OF ILLUSTRATIONS

All films originally released by RKO Radio Pictures unless otherwise indicated. Bold numbers in the text refer to illustrations.

Photo source credits

British Film Institute: 2, 4, 6, 8, 1.1, 1.2, 1.3, 1.4, 2.1, 2.2, 2.3, 2.4, 2.6, 2.8, 2.10, 2.13, 2.14, 3.1, 3.4, 3.5, 3.7, 4.4, 5.3, 6.1, 6.2, 6.4, 7.5, 7.6, 7.8

The Kobal Collection: 3, 5, 7, 10, 2.5, 2.11, 3.2, 3.6, 4.5, 5.1, 5.2, 5.5, 6.3, 6.6, 7.2, 7.10

The Kobal Collection/John Miehle: 7.7

The Ronald Grant Archive: 3.8, 4.3

Cover photo/7.9: Courtesy of Phil Hyam

All other photos are from the author's collection

LIST OF TABLES

ACKNOWLEDGEMENTS

It's a scary thought that if the dedicatee of this book had not urged her sceptical daughter, one afternoon some twenty years ago, to 'Come and watch this', I might never have discovered Fred and Ginger. But happily she did. I'm not sure if it was *Top Hat* or *Swing Time* that was being shown, but I was instantly hooked, and many hundreds of viewings later I am as confirmed an addict as ever.

This book started life, in a very small way, not long after that first encounter, and I tinkered with it at intervals over the years. It would not have reached this stage without the advice, assistance, encouragement and support of a number of people.

My greatest debt is to my friend Pat Tatspaugh, whose perceptive criticism prompted me to expand what was, until relatively recently, still a brief and inadequate text into a full-length book. *Fred and Ginger* would simply not exist were it not for her. Reading and commenting on each chapter as I wrote it, she was an invaluable critic and mentor then and has been an unfailing source of support and encouragement ever since.

Very grateful thanks to the literary agent Jeffrey Simmons, for his faith in my book, his invariably sound advice and his unstinting efforts on my behalf, without all of which I doubt that the book would ever have appeared in print.

From the moment he heard that I was writing this book my friend and colleague Alan Evans has gone out of his way to be helpful, not only offering advice and moral support on the several occasions I needed it, but putting his ever-fertile imagination to work on ways of securing the book's publication and, latterly, of promoting its sales – in which generous endeavour he is still actively engaged at the time of writing.

Arlene Croce was kind enough to read my embryo manuscript many years ago, and gave me much encouragement as well as valuable advice. As will be evident, in writing the present book I had frequent recourse to her classic text *The Fred Astaire and Ginger Rogers Book*. I also relied a good deal on Stanley Green and Burt Goldblatt's *Starring*

Fred Astaire, Larry Billman's *Fred Astaire: A Bio-Bibliography* and (most especially) John Mueller's invaluably comprehensive and illuminating *Astaire Dancing: The Musical Films*. My principal source, however, was of course the films themselves.

Selecting and obtaining the illustrations for this book was a lengthy process, which I could not have undertaken without the cooperation and assistance of Nina Harding of the British Film Institute Stills Department; Phil Moad and his colleagues at the Kobal Collection; and Martin Humphries of the Ronald Grant Archive. My thanks also to Tim Nicholson of DN-Images for his efforts on my behalf.

For her expert advice on copyright I am extremely grateful to Nancy E. Wolff, of Cowan, DeBaets, Abrahams & Sheppard LLP, New York.

Phil Hyam, my brother, who shared my passion in the early days and was my first critic, obligingly donated to me his out-of-print books on Astaire and Rogers and also, more recently, entrusted to me his precious copy of the cover photograph.

My friend Sue Hourizi's thoughtful comments on the manuscript were both helpful and encouraging. Many other friends, colleagues and members of my family have offered encouragement, support and advice during the lengthy gestation of this book; I am especially grateful, for very specific acts of kindness, to Margaret Bartley, Shirley Darlington, Hilary De Lyon and Martin Webster, and Miriam Gilbert.

The online Astaire group, a 'forum for fans of Fred Astaire' managed by PJ Thum and Chris Bamberger and hosted by Yahoo! Groups, has been a source of all sorts of helpful information, and it has been both a pleasure and an education to 'sit in' on the discussion of its many knowledgeable and devoted members. Special thanks to Dermot Bowers for enabling me to view the French documentary *L'Art de Fred Astaire*, and to John Funnell for his assistance at what proved to be an important stage in this project.

Finally, my thanks to my publisher, Lynn Ashman, for all her help and support, and to her team at Pen Press – in particular reader and editor Linda Lloyd for her perceptive comments on the manuscript, and art director Jacqueline Abromeit and typesetter Kathryn Harrison for their sterling work in the design and production stages.

Hannah Hyam

INTRODUCTION

Fred Astaire and Ginger Rogers danced together for a total of only fifty minutes in the seven films that are the subject of this book: a series of Hollywood musical comedies, beginning with *The Gay Divorcee* in 1934 and ending with *Carefree* in 1938, that contains the cream of their work. They danced together in three other films as well, one before and two after this series, but it is those fifty minutes, comprising twenty-two individual dance duets, that represent their most remarkable achievement, and that established Astaire and Rogers as one of the supreme dancing partnerships of the twentieth century.

They did much more than dance together in those seven films, and the phenomenon of 'Fred and Ginger', that indivisible entity that is the manifestation on screen of the Astaire–Rogers partnership at its most typical and memorable, owes as much to their acting and singing as it does to their dancing together. The three components are in important respects inseparable, and all three have a central place in a book devoted to their partnership. What has only a marginal place in this book is Astaire's solo work: the many song and dance routines he performed without Rogers, brilliant and rightly celebrated though they are. For it is only as a *partnership* in dance that Astaire and Rogers become 'Fred and Ginger' – a whole that is greater than the sum of its two parts. As Arlene Croce observes in *The Fred Astaire and Ginger Rogers Book*:

> In their dance [Fred and Ginger] grow suddenly large and important in a way that isn't given to Fred alone or to Fred with someone else. When Fred dances alone, he's perfect . . . simply Astaire, *the* dancing man, self-defined. He is his own form of theater and we ask nothing

more. But when he dances with Ginger we suddenly realize what further revelations that theater can produce: it can encompass the principle of complementarity.[1]

That 'complementarity' is the very essence of the Astaire–Rogers partnership, and it is a defining element of the Fred and Ginger series: a rapport and emotional richness that infuses virtually all their scenes together, whether comic or serious, musical or non-musical. It is the comic that prevails, of course, for only rarely do any of these seven films strike a serious note, and the humour between Fred and Ginger is a second defining element of the series. Manifested in speech, song and dance alike, it is predominantly of the gently teasing variety, stemming from a delightful, irrepressible sense of fun.

The remarkable rapport between Astaire and Rogers (though not the gently teasing humour) is evident even in the two films they made after *Carefree* (*The Story of Vernon and Irene Castle* in 1939 and *The Barkleys of Broadway* ten years later), but in these, as in the very first one they appeared in together (*Flying Down to Rio*, 1933), a third defining Fred and Ginger element is missing: the element of romance. Fred and Ginger are essentially partners in romance. In five of the seven films in the series (*The Gay Divorcee, Top Hat, Swing Time, Shall We Dance* and *Carefree*) they meet, fall in love (though not at the same time – that would be much less entertaining), overcome the various difficulties or misunderstandings that stand in their way, and are finally, joyously, united. In each of the five their courtship is pursued, at least partly, through dance, and these dances of courtship are among the major highlights of the films. The pattern changes in the other two films (*Roberta* and *Follow the Fleet*), but the essentials remain. Here the pair meet as former sweethearts, reunited after a lengthy separation, and the main romantic complications revolve around a second couple. Romance between Fred and Ginger is less central to the plot, and they do not court each other through dance, but marriage is still the happy outcome, and romance in dance is still one of the major highlights of each film. Romance in dance is almost entirely absent from the three films outside the series, and romance in any form features only briefly in one of them.

Drama in dance, the fourth defining Fred and Ginger element, is equally absent from those three films. Drama in dance is closely allied to romance: while not all the romantic dance duets in the series have a dramatic purpose, all the duets in which a drama is played out are highly romantic, for the drama is one of seduction, or (in one case) of unwilling separation. Sometimes the drama is of a playful kind (as in 'Isn't This a Lovely Day', from *Top Hat*), sometimes it is deeply serious (as in 'Change Partners', from *Carefree*), and nearly always the dance itself is preceded by a stretch of dialogue and a song that set the mood of the scene; but in all cases the dance fulfils its dramatic function more vividly, and more eloquently, than dialogue or song alone could ever do.

The fifth and final defining element of the Fred and Ginger series is most closely allied to the first. The complementarity between Astaire and Rogers, the emotional richness of their on-screen relationship, is manifested in both dialogue and song throughout the seven films, but – as the quotation from Arlene Croce suggests – nowhere more memorably than in dance. The expression in dance of this emotionally rich relationship is the greatest and most original legacy of the Astaire–Rogers partnership, and it is seen in almost all the duets they perform together in the series, whether playful or serious in mood, and whether or not there is a dramatic or romantic element. Before the start of the series, in *Flying Down to Rio*, there is no emotional relationship between Astaire and Rogers, and hence no place for this fifth defining element; after its close, in *The Story of Vernon and Irene Castle* and *The Barkleys of Broadway*, while the complementarity between the pair is still very evident, it receives only limited and (in the case of the latter film) much less successful expression in dance.

In dance, as Fred and Ginger, Astaire and Rogers explore a range of emotional and dramatic expression far wider than is allowed for in the predominantly lighthearted, sometimes downright silly or dull scripts; yet the dance always springs from the script, and often has a vital role to play in the action of the film. In dance, too, they attain a level of artistic achievement which, in their more serious numbers, so transcends the bounds of musical comedy that it might almost seem incongruous were it not so firmly rooted in its context, so wholly unaffected and compelling. Nowhere is the power of the Astaire–Rogers duet to turn base metal into pure gold more clearly demonstrated than in *Follow the Fleet*, a film that labours under the dullest script of the series, but whose closing number, 'Let's Face the Music and Dance', which Fred and Ginger perform as the star turn in a fundraising show, enters the world of high drama and emotion, high glamour and romance, and presents a spectacle of quite dazzling beauty and accomplishment that ranks alongside the masterworks of dance in any genre (**1**).

Such a level of technical proficiency and expressive power was unheard of in the Hollywood musical before the advent of Astaire and Rogers, and their achievement in the dance duets of the Fred and Ginger series remains unmatched in the history of musical film. Subsequent chapters of this book will explore that achievement, and the other elements of their partnership, in detail. To place the seven Fred and Ginger films in context this introduction takes a closer look at the 'before' and 'after' of the series. 'Before Fred and Ginger' considers (1) the nature of dance in the Hollywood musical and (2) the careers of Astaire and Rogers themselves (including their first appearance together in *Flying Down to Rio*) before the start of their partnership proper in *The Gay Divorcee*. 'After Fred and Ginger' examines more fully why *The Story of Vernon and Irene Castle* and *The Barkleys of Broadway*, though products of the Astaire–Rogers partnership, are not Fred and Ginger films and are consequently excluded from the main discussion in this book.

Before Fred and Ginger (1):
Dance in the Hollywood musical before *The Gay Divorcee*

In the age of the early sound musicals, beginning in the late 1920s, dance featured in film in a very primitive form, reflecting the primitive recording equipment of the time. With a stationary microphone and a camera that had to be enclosed in a soundproof booth to mask the noise of its motor, only the simplest of routines could be attempted. Originally the musical soundtrack was recorded simultaneously (and expensively) with a live orchestra, but later, when dances were filmed to a piano accompaniment, the process of matching the separately recorded orchestral soundtrack to the filmed routine was fraught with technical difficulties, necessitating clumsy expedients such as frequent cutting and inserted reaction shots to paper over the cracks. Moreover dance directors, most of whom were recruited by Hollywood from stage backgrounds, had little interest, and no expertise, in developing dance specifically for the medium of film, or in integrating dance with the dramatic action. Few individual dancers of note appeared in musical films, and in a typical

1 High glamour and romance: the Astaire–Rogers dancing partnership transforms the prosaic *Follow the Fleet* in the film's dazzling closing number, 'Let's Face the Music and Dance'.

number rows of lumpy chorus girls would perform stolid choreography adapted from Broadway stage shows. The period 1929 to 1930, which saw more than a hundred musical films released in Hollywood, was notable for the quantity rather than the quality of its product, and the initial popularity of the genre began to decline the following year.

It was revived by Busby Berkeley, a successful Broadway dance director (despite his lack of training in either dance or choreography) who came to Hollywood in 1930 to work on a musical film for producer Samuel Goldwyn, and was later contracted to Warner Brothers to direct the dances in *42nd Street* (1933) – a huge success that began a new era in musical film. From the start of his career behind the camera Berkeley, abandoning the limitations of the theatrical stage, set about revolutionising the filming of dance. His chorus girls were far from lumpy, and he frequently showed their faces in close-up, but it was not the showcasing of individual dancers that would become his trademark. Using a single camera mounted high above the stage, he created spectacular patterns and formations of geometric precision, his 'dancers', unrecognisable as individual human beings, moving in unison to simulate images limited, apparently, only by Berkeley's imagination. A giant flower opens and closes (*Gold Diggers of 1933, Fashions of 1934*); black and white stars – and stars within a star – take shape before our eyes, in formations as precise and complex as a snowflake (*Dames*, 1934) (**2**); two huge water snakes slowly uncoil side by side in perfect symmetry – and metamorphose, breathtakingly, into the total abstraction of four concentric circles (*Footlight Parade*, 1933). In the course of a single number, lasting up to ten minutes, Berkeley will present an astonishing sequence of such images, many easier to draw than to describe, and all conceived expressly for the black and white cinema screen. The celebrated 'Shadow Waltz' from *Gold Diggers of 1933*, in which each of about fifty chorus girls 'plays' a violin, progresses from a flower formation (the girls' swirling, hooped white skirts forming the petals) to one of Berkeley's most extraordinary effects: the stage darkens, the shape of each violin is outlined in neon light, and the figures of the girls disappear altogether as the individual

2   Dance, Busby Berkeley style (1): This overhead shot shows just one of a sequence of stunning formations seen in the latter part of the title number from *Dames* (1934). The snowflake-like star (slightly truncated here) is composed of nearly eighty chorus girls, costumed in black tights, frilly white tops and circular head-dresses. What this image cannot convey is the dynamic nature of the formation, as the girls cross and uncross their arms, or the magical way in which the star takes shape, swiftly opening out from a squarish huddle of white.

white violins take the shape of one giant violin, 'played' by an equally
giant neon bow.

Like all Berkeley's trademark overhead shots, the neon violin is a
stunning spectacle, but it has little to do with dance as such. In these
kaleidoscopic sequences, involving dozens of elaborately costumed
performers, Berkeley is concerned not with choreography but with the
precise manipulation of his forces to achieve a purely visual effect. And
though his numbers are ostensibly performed before theatre audiences,
with the curtain rising as they begin, these effects could never be achieved
on the theatrical stage. In 'Young and Healthy', from *42nd Street*, there
are brief shots from the audience's perspective of the chorus members as
they begin and end their typically spectacular circular formations, and
they appear no more than a muddle of bodies. Many numbers use vast
sets, impossible to replicate in any theatre – the immense columns and
mirrors in 'Don't Say Goodnight' (*Wonder Bar*, 1934), the huge pool
and fountains in 'By a Waterfall' (*Footlight Parade*) (**3**); and lavish props
are equally characteristic – the surreal, human-adorned harps in 'Spin a
Little Web of Dreams' (*Fashions of 1934*), the luxury beds, foam-filled
bathtubs and dressing tables (one for each member of the large chorus)
of the title number from *Dames*. Berkeley's extravagant use of props
would culminate a year later in 'The Words Are in My Heart', from
Gold Diggers of 1935, where (rather like the more modest violins of
the 'Shadow Waltz') the fifty or so white grand pianos, 'played' by the
chorus girls, eventually take over the scene, gliding across the black
stage, seemingly without human intervention, in typically astonishing
formations.

Not surprisingly, these fantastic creations have little to do with the
concept of dramatic relevance and the integration of musical numbers into the plot of the film. Berkeley was especially associated with
'backstage' musicals – films that revolve around the putting on of a
show – and the numbers are simply presented as part of the show (however wildly improbable they might appear), usually concentrated in the
latter part of the film when the show finally comes to fruition.

3 Dance, Busby Berkeley style (2): A human pyramid, reflected in the huge, darkened
swimming pool where a few moments earlier the astonishing 'water snake'
sequence was staged – one of many to be seen in 'By a Waterfall', from *Footlight
Parade* (1933). On screen, the first four levels of the pyramid slowly revolve in
opposite directions (with an additional, stationary circle of swimmer-dancers at its
base, kneeling in the water of the small pool in which the structure stands), and
the sequence, with dynamic effects, is also shown from above. It is followed by
torrential jets of water over the main pool, and yet more formations.

Where dance is recognisable as such in a Berkeley film, whether individual or chorus work, it is unimpressive as dance, though often effective as spectacle. Ruby Keeler, the tap-dancing female lead in several Berkeley vehicles, is no Ginger Rogers, and appears terribly heavy-footed and lumbering in the title number from *42nd Street* – a routine that is essentially unvaried in her subsequent appearances; while the large tap-dancing chorus (brilliantly transformed in the closing moments of the number into a glittering cityscape) is enthusiastic but regimented, moving in unison with military precision. Berkeley had a military background, and some of his 'realistic' numbers, dramatic depictions of life in the America of the Depression, feature explicitly military parades, with marching rather than dance, as in 'Remember My Forgotten Man' from *Gold Diggers of 1933* and 'Shanghai Lil' from *Footlight Parade*. Elsewhere, the array of dancing couples in 'Don't Say Goodnight' (*Wonder Bar*) waltz unremarkably, and the tap-dancing of the chorus girls in the title number from *Dames* is equally unexceptional. It is the overall spectacle that counts, not the choreographic skill of any of the participants, whether individually or as a group.

Moreover, although Berkeley used a single camera and no editing for his kaleidoscopic overhead sequences, Keeler's solo routines are invariably disfigured with a close-up shot of her legs. This and other similarly distracting techniques would be taken to their limits in Berkeley's most massive dance sequence, in 'Lullaby of Broadway' from *Gold Diggers of 1935*, where the huge ranks of male and female dancers who perform a thunderous tap routine are shown from above, from below, from the side, from anywhere, with close-up shots of legs and feet and faces, and rapid cutting from one group or angle to another.

Two years before *Gold Diggers of 1935* was released, Fred Astaire arrived in Hollywood, and at the studios of RKO Radio Pictures he set about developing a very different kind of dance, and an unobtrusive, altogether more sensitive technique for filming it. Within a year he would demonstrate, as Croce puts it, 'that screen choreography could consist of a man dancing alone in his living room',[2] and, with Ginger Rogers, that a man and a woman dancing together on a bare stage could be more thrilling than the most elaborate of special effects. Berkeley transformed the Hollywood musical, but it was Astaire, first and foremost a dancer and choreographer, who would truly transform the nature of dance in film.

Before Fred and Ginger (2):

Astaire, Rogers and *Flying Down to Rio*

Fred Astaire was thirty-four years old when he appeared in *Flying Down to Rio*, his second film. He was already a celebrity, having enjoyed a long and extremely successful career on the Broadway and London stages, partnered by his sister Adele. The pair had started out in vaudeville as young children, and appeared in their first musical in New York in 1917, when Fred was eighteen and Adele twenty. In 1923 they opened in their first London show, and for the next nine years appeared together in a succession of musicals on both sides of the Atlantic. Astaire began choreographing their material in the early 1920s, and his characteristic dancing style, influenced by tap, ballet and especially ballroom dancers of the time, was largely formed in this period.

The brother–sister partnership came to an end when Adele married in 1932, after which Astaire appeared solo in his last stage show, *Gay Divorce*, first on Broadway and then in London. Before the London opening in 1933 Astaire, who had expressed interest in appearing in films, came to Hollywood to do a screen test for RKO and signed a contract to make *Flying Down to Rio*. As the studio was not yet ready to begin filming he was able to fit in another assignment, and made his film debut in MGM's *Dancing Lady* (1933), a romantic drama cum backstage musical in the *42nd Street* mould, starring Clark Gable and Joan Crawford. He had a small but prestigious part, playing himself – helping Crawford in a dance routine she is rehearsing and later partnering her in two numbers during the musical extravaganza that forms the latter part of the film. It was not an especially remarkable debut (and Astaire looks quite ridiculous in the Bavarian costume he is obliged to wear for the second number), but it was favourably received and served to introduce Astaire to film audiences before he appeared in a more substantial role.

Like Astaire, Ginger Rogers had enjoyed a successful career in vaudeville and Broadway before she appeared in *Flying Down to Rio*, but she was also familiar to film audiences, having already made nineteen feature films. Twelve years younger than Astaire, she had started out in vaudeville at the age of fourteen and appeared in her first Broadway show four years later, in 1929. The following year she and Astaire met for the first time (and became friends), when he was called in to choreograph a dance for her and her partner in the George and Ira Gershwin show *Girl Crazy*. Rogers was not a trained dancer but had won Charleston contests as a youngster, and had both sung and danced on stage and on the screen before she was first teamed up with Astaire. Her nineteen films in this period, beginning in 1930 with *Young Man of Manhattan* for Paramount, were mostly non-musical, including both comedy, straight drama and romance; but several gave her the opportunity to perform one or more musical numbers, and she appeared in both *42nd Street* and *Gold Diggers of 1933* – memorably opening the latter (scantily clad in an eye-catching costume made of gold coins) with a song that included a verse in pig Latin.

Rogers was a popular screen actress, in a variety of not terribly demanding roles, both leading and supporting. She played (amongst others) the romantic ingenue, somebody's sassy girlfriend, a carnival-boat entertainer, a wisecracking flapper, and a chorus girl, and she was always very much at home at the wisecracking end of the scale. She was funny, warm and likeable, but essentially unpolished. As Croce remarks, 'Astaire, when he came into movies, was already formed as a personality and as an artist, but movie audiences watched Ginger Rogers grow up.'[3]

Flying Down to Rio

Flying Down to Rio was RKO's first full-scale musical to use the revolutionary and by now fully developed playback system which enabled numbers to be staged using a pre-recorded soundtrack instead of a live orchestra or a piano substitute. Astaire was fortunate to arrive in Hollywood at just this time, avoiding the very earliest years of the musical with all the technical problems they posed. It was originally intended that he would have a leading role in the film, but after a number of changes in the planned cast he ended up with fifth billing. Rogers, under contract to RKO at this time, was brought in as his dancing partner at a late stage, after the actress intended for the part dropped out to get married; as only an incidental dancer, not in his style, she was not the most obvious of choices to partner Astaire, but she was certainly well equipped for the wisecracking comedy of her role. She was given fourth billing, while the star of the show was the Mexican actress Dolores Del Rio and the two male leads Gene Raymond (blond, North American) and Raul Roulien (dark, Brazilian). The film also featured the British actor Eric Blore, who was later to appear in no fewer than four of the Fred and Ginger series, in a brief but typical role as head waiter in a hotel. Off screen two further stalwarts of the series contributed to the musical numbers: rehearsal pianist and arranger Hal Borne, and Astaire's dance assistant (later dance director) Hermes Pan, both working with him for the first time.

The plot of *Flying Down to Rio*, not its most memorable feature, revolves around the love triangle of Del Rio and the two men in her life – Raymond, a bandleader whom she meets for the first time at the start of the film in a North American hotel, and Roulien, her fiancé back home in Rio de Janeiro. Astaire plays Raymond's sidekick and a member of his band, a sort of juvenile version of the role he would later play opposite Randolph Scott in *Roberta* – much less in control of the situations he finds himself in (at one point he is literally thrown out of a restaurant, in a most undignified fashion), and with little hint of the suave, elegant character he would assume from *The Gay Divorcee* onwards. Even his one appearance in his familiar costume of top hat, white tie and tails is attended by awkwardness, as he is loftily ignored by the doormen to whom he proffers his hat and cane. Rogers, much more at home, plays the band's singer, and gets to deliver several entertaining one-liners in her laconic style ('You're looking for a noodle in a haystack,' she tells Raymond, as he searches the streets for Del Rio). She makes an early first appearance, fixing her makeup before greeting the pompous hotel manager with a cheeky 'Good morning, Popeye', and filing her nails while he lays down the law to the assembled staff (4), and she sails through the rest of the film with cheerful unconcern. But though she has a much happier and more relaxed time than Astaire she gives equally little hint of the refinement and occasional haughtiness she would bring to her roles in *The Gay Divorcee* and subsequent films in the series.

The romantic interest in the film is strictly confined to the three leads, and there is not even the faintest hint of a romance between Astaire and Rogers, who have only the most casual friendship arising from their common involvement with Raymond's band. They are each assigned one song (in a tuneful score by Vincent Youmans), Rogers singing 'Music Makes Me' in the first few minutes of the film, and Astaire the closing title number; he also performs a tap dance to 'Music Makes Me'. Rogers, clad in a low-cut, slinky black dress, transparent

4 Ginger Rogers, making her first appearance in *Flying Down to Rio*, blithely continues to file her nails in the presence of hotel manager Franklin Pangborn (centre) and head waiter Eric Blore. There will be no trace in the Fred and Ginger series of the brassiness she displays in this early scene.

from the waist down, that reveals her very slim and shapely figure, delivers the suggestive lyric of the song (declaring that music makes her do the things she 'never should do') in an appropriately suggestive manner; both her dress and her manner would be altogether more decorous throughout the Fred and Ginger series. Astaire's tap solo, however, is entirely in character – an energetic, fast-moving, impromptu display that is marred only by the inserted close-up shots of his legs. He is also seen, in his white tie and tails, performing a brief tango with Del Rio (at her instigation, to escape her two suitors) – an unremarkable piece of purely social dancing fragmented by some distracting non-musical business.

The title number is what *Flying Down to Rio* would be solely remembered for today if Astaire and Rogers had not happened to appear in the film. An extravaganza as spectacular in its way as anything Busby Berkeley produced, and astonishingly ambitious for its time, it involves large numbers of attractive young women (including Rogers), gamely secured in diverse configurations to the wings of several light aircraft flying high above a Rio hotel, who perform with great enthusiasm various synchronised manoeuvres in time to the music supplied by Raymond's band below (conducted by Astaire, as Raymond is flying one of the planes). It's an enjoyable and very endearing spectacle (albeit immensely improbable), much less mechanical and more human in its appeal than Berkeley's clinically precise formations.

But what made *Flying Down to Rio* an enormous box-office success, rescuing the ailing RKO from bankruptcy and ensuring the film's immortality, is a two-minute sequence in the middle of a lengthy production number that saw Fred Astaire and Ginger Rogers dance together for the very first time. 'The Carioca' is performed by a Brazilian band in a Rio casino while Astaire and Rogers watch in the company of their own band, who are anxiously sizing up the competition. The pair, intrigued by the sight of couples pressing their foreheads together while they dance to the infectious music,[4] decide to have a go themselves. 'We'll show them a thing or three!' says Rogers, as Astaire casually takes her by the hand and they get up from their table. As they start to dance on a small vacant spot near the bandleader, he gestures to them to move down to the centre of the stage – a circular area composed, extravagantly, of seven white grand pianos, which contrast nicely with their black costumes (a suit for Astaire and a close-fitting, low-cut dress with a full skirt for Rogers). So begins their duet proper, an engaging routine which involves – in addition to, and sometimes simultaneously with, the forehead pressing (5) – a combination of tap and ballroom-style spins and lifts; and which ends comically as the pair audibly bump their heads together and stumble disorientedly about the stage. The duet is, unfortunately, disfigured by some particularly inane reaction shots, but it is otherwise presented reasonably intact, and is enthusiastically received by the audience. Later in the eleven-minute sequence of chorus dancing and miscellaneous singing Astaire and Rogers do another nineteen seconds of Carioca-ing atop the (now revolving) grand pianos, this time encircled by the chorus.

This first Astaire–Rogers duet, unremarkable though it is in comparison with their later work, remains freshly appealing today, and it is not difficult to understand why it caused a sensation at the time. Nothing like it had been seen on the cinema screen before, and the sight of such

a youthful, well-matched, engaging young couple dancing together so stylishly, so apparently spontaneously, with humour and with such obvious rapport, must have come as a breath of fresh air after the plodding efforts of performers such as Ruby Keeler and the massive, impersonal Berkeley displays. Hermes Pan recalls that audiences cheered and applauded the number at previews (an unprecedented event),[5] and it was immediately obvious that Astaire and Rogers had stolen the show.

RKO rushed to capitalise on their success, buying the rights to *Gay Divorce*, and posters for the subsequent film billed the pair as 'The King and Queen of "Carioca" '. Rogers was still on their books, and in 1934 Astaire's further services were secured with a new, more favourable contract. For the next five years, until their last appearance together for RKO, he would be teamed almost exclusively with Rogers, making only one film without her (*A Damsel in Distress*, with a young Joan Fontaine, in 1937), whereas Rogers would continue to pursue a separate career, making several films without Astaire (some extremely successful) in the same period.

Flying Down to Rio saw the birth of the Astaire–Rogers partnership, but it was in *The Gay Divorcee* that Fred and Ginger were born. Here for the first time the pair became partners in romance, and their dances a vehicle for the pursuit of that romance and the expression of the new depth of their relationship and rapport. Here too was introduced the element of humour between them that would be more fully developed as mutual teasing in *Roberta* and subsequent films. In *The Gay Divorcee* Astaire shed the awkwardness that had attended his role in *Flying Down to Rio* and assumed the suave, charming, breezily self-assured persona that would prove so irresistible to Ginger; while Rogers, in a much classier role than any she had played before, shed her brassiness – though not her lively spirit – and acquired a new refinement, tinged with a certain haughtiness but leavened with a touching vulnerability that (coupled with her natural beauty) would be equally irresistible to Fred. They were ideally matched, and in the course of the seven films they made together between 1934 and 1938 they became one of the most popular box-office attractions of the day, and the most successful dance team ever to be seen on the cinema screen.

5   Fred Astaire and Ginger Rogers dance together for the first time in 'The Carioca', foreheads pressed together in the dance's characteristic feature.

Their winning formula could not be repeated indefinitely, however, and in 1938, with *Carefree*, Fred and Ginger made their final appearance. It was not the end of the partnership between Astaire and Rogers, which would be seen in action again in two further films, the first immediately following *Carefree* (in 1939) and the second ten years later; but neither of these films would make a comparable impact or recapture the special qualities that made their previous collaboration so uniquely memorable.

After Fred and Ginger:
The Story of Vernon and Irene Castle and The Barkleys of Broadway

The Story of Vernon and Irene Castle (1939) and *The Barkleys of Broadway* (1949) stand apart from the Fred and Ginger series for very different reasons. In the first, Astaire and Rogers portray real-life characters from an earlier age, in a story that ends tragically. In the second, they return to musical comedy but in the roles of a married couple, no longer in the first flush of either youth or romance. They have not lost their remarkable rapport, but the other defining elements of the Fred and Ginger series are essentially missing from both films. Moreover, while both partners are still youthful and on top form as a dance team in 1939, ten years later Rogers is no longer the ideal partner for Astaire that she was in the 1930s.

The Story of Vernon and Irene Castle

Vernon and Irene Castle were the Astaire and Rogers of their day, a hugely popular dance team who, as Astaire recalls in his autobiography, 'were easily the most potent factor in the development of ballroom dancing as a public pastime'. He and his sister Adele saw them perform many times, and 'they were a tremendous influence on our careers, not that we copied them completely but we did appropriate some of their ballroom steps and style for our vaudeville act'.[6] The Castles first came to prominence in 1912, and had a relatively short career together before Vernon was killed in a flying accident in 1918; the film is a straightforward and reasonably faithful depiction of those six years in their lives,[7] and captures the period feel nicely, especially in its use of a great many popular songs of the time.

Astaire and Rogers were clearly ideally suited to portray the couple (though Irene Castle did not want Rogers to play her), and they do so as well as anybody might expect, bringing a great warmth and tenderness to their non-musical scenes together and convincingly re-creating the dances that the Castles made famous. But it is all, of course, a very far cry from their partnership as Fred and Ginger. Vernon and Irene meet, fall in love and marry within the first half-hour of the film, in utterly conventional style and without any of the obstacles or misunderstandings that typically beset, and add such zest, to Fred's courtship of Ginger. There is humour in the story, especially in the early part when the couple first meet and start courting (under the watchful eye of Irene's faithful family servant, engagingly played by Walter Brennan), but once they are married their relationship is essentially serious – deeply affectionate, but serious – and there is certainly no teasing on either side. They experience much anxiety and disappointment before they finally attract the attention of an agent (an enjoyable performance by Edna May Oliver) and achieve overnight success, and the outbreak of war, with the English-born Vernon deciding to enlist in the Royal Flying Corps, brings a sombre note to the proceedings. Finally it all ends in tragedy, with his sudden and untimely death in a freak flying accident, just as the couple were to enjoy a long-awaited reunion. Rogers acquits herself well enough in the difficult scene when she receives the news, but she is more affecting on the rare occasions in the Fred and Ginger series when the scripts touch a serious note.

The film contains no fewer than seven dance duets for Astaire and Rogers, more than twice the number to be found in most of the Fred and Ginger series, but some are very short or just a fragment, lasting under a minute. All are exhibition pieces, re-creations of dances from the past, and performed in front of an audience; consequently none has any intrinsic dramatic function, and only the last bears any emotional significance. The performances are, needless to say, very fine, but the dances themselves are rather variable in quality. The most enjoyable are 'Too Much Mustard', a brisk number in which Vernon and Irene introduce their famous 'Castle Walk' in the Café de Paris and become instant sensations; and 'The Maxixe', a seductively beautiful piece included in a montage of several different dances showing the Castles at the height of their fame. Less memorable are the first number, 'Waiting for the Robert E. Lee', an audition dance for which Rogers wears a rather dowdy hairstyle and dress (**6**); and other pieces from the montage, including a tango which sees both partners in Spanish costume (Astaire always looks uncomfortable and a bit silly in fancy costumes, and this is no exception).

The last dance of the film (apart from a brief closing sequence) is the only one that attains the emotional depth of the Fred and Ginger duets. 'The Last Waltz' brings the couple together in the crowded Café de Paris after a long separation, and a period of great anxiety for Irene occasioned by Vernon's wartime duties, and Astaire and Rogers convey beautifully their quiet joy in their reunion and their rapt absorption in each other (**7**). The duet is reminiscent in mood of the serene togetherness of 'Smoke Gets in Your Eyes', from *Roberta*, but it lacks the coherence and the sheer visual beauty of that early gem. A medley of three different waltzes, the whole lasting barely two minutes, it is frustrat-

6   A dowdy-looking Rogers partners Astaire in 'Waiting for the Robert E. Lee', which the newly married Irene and Vernon Castle perform as an audition in the hope of starting a career as a dance team. 'Well now, who's going to pay money to watch a man dance with his wife?' is the unencouraging response.

7   The newly reunited couple dance 'The Last Waltz', their quiet joy and absorption in each other beautifully conveyed by Astaire and Rogers. The setting is the Café de Paris, scene of their first triumph, and this moment comes just before the lilting music changes to a more upbeat tempo for the second section of the medley. Astaire, wearing his Royal Flying Corps uniform, copes as well as can be expected with those enormous fur cuffs.

ingly brief and fragmented; and the absurdly exaggerated sleeves, with enormous dangling fur cuffs, on Rogers' otherwise simple and elegant dress (a copy of Irene Castle's original) are an unwelcome distraction.

The film comes to a touching close as the couple, in ghostly double exposure, dance their way down a tree-lined path (to the music of the love song that Vernon had sung to Irene before he proposed to her) and gently fade away. It is a graceful exit for Astaire and Rogers, at the end of what was to prove their final film for RKO and their last appearance in their prime as a dancing partnership. And it is certainly ironical that *The Story of Vernon and Irene Castle*, a sympathetic and sensitive portrayal of a renowned dance team, should fall far short of their previous seven collaborations as a *dance* film. Yet it is also inevitable, for the purely social dances of the Castles, never intended to feature in musical film, are no match for the masterpieces of dramatic and emotional expression that distinguish the Fred and Ginger series. In doing the Castles full justice in this re-creation of their partnership Astaire and Rogers demonstrate nothing so clearly as the transformation that they themselves had wrought in the art of dance in the five preceding years.

The Barkleys of Broadway

There had been no firm plans for a revival of the Astaire–Rogers partnership after *The Story of Vernon and Irene Castle*, and MGM's *The Barkleys of Broadway* was originally intended as a vehicle for Astaire and Judy Garland, after their great success in *Easter Parade* in 1948. When Garland failed to turn up for rehearsals Rogers was called in to replace her, and the result was both a box-office and a critical success. It is certainly an entertaining film, with a strong script by the top team of Betty Comden and Adolf Green, and witty support from pianist and humorist Oscar Levant (more or less playing himself, in typically acerbic style). Ten years after their last appearance together it provides Astaire and Rogers with an appropriate vehicle for their older selves; at the ages of forty-nine and thirty-seven respectively they could hardly be expected to resume the roles of romantic young lovers, and in place of Fred and Ginger we find a middle-aged husband and wife, a successful musical comedy team who, although warmly attached to each other, spend much of their time offstage bickering and fighting (**8**). Astaire and Rogers are both equally convincing and appealing in their roles, their old rapport clearly undiminished, but while it is easy enough to accept them in this new incarnation and enjoy the resulting comedy, it is much harder to come to terms with the loss of the Fred and Ginger of the dance floor.

We are given a very early opportunity to see how the Astaire–Rogers dancing partnership has weathered the ten-year gap (during which Rogers did not appear in a single musical), the film's opening titles being superimposed on a sparkling duet, the 'Swing Trot'.[8] Here, as the camera pulls back from the tantalising opening shot of the couple's feet, are Astaire and Rogers dancing in Technicolor for the very first time, with Rogers resplendent in a gold gown. But her hair is done up in an elaborate sort of bun, and she is not as slim as she was; though she dances with all her usual verve she looks a little matronly, like the mother of her younger self (**9**). She wears a rather fixed smile on her face, too, her expression not as spontaneous-seeming or

8 Marital strife: after a flaming row less than twenty minutes into *The Barkleys of Broadway*, when she hurled a bottle at Astaire's head, drawing (a little) blood, a contrite Rogers tells him to hit her in return. The romantic days of Fred and Ginger are well and truly over.

subtly varied as it used to be. By contrast Astaire, who unlike his partner has been dancing in one musical after another since 1939, has merely acquired a few lines on his face; he looks older but otherwise unchanged. The audience, at this the first night of the couple's new show, applauds enthusiastically, but the viewer is left wondering whether an Astaire–Rogers reunion was such a good idea after all.[9]

Twenty minutes later it is as if the years have fallen away, and Rogers is back to her old self. The pair are rehearsing a number for their show, and Rogers, in loose-fitting slacks and top, her hair left long in a much younger and more flattering style (seen in **8**), is beautifully relaxed.

9 A rather matronly-looking Rogers, dressed all in gold, dances with Astaire for the first time in ten years. In this posed still, showing the very end of 'Swing Trot', just before they exchange a brief kiss on the final beat, Rogers' smile appears more natural than the rather fixed expression she wears for the greater part of the number.

'Bouncin' the Blues', a fast-moving tap routine, was introduced into the film for Rogers' benefit, and it brings to mind the very first playful duet in the Fred and Ginger series, the wonderful 'I'll Be Hard to Handle' from *Roberta*. It does not appear as spontaneous as that seemingly improvised number – in part understandably, since 'Bouncin' the Blues' is explicitly a prepared performance; in part unfortunately, as Astaire's intermittent (and uncharacteristic) exclamations and laughter sound irritatingly artificial – but it is richly enjoyable nonetheless. Now it is Rogers who comes off best, unaffected as well as relaxed, obviously enjoying herself and fully a match for Astaire in this high-spirited and energetic routine. It's not quite Fred and Ginger – in more ways than one (Rogers' very sexy exit, covering herself with the curtain 'like a stripper who has just dropped her last bit of drapery',[10] would be out of character for the chaste Ginger) – but it certainly comes close, and is by far the best duet of the film.[11]

The next two numbers don't even come close: both clearly intended for Judy Garland, they are highly untypical of Astaire and Rogers. The first, 'My One and Only Highland Fling', sees them wearing kilts and singing in exaggerated Scottish accents in a harmless comedy routine, performed as part of their show. Rogers gamely enters into the spirit of the thing, and is amusing and rather endearing as the adoring wife, steadfastly ignored by her dour husband; but both are wasted in this material, which includes only the most elementary of dances. In 'A Weekend in the Country', which follows shortly after, the couple, accompanied by the unenthusiastic, town-loving Oscar Levant (their composer and friend), sing cheerfully of the joys of country life while walking briskly along the road to the house where they are to take a weekend break.

It is at this stage in the proceedings that the film starts to take a turn for the worse. Rogers, resenting Astaire's claim that he has taught her everything she knows, is seduced by a young French playwright (one of the house guests) into believing that she can be a great dramatic actress. She abandons musical comedy to take on the part of the young Sarah Bernhardt in his new play and, after a disastrous start, is a triumphant success – thanks to some telephone coaching by a concerned Astaire, impersonating the playwright/director. The scene in which Rogers, as Bernhardt, recites the Marseillaise at her audition for entry to the French Conservatoire, in atrocious French and with the most ludicrously exaggerated, supposedly highly dramatic expression, makes truly excruciating viewing. The Rogers of the Fred and Ginger series, always admirably economical of both expression and gesture, is unrecognisable in this new guise.

As a result of her dramatic aspirations, and before her so-called triumph, Rogers and Astaire have a furious row and split up, but they are tricked by Levant into dancing together in a benefit show – a device very similar to one that was used twelve years earlier in *Shall We Dance*. And it is a song from that film that they dance to now, George Gershwin's classic ballad 'They Can't Take That Away From Me' (which outclasses by a long way all the new songs composed for *The Barkleys of Broadway* by Harry Warren). It was Rogers' idea to reuse the song, whose obvious potential as the basis of an Astaire–Rogers romantic dance duet had, most regrettably, not been realised in *Shall We Dance*, and Astaire choreographed a duet for the occasion that was intended to repair the omission. But, sadly, 'They Can't Take That Away From Me' is the biggest disappointment of the film, the number in which the difference between the Rogers of 1949 and the Rogers of the Fred and Ginger series is most keenly felt. Again she appears in a matronly hairstyle, and her dress, a white, low-cut gown that would have enhanced the young Rogers' slim figure and supple back, now exposes, unflatteringly, her heavier, more muscular upper body and arms (**10**). As Astaire sings to her she stands rather awkwardly, as if not knowing what to do with her arms; her facial expressions are unconvincing and she moves stiffly. Much of her former appeal as a dancing actress – in Mueller's words 'the way she would react with subtle liveliness to the singing and inflect the dance with mood and poignance by acting through the dancing'[12] – has been lost, along with her beautifully supple back. With the young Rogers in her place this duet would be quite exquisite; as it is, it inspires only renewed regret that the pair did not dance to the song in the heyday of the 1930s.

Their final performance together, 'Manhattan Downbeat', which begins in the newly reconciled couple's apartment and ends as a garish production number in their show, is at best undistinguished. Rogers, her hair once again in that unflattering bun, and wearing a mauve dress as garish as the production, does not enhance the spectacle, and for all its glitz the number does nothing to erase the dispiriting effect of the previous duet.

The Barkleys of Broadway has saved generations of Astaire–Rogers fans from wondering 'what if . . . ?', and for all its flaws we cannot wish that it had never been made. There is much to enjoy in it, including one really first-rate dance duet (not to mention a clever, especially inventive Astaire solo in which he dances with several pairs of disembodied

10 Not Rogers' finest moment on the dance floor: the heaviness of her upper body (compare **1**) and general stiffness of movement and demeanour make 'They Can't Take That Away From Me' a disappointing experience. The hairstyle doesn't help.

shoes), and its very deficiencies heighten our appreciation of what made the Fred and Ginger series so special. Like *The Story of Vernon and Irene Castle* it does not merit any further consideration in this book, but it is by no means a negligible product of the Astaire–Rogers partnership.

About this book

Most books about the films of Astaire and Rogers adopt a chronological approach, typically devoting one chapter to each of the ten films they made together. Such an approach can be extremely valuable (especially to readers new to the films), as it certainly is in the case of the three most important studies – those by Arlene Croce, Stanley Green and John Mueller (all sadly now out of print). But a chronological approach, focusing as it does on one film at a time, with a usually sequential dis-cussion of the plot and the musical numbers, also has its limitations. The primary purpose of this book is not to describe and appraise indi-vidual films but to define, analyse and assess the distinctive qualities of the Astaire–Rogers partnership in all its manifestations – acting and singing as well as dancing; and to that end I have adopted a thematic approach, focused on these three aspects rather than on the individual films. Because of the limitations and untypical nature of the three 'before' and 'after' films discussed above, I do not devote further space to the partnership outside of the period 1934 to 1938, and accordingly the remainder of this book is concerned exclusively with the seven films of the Fred and Ginger series.

A thematic approach of course has its disadvantages, apart from the obvious lack of convenience for readers wishing to find out all about one particular film, or to look up a specific scene or musical number. In considering separately the three elements of dialogue, song and dance I necessarily fragment what is in many cases a continuous process, and indeed one of the most distinctive features of the seven films. The dis-cussion of the great 'Pick Yourself Up' sequence from *Swing Time*, for example, in which dialogue leads seamlessly to song, and song leads very swiftly to dance, will be found divided between three different chapters, each focusing on one stage in the sequence. Moreover this particular sequence also makes an appearance in a previous chapter, in the discus-sion of the qualities that distinguish *Swing Time* from *Shall We Dance*. Some purely non-musical scenes are also dissected and approached from different angles within a single chapter, illustrating different features of the romantic partnership between Fred and Ginger. Consequently there is a certain degree of overlap and repetition both within one or two chapters and from one chapter to another, but only as much as is necessary to establish a context for the discussion in each case.

What is gained from this fragmentation, what my thematic approach achieves that a chronological and sequential discussion could not, is, I hope, a fuller and sharper appreciation of distinctive and recurring features that unite the seven films and illuminate the special qualities of the Astaire–Rogers partnership (for example the typical characteristics of the first meetings between Fred and Ginger, and the anti-romantic nature of much of the dialogue between them); of similarities and differences between individual films and individual scenes and musical numbers, and between Astaire and Rogers themselves; of the development of the partnership in its three manifestations from the start of the series to its close; and of the overall achievement of Astaire and Rogers in the seven films.

In focusing very specifically on the Astaire–Rogers *partnership* I have all but excluded from the discussion Astaire's solo work (by which I mean songs and especially dances that do not involve Rogers in any capacity), according it only brief space in the broad survey of all the musical numbers in chapter 3. This work has been amply covered in other books, most notably in John Mueller's monumental study of all Astaire's musical films, *Astaire Dancing*. And while I highlight throughout the book the qualities that each performer brings to the respective aspects of the partnership, I place particular emphasis on Rogers' contribution to the dance duets – a contribution that, though absolutely equal to Astaire's in terms of the finished result, has sometimes been unjustly overshadowed by his greater renown as a dancer and choreographer. For the greater part of the book I concentrate on what is actually seen and heard *on screen*, keeping to a minimum any reference to external factors; hence I include only such background information about the productions and the people involved in them as is relevant to the central discussion. Again, this sort of material has been amply covered elsewhere, most usefully in the studies by Croce, Green and Mueller already cited.

The book is intended to be read in sequence, essentially the dialogue–song–dance sequence characteristic of the films themselves. Just as each of these three stages in a typical musical number prepares for the next and gains from the last, so each chapter in this book provides a foundation for the next and follows on from the last, building up to the culmination of the partnership in the four chapters on the dance duets. Only by following this sequence will readers be able to reap the full benefits of the thematic approach; however, readers who know the films well may choose to find their own way around the book, or to dip into it (with the help of the index) to read about a particular musical number or other sequence.

In keeping with the overall approach, the discussion within each chapter does not necessarily follow a chronological order. The introductory first chapter on the seven films of the Fred and Ginger series considers them mostly in pairs, a structure that – especially in the case of *Swing Time* and *Shall We Dance* – enables comparisons and distinctions to be made that might otherwise go unremarked. In the subsequent chapters the musical numbers and the dance duets are grouped, respectively, according to performer(s) and to type of duet. Tables in chapters 1 and 4 give a chronological listing of the films and the dance duets, and a further table in chapter 4 lists the duets according to the three groups in which they are discussed in chapters 5 to 7. Likewise the table in chapter 3 groups the musical numbers according to the headings under which they are discussed in the text, while the appendix gives a chronological listing, with an indication of the different guises in which each number appears.

The chapter on the musical numbers, while surveying all those in the series, concentrates chiefly on song and on those numbers that involve both Astaire and Rogers in some capacity. The discussion focuses not so much on the purely musical aspects of the numbers as on their distinguishing features and overall quality and impact in performance, and the degree of success with which they are integrated into the dramatic action of the films. The chapters on the dance duets take a similar approach, being chiefly concerned not with a step-by-step choreographic analysis (which Mueller has definitively provided in *Astaire Dancing*) but with the distinguishing features of the duets in performance and the visual, emotional and dramatic impact of each individual dance in this unparalleled body of work.

1

THE FRED AND GINGER FILMS

From *The Gay Divorcee* to *Carefree*

While the three 'before' and 'after' films have nothing in common but the presence in them of Astaire and Rogers, the seven films in this series share a great many common features quite apart from the defining elements discussed in the Introduction and the perennial characters of Fred and Ginger themselves. Each of the films is nonetheless wholly individual, and even the two that share a key plot device and three-quarters of their supporting casts (*The Gay Divorcee* and *Top Hat*) are very different in other respects.

The basic ingredients of the seven films are essentially the same: an improbable though generally entertaining plot that eventually ends in marriage between Fred and Ginger; three (or in one case four) dance duets for Astaire and Rogers, most of which are preceded by a song by one or both performers, and are well integrated into the dramatic action; and one or more solo song and dance routines for Astaire. All the films except *Carefree* also feature musical numbers involving other performers, though in *Top Hat* and *Swing Time* these are limited to an accompanying chorus of dancers. The musical content takes up a fairly small proportion of the running time of each film – typically about a quarter to a third (twenty-five to thirty minutes or so); *Roberta*, which features a lengthy musical fashion show, has the highest proportion at over a third (nearly thirty-eight minutes), while in *Carefree*, with the fewest musical numbers (and by far the shortest running time), the proportion is as little as a fifth, or about fifteen minutes.

Carefree, an untypical film in many respects, is also the only one of the series to be set in an indeterminate location – an unnamed American city and a nearby country club. By contrast *Roberta*, whose plot revolves

The Fred and Ginger films

All films black and white and produced by Pandro S. Berman for RKO Radio Pictures.

Film Date of release	Director Music by	Principal supporting players	Running time (min.)[a]
The Gay Divorcee October 1934	Mark Sandrich Cole Porter Harry Revel Con Conrad	Alice Brady Edward Everett Horton Erik Rhodes Eric Blore	105
Roberta March 1935	William A. Seiter Jerome Kern	Irene Dunne[b] Randolph Scott	106
Top Hat August 1935	Mark Sandrich Irving Berlin	Edward Everett Horton Erik Rhodes Eric Blore Helen Broderick	100
Follow the Fleet February 1936	Mark Sandrich Irving Berlin	Randolph Scott Harriet Hilliard	110
Swing Time August 1936	George Stevens Jerome Kern	Victor Moore Helen Broderick Eric Blore Georges Metaxa	104
Shall We Dance May 1937	Mark Sandrich George Gershwin	Edward Everett Horton Eric Blore Jerome Cowan	109
Carefree September 1938	Mark Sandrich Irving Berlin	Ralph Bellamy Luella Gear Jack Carson Clarence Kolb	83

[a] Running times (stated and/or actual) vary somewhat according to the source. The times given here are as in the Warner Home Video DVD release (2006).
[b] Not strictly a supporting player, as she received top billing above Astaire and Rogers.

around a fashionable couturière's salon, is located very firmly in Paris; and both *The Gay Divorcee* and *Shall We Dance* open in the same city – the first with a very French chorus routine in a nightclub, the second with a sequence that could be set almost anywhere, except that the plot requires Fred and Ginger to meet (again) on the long sea voyage to New York, where the greater part of the action takes place. There is less excuse for the move from London to Venice in *Top Hat*, and when we get there it's a thoroughly improbable Venice, all decorative bridges and gleaming white gondolas, in the fantastically lavish setting of a Lido hotel (seen in **5.3**, p. 164). The London of *Top Hat* is more realistic, and the film opens with an entertaining scene that pokes fun at the stuffy old members of a gentlemen's club. London also features briefly in *The Gay Divorcee*, before the action moves to an English seaside resort. Both *Follow the Fleet* and *Swing Time* (like *Carefree*) eschew European locations: the fleet in question drops anchor in San Francisco, where – contrary to what the title suggests – the main action stays even when the sailors are obliged to depart; and in *Swing Time* Fred the gambler seeks his fortune (finding both it and Ginger) in New York, leaving his fiancée back home, a freight train's journey away. Most of the films (the exception is again *Carefree*) feature glamorous, often improbably luxurious art deco sets, typically used for the interiors of hotels and nightclubs.

Five of the films feature a plot in which Fred and Ginger meet and fall in love as strangers, and the plot revolves around their romance. This invariably involves initial hostility on the part of Ginger, subsequent misunderstandings or other obstacles, and the not always helpful intervention of one or more secondary characters – including a male friend or professional associate of Fred's and an older female friend of Ginger's or her chaperoning aunt, or exceptionally, in *Shall We Dance*, her male manager. In the two other films (*Roberta* and *Follow the Fleet*) the pair meet as former sweethearts and it is a second couple who are, much less entertainingly, the focus of the main romantic complications. In the case of *Roberta* one half of the second couple, Irene Dunne, receives top billing; in *Follow the Fleet*, as in all the other films, top billing goes to Astaire and Rogers.

Both *Roberta* and *Follow the Fleet* are adaptations, respectively of a Broadway musical (Jerome Kern and Otto Harbach's *Roberta* of 1933–4) and a Broadway play (*Shore Leave*) dating from 1922 and already adapted as a stage musical (*Hit the Deck*), which was in turn made into a musical film by RKO in 1930. *The Gay Divorcee* is also an adaptation, this time of the stage musical of (nearly) the same title[1] (with music and lyrics by Cole Porter) in which Astaire had recently starred, with great success, both on Broadway and in London. John Mueller, in *Astaire Dancing*, points out that the initial, humorously acrimonious encounter between Astaire and Rogers, which was to become such a trademark of the Fred and Ginger series, did not feature at all in the stage version of the story.[2] The film (which used only one of Porter's songs, 'Night and Day', the show's biggest hit) was an even greater success than the stage musical, and instantly established Astaire and Rogers as RKO's premier box-office attraction.

The scripts of the remaining films, of which *Top Hat* is the first, are all original (albeit drawn from existing sources), and the work of several different hands, though one writer, Allan Scott, contributed to all of them, and indeed also to those of *Roberta* and *Follow the Fleet*. The scripts and the plots of the series as a whole are of very variable quality, ranging from the consistently enjoyable, witty and well controlled (*Top Hat, Carefree*) to the dull (*Follow the Fleet*) and the occasionally incoherent (*Swing Time*). The quality of the supporting casts is equally variable, and often reflects that of the script; hence the expertly funny quartet of players in *Top Hat* (all of whom fortunately appeared in at least one other film in the series) and the dull, distinctly unappealing pairing of Harriet Hilliard and Randolph Scott in *Follow the Fleet*. But all the films, however variable, are enduringly appealing and entertaining at least in part, and irrespective of their musical content – as audience reaction at a 2004 screening of all seven in the series at the National Film Theatre, London, amply demonstrated.[3] The happy world of Fred and Ginger – which, as Stanley Green amusingly details in his introduction to *Starring Fred Astaire*, bears only a tenuous connection with real life[4] – continues to exert a very special charm, and all the films enjoy a proportion of non-musical scenes which never seem to date or grow stale, remaining today as fresh, amusing and often touching, even after innumerably repeated viewings, as they must have seemed on their first release.

The Gay Divorcee and Top Hat

The plots of *The Gay Divorcee* and *Top Hat* are closely related, both hinging on a case of mistaken identity, and their supporting casts are almost identical.[5] In *The Gay Divorcee*, Rogers, chaperoned by her dotty aunt (amusingly played by Alice Brady), mistakes Astaire for the professional co-respondent hired to help her secure a divorce; in *Top Hat* she mistakes him for the husband of her older friend (the wittily sharp-tongued Helen Broderick). The three men who complete the quartet of supporting players, in roles that change hardly at all from one film to the other, are a priceless trio: Edward Everett Horton, as bumbling lawyer and old flame of Rogers' aunt in the first, bumbling impresario and husband of Rogers' friend in the second; Erik Rhodes as an endearingly absurd Italian, respectively the honourable co-respondent ('My slogan – "Your wife is safe with Tonetti. He prefers spaghetti"') and Rogers' ineffectually protective dress-designer and would-be husband; and the quintessentially English Eric Blore, progressing rather more than the other two, from modestly obliging hotel waiter to distinctly superior valet to Horton. (Horton and Blore would both reappear in *Shall We Dance*, to much the same effect, and Blore also in its predecessor *Swing Time*, though in a briefer, rather different role.) In both films Astaire plays a professional dancer, while Rogers' role is less well defined; she is simply Brady's unhappily married niece in *The Gay Divorcee*, a socialite (and wearer of Rhodes' dresses) in *Top Hat*.

The mistaken-identity device is the mainspring of the plot in *Top Hat*, but in *The Gay Divorcee* it features relatively briefly and is far less contrived: after Astaire, to Rogers' dismay, unwittingly utters the password that is intended to identify her co-respondent, he is duly summoned to her bedroom, where he takes an early opportunity to set the record straight. But this early film is much less consistently entertaining than *Top Hat*, largely (and unusually) because of the high proportion of musical content it includes for performers other than Astaire and Rogers. Marking as it does their first appearance as Fred and Ginger, *The Gay Divorcee* seems to have a lack of confidence in the power of its two new stars to carry the film without substantial contributions from miscellaneous others; hence the unlikely spectacle of Horton, in shorts, taking part in a song and dance routine (the absurd 'Let's K-nock K-neez', with a young Betty Grable and assorted extras), and the seemingly interminable 'Continental' sequence, in which two all-too-brief duets by Astaire and Rogers are separated by several minutes of distractingly edited chorus dancing and renditions of the song by supporting players. (Later films in the series would waste much less time on such extraneous material.) But *The Gay Divorcee* is an otherwise delightful film, establishing with humour and charm the essential features of Fred and Ginger's romantic partnership: the initial clash, when Astaire carelessly tears Rogers' dress while trying to be helpful; the pursuit (which takes on this occasion the quite literal form of a car chase, for which Astaire has with great foresight armed himself with both a 'Road Closed' sign and a picnic basket); the gradual winning over, first in speech and then in song and dance; the setbacks and the final resolution.

The strong supporting cast adds a good deal to the general gaiety, providing some enjoyably farcical comedy; Rhodes especially is a treat as, searching for Rogers in the seaside hotel chosen for their assignation, he accosts various unsuspecting women with mangled versions of his password. And though the tiresome superfluity of some of the musical numbers lets the film down, it is more than redeemed by those performed by Astaire and Rogers themselves. 'Night and Day' is the first in the great series of romantic song and dance-duet sequences, and the pair's two appearances to the music of 'The Continental' bring true class to the proceedings; while Astaire's main solo, the song and dance routine 'A Needle in a Haystack', in which he taps his way around his living room while completing his dress, sets the standard for a whole series of Astaire solos to come, with its casual grace and effortless incorporation of everyday objects and actions into the choreography.

Released just a year after *The Gay Divorcee*, *Top Hat*, the third film in the series, brings close to perfection the formula established rather tentatively at the start of it. With a first-rate supporting cast, a clever, witty script (significantly the first one to be written specially for Astaire and Rogers),[6] a well-controlled plot and a matchless score by Irving Berlin it could hardly fail, and it is undoubtedly the most consistently entertaining and successful of the series. The supporting cast (seen in **2.12**, p. 84) is exceptionally strong: the three already-familiar men now play more substantial roles – especially Blore, who truly comes into his own, both as Horton's lofty valet ('We are Bates,' he informs Astaire grandly) and as the resourceful engineer of the happy denouement – and are joined by the deliciously laid-back Helen Broderick, whose laconic put-downs of her inept husband are especially enjoyable. (Horton, after Rhodes has threatened to kill him for what he believes to be his philandering with Rogers: 'Madge, explain to this maniac that he's making a very serious mistake.' Broderick: 'Well, he may be making a mistake, but it's not serious.') All four serve as excellent foils to the leading players, and spar expertly and hilariously with each other. The early scene in which Horton and Blore, who have a difference of opinion over neckties, exchange silent, venomous glares, is the first of several such entertaining clashes, and the cowardly Horton's encounters with the hot-tempered, sword-wielding Rhodes are equally diverting.

Whereas in *The Gay Divorcee* the case of mistaken identity was over and done with in a mere ten minutes, in *Top Hat* Rogers spends almost half the film under the impression that Astaire is Broderick's husband, following a moment of confusion in a hotel lobby. It is a mystery how she could imagine that someone of Astaire's grace and aplomb would have so pedestrian a name as Horace Hardwick, and the script, rather improbably, does not allow Astaire the simple expedient of revealing his real identity and clearing up the confusion until a mere quarter of an hour before the end of the film – by which time Rogers has impulsively married Rhodes (or so we are led to believe). Nevertheless, the quality of both the script and the acting are such that we willingly suspend our disbelief almost throughout; only in one brief, rather silly scene between Astaire and Rogers, when she attempts to compromise him by 'reminding' him of a former illicit assignation in Paris – and he scares her off by calling her bluff – do we begin to lose patience. That, and a wholly dispensable scene between Blore and an Italian policeman, are the only real weaknesses in the entire film. Certainly there are none on the musical front, for *Top Hat* boasts both songs and dances that are among the very best of the series: the title number is one of Astaire's most brilliant solo routines; 'No Strings', a spontaneous song and tap dance which precipitates his first encounter with Rogers, is another Astaire classic; and the song and dance-duet sequences, especially the playful 'Isn't This a Lovely Day' and the romantic 'Cheek to Cheek' (in both of which Astaire successfully woos Rogers only to have his face slapped shortly afterwards), are superlative examples of their kind. By any standards, *Top Hat* is first-class entertainment; it was enormously successful on its release and has (deservedly) remained the most popular and widely known of all the Astaire–Rogers films.

Roberta and Follow the Fleet

Respectively the second and fourth films of the series, *Roberta* and *Follow the Fleet* invite comparison because of the 'two couple' formula they share, and especially because the same actor, Randolph Scott, plays one half of the second couple (and Astaire's buddy) in both films. In *Roberta* he is fortunate to be paired with the very classy Irene Dunne, and his character, though dull, is honourable and not unlikeable. In *Follow the Fleet* his other half is the colourless Harriet Hilliard, and the selfish, conceited sailor he plays is wholly unappealing. The film, following close on the heels of *Top Hat*, not only falls far short of its illustrious predecessor in wit, sophistication and sheer entertainment value, but also fails conspicuously to match the gaiety and charm of *Roberta*. Though wit and sophistication are not its most obvious attributes, this once neglected and underrated film sparkles – despite the fact that, uniquely in the series, one of the characters dies.

The character in question is the eponymous Madame Roberta, Scott's elderly aunt (an engaging performance by Helen Westley) and the owner of a Parisian fashion salon, which is run by Dunne, her assistant. Dunne is no ordinary assistant, however, being an emigré Russian princess, no less; the clientele of the salon and the adjoining Café Russe clearly value the eastern European aristocracy, for Rogers, who had left her home in America as plain Lizzie Gatz, finds it necessary to fake the title of a Polish countess (and the accent that goes with it) to be accepted as a singer in this milieu. Using her influence with the café owner, she secures an engagement for Astaire and his band, newly arrived in Paris, but not before he has taken the chance to tease her about her new identity. They are old friends and clearly fond of each other; before their fortuitous meeting Astaire mentions that he used to be crazy about Rogers, and later they reminisce about the happy times they shared back home, each admitting that they were in love with the other then.

Their roles are no more than incidental to the main storyline, which centres on the complications that ensue when Scott inherits his aunt's salon on her death and his former girlfriend arrives on the scene. But despite their second and third billing below Irene Dunne, Astaire and Rogers steal the show. Separately and together, the two of them provide most of the comedy, leavening the rather sober mix of Dunne and Scott (**1.1**), and their affectionate banter is one of the joys of the film.

1.1 'I beg your pardon,' says Randolph Scott to a surprised Irene Dunne, whom he has rather clumsily manhandled in order to rescue her from a tantrum-throwing Rogers (masquerading as a Polish countess) early on in *Roberta*. Scott's character in *Follow the Fleet* (**1.2**) is neither so gallant nor so scrupulous.

Dunne is unquestionably a star, both spirited and dignified, and always appealing, but her relationship with Scott is much less interesting and entertaining than that of the two old friends, despite the absence, until shortly before the end, of any explicit romantic attachment between them. The rapport that distinguished the first appearance of Astaire and Rogers as a partnership in *The Gay Divorcee* has deepened to a remarkable degree and is now complete in every respect; as Mueller notes, it is in *Roberta* that the pair fully achieve 'the spirited gaiety, the irrepressible charm, and the emotional depth that became the trademarks of their collaboration'.[7] It seems astonishing now that this film could have been dismissed by a previous commentator, noting (in 1973) that it had never been shown on television, as 'not really a serious loss'.[8]

Some parts of *Roberta* are, indeed, expendable, in particular the silly scene in which Astaire and Scott over-enthusiastically display their knowledge of basic French vocabulary. Elsewhere, several long minutes are given over to the modelling of Roberta's latest creations, and tedium also sets in when Scott's former girlfriend turns up to disrupt his slow-burning romance with Dunne; Claire Dodd is as unappealing in this role as Scott himself would be in *Follow the Fleet* a year later, and it's a relief all round when he sends her packing.

Musically, however, the film scores very highly, with several fine Jerome Kern songs, a couple of enjoyable numbers for Astaire – the first ('Let's Begin') with comic support from his band, the second (an energetic tap routine to 'I Won't Dance') preceded by a terrific piece of piano playing on his part – and three outstanding dance duets. No fewer than four of the songs, including the classic 'Smoke Gets in Your Eyes', are given to Irene Dunne, who is an attractive and sensitive performer, though her clear soprano has a tendency to shrillness on high notes. Rogers' more robust tones are heard in two numbers (both of which she sings in her Polish accent), the second as a duet with Astaire in the 'I Won't Dance' sequence.

Three of the four songs given to Dunne are featured in the interval of over an hour between Astaire and Rogers' first and second dance duets. It is a very long time to wait after our appetites have been whetted by 'I'll Be Hard to Handle' – the first in the wonderful series of playful duets – but then, like buses, two come along one after the other, and the sumptuous duet to the music of 'Smoke Gets in Your Eyes' is followed after only a couple of minutes (sufficient time for the question of marriage to be happily settled) by the ebulliently joyful 'I Won't Dance', this versatile music making its final, infectious appearance in the film's closing moments.

In purely musical terms *Follow the Fleet*, with a score by Irving Berlin, is fully the equal of *Roberta*, and indeed of *Top Hat*, for which Berlin also wrote the score. But its inferior script, leaden plot and unappealing supporting cast make *Follow the Fleet* the least successful film of the series in non-musical terms.

1.2 In this early scene from *Follow the Fleet* Randolph Scott chats up a newly made-over Harriet Hilliard, unaware that this is their second meeting. 'Watch my manoeuvres – you can't beat the navy,' he says modestly, ignoring the 'line of defence' she has set up between them, and Hilliard promptly surrenders.

Matters are not helped by the transformation of the innately suave and elegant Astaire into a low-ranking, gum-chewing sailor, though mercifully he drops this irritating habit after the early part of the film. But the main fault lies with the pairing of Randolph Scott and Harriet Hilliard and the tedious, rather distasteful progress of their liaison. Hilliard, playing Rogers' dowdy sister, instantly falls for the boorish Scott when they meet in a dance hall frequented by the fleet on their shore leave, but he is not interested – until he meets her again, unrecognisable after she has undergone a glamorous makeover at Rogers' suggestion (**1.2**). His interest is short lived, however, for he is only out for a good time, and shies off as soon as he discovers Hilliard's marital aspirations. In *Roberta* the spirited and dignified Irene Dunne attracted both sympathy and admiration when Scott behaved badly, but the foolish, duped Hilliard only provokes impatience and exasperation, and it is left to Astaire and Rogers to supply both the comedy and the emotional depth that are conspicuously absent from the Scott–Hilliard storyline.

Their roles in this film are far from incidental, however, involving just as much misunderstanding and machination as are to be found in any of their more typical pairings, and a romantic interest that was all but absent from their comradely partnership in *Roberta*. Their former relationship is clearly established and provides a firm foundation for a continuing attachment; we learn very early on that they were once 'Baker and Martin', a team offering 'High Class Patter and Genteel Dancing', and that Astaire joined the navy after Rogers refused to marry him – for professional rather than personal reasons, it transpires later. Their mutual fondness is apparent from the moment they meet again at the Paradise Ballroom in San Francisco (scene of Hilliard's meeting with Scott), where Rogers is engaged as a singer, and this happy reunion is one of the most touching and engaging scenes in the film. Unlike the gum-chewing Astaire, Rogers is not handicapped by anything other than the patchy script, and, with the exception of a rather wicked, though well-deserved, prank she plays on him, is sweet and natural throughout (even towards her foolish sister), in one of her most sympathetic parts.

The nautical theme is appropriately reflected in the jolly opening number, 'We Saw the Sea', which, like 'I'd Rather Lead a Band' later in the film, Astaire performs with a male chorus of sailors on board ship. For the first time in the series there is no purely solo dance for Astaire, though we are treated again to the sight and sound of his piano playing, a lively rendition (on a battered upright) of 'I'm Putting All My Eggs in One Basket', which precedes his and Rogers' winning performance of the song and their comic dance routine to the same music. Rogers, however, does dance solo, for the first and only time in the series, with a deservedly well-received audition piece (one of the few numbers in the film to fulfil a dramatic function) to the music of 'Let Yourself Go' – a number which she had earlier sung, in equally captivating style, to the audience of sailors in the Paradise Ballroom. Hilliard also gets her solo spots, with two of Berlin's less memorable songs; she performs them adequately, but her musical musings are no more arresting or engaging than the rest of her performance.

'Let Yourself Go' also features as the first of the film's three dance duets, one of Astaire and Rogers' most exuberant and technically brilliant playful routines. This number, and the climactic 'Let's Face the Music and Dance', are the twin glories of the film – but they could not be more different in style and mood. Finally escaping the confines of the prosaic plot, by the device of an on-board fundraising show, Astaire and Rogers step completely out of their screen roles to perform one of the very finest duets of the series, a number which magnificently redeems the film's failings on other fronts. Followed by a brisk settlement of romantic matters – Hilliard and Scott (who has now seen the error of his ways) for once not outstaying their welcome as they briefly clinch their union, and Astaire and Rogers stepping seamlessly back into their roles to follow suit – 'Let's Face the Music and Dance' brings this curate's egg of a film to a triumphantly successful conclusion.

Swing Time and Shall We Dance

Swing Time and *Shall We Dance* are not an obvious pair, and indeed they are streets apart in many important respects, both musical and non-musical. Significantly, they had different directors, George Stevens making his sole contribution to the series with *Swing Time* and Mark Sandrich his fourth with *Shall We Dance*, and their different directing styles heighten the films' inherent contrasts in plot, script and characterisation. No two films in the series are more unlike each other, yet there are parallels between them, and an examination of both parallels and differences helps to illuminate their individual strengths and weaknesses, and to define their individual styles.

The most obvious, though purely superficial, parallel between the two films is that they share a familiar member of the supporting cast, Eric Blore, making his third and fourth appearances in the series. In *Shall We Dance* he has a substantial and typical role as an ingratiating hotel manager, and is joined once again by Edward Everett Horton, with predictably entertaining results, but in *Swing Time* his role as the rather irascible owner of a dancing academy is much shorter and has little of the usual comic potential.

More importantly, the films also share a key plot device, whereby Astaire conceals his true dancing ability from Rogers only to reveal it to spectacular effect in a playful duet during which he completely conquers her initial hostility. In *Swing Time* he is a hoofer by profession, gambler by inclination, who contrives to receive a dancing lesson from Rogers, a teacher at Blore's academy, after an acrimonious encounter on the street outside. In *Shall We Dance* he is a ballet dancer by profession, hoofer by inclination, while she is a tap-dancing musical comedy star, and after their unsteady relationship has taken a turn for the worse they are tricked by her manager into performing together in front of a night-club audience. The resulting dance duets, 'Pick Yourself Up' and 'They All Laughed', are brilliantly successful both as drama and as dance. But though they follow a similar pattern they also illustrate some of the different qualities of the two films.

'Pick Yourself Up' is a very homely affair. Rogers is in her working clothes, going about her daily job as a low-level employee in an obscure dancing school. She believes (mistakenly) that Astaire has stolen a quarter of a dollar from her purse after asking her for change for a cigarette machine, and rejects his attempts to explain the truth in the course of the dancing lesson she finds herself obliged to give him. Reluctantly she attempts to teach him some very basic steps, but she gives up when his feigned clumsiness brings them both toppling to the floor. Advising him to save his money, because 'No one could teach you to dance in a million years', she is promptly fired by Blore (**1.3**), whereupon Astaire comes to her rescue and shows Blore what a marvellous teacher she really is. Her hostility turns to delight, and their joyous duet marks the beginning of their romantic attachment.

'They All Laughed' takes place in quite different circumstances and in the quite different, very public setting of a glamorous night-club. We are already over fifty minutes into the film, and Astaire and Rogers, who are both famous stars, are well known to each other, and indeed are commonly believed to be married to each other (more on the intricacies of the highly implausible plot later), though she is unaware that he is anything other than a ballet dancer. Once again he has incurred her hostility – this time through a false report that he claimed to be married to her purely to escape the clutches of another woman. Generally disillusioned with life, she has vowed to give up her career and marry her fiancé, and in order to spike her plans her

1.3 A furious Eric Blore, appearing in *Swing Time* in an untypical role, fires Rogers from her job as dancing instructor in his academy after overhearing her advise the hopelessly clumsy Astaire to save his money.

manager has conspired with the nightclub bandleader to announce (to Rogers' dismay) that she and Astaire have agreed to dance together. This time, instead of feigning clumsiness Astaire goes into full ballet mode, leaving Rogers initially at a loss, but then he astounds her by switching to tap. The outcome, like that of 'Pick Yourself Up', is a foregone conclusion, and the dance ends with the two of them joyfully reconciled – though only for the moment, as soon their relationship will be sabotaged for a second time by further devious plotting on the part of Rogers' manager.

Deception plays a key role in both these duets, but it is of a different kind in each. In 'Pick Yourself Up' Astaire conceals his dancing ability simply in order to gain some time with Rogers and clear up a misunderstanding (and to have some fun in the process), and when his little ruse has unfortunate consequences he saves the day and earns her gratitude. In 'They All Laughed' they have both been deceived by a third party and are obliged to perform together in public, and Astaire deliberately (though, again, mischievously) adds to Rogers' evident embarrassment by a pretentious display of his balletic prowess. Only when she counters with a little display of her own does he switch to tap and allow the dance to proceed on equal terms.

This difference in kind is reflected more widely in the plot and general tone of each film. *Swing Time* is essentially a down-to-earth sort of film, in which the main characters are ordinary people, motivated by genuine emotions for each other. *Shall We Dance*, whose main characters are stars in the public eye and their not entirely altruistic managers, has a veneer of sophistication and glamour, and deliberate deception of one character by another is the dominant feature of the plot.

In *Swing Time*, Astaire, who in the opening sequence misses his own wedding through a ruse on the part of his friends and fellow hoofers (for he is not quite the only character in this film to engage in a little light deception), leaves his fiancée, and his home town, to seek his fortune in New York, having been told by his prospective father-in-law that he can make her his bride if he comes back with twenty-five thousand dollars. Known as 'Lucky' for his success at gambling, Astaire soon starts to amass a fortune, but by now he has met and fallen in love with Rogers. Mindful of his obligations, he does not at first allow himself to pursue a romantic relationship with her, but at the same time he deliberately stops short of winning the stipulated sum so that he does not have to go back home and marry his fiancée. When Rogers finds out about Astaire's engagement through a third party she is deeply hurt, and when his fiancée turns up in New York Rogers supposes the worst and promptly decides to marry someone else. All ends happily after the fiancée (played by the likeable Betty Furness) announces that *she* is in fact marrying someone else.

The plot, as John Mueller observes, is 'riddled with inconsistencies, implausibilities, contrivances, omissions, and irrationalities'.[9] The biggest implausibility of all comes at the end, when Astaire's super-smooth and deeply unappealing rival (Georges Metaxa) suddenly decides to act the nice guy after Astaire has stolen both his trousers and his fiancée. Metaxa's transformation, complete with a cheerful snatch of song to send the lovers on their way, is as unconvincing as the hysterical laughter into which the other main characters lapse, one after the other, in the concluding scenes. Other weaknesses include a patchy script: not even Helen Broderick (making a welcome reappearance as

Rogers' older friend) can raise a laugh with a line like 'You know, I often talk to myself. You see, I'm my own grandmother, and I have to keep the old girl interested.' But elsewhere both she and Victor Moore, Astaire's faithful friend, give strong support to the two leads. Broderick more or less reprises her role in *Top Hat*, while the rotund and balding Moore (seen in **2.3**, p. 62), a loyal, affectionate, simple sort of fellow who likes playing card tricks (well, one trick) and making coins disappear, is an interesting change from Astaire's usual partners, the farcical Edward Everett Horton and the dull Randolph Scott. Moore and the quick-witted Broderick, thrown together by circumstance, make an unlikely sort of couple, and have a rather grumpy relationship, but they are responsible for much of the comedy in the film after 'Pick Yourself Up' (and indeed contribute their own amusing counterpoint to this sequence).

Astaire and Rogers themselves have some more than usually serious scenes to play, and, thanks to some sensitive scripting and the equally sensitive direction of George Stevens – less slick but yielding much richer results than that of Mark Sandrich in *Shall We Dance*[10] – *Swing Time* touches greater emotional depths than any other film in the series. Most notable are the 'Fine Romance' sequence, when Rogers first discovers that Astaire is engaged to another woman; and the prelude to 'Never Gonna Dance', when they meet for what they believe is one last time before they part for good. For once the unhappy situation in which they find themselves is wholly believable, and not the result of devices such as mistaken identity or (as in *Shall We Dance*) contrived reports of marriage.

These two scenes alone make *Swing Time* something special – but we have yet to consider its musical credentials. All six individual numbers in Jerome Kern's richly melodic score are of high quality, among them two outstanding songs ('A Fine Romance' and 'The Way You Look Tonight') and a groundbreaking solo routine for Astaire (with female chorus), 'Bojangles of Harlem', in which he uses special effects for the first time and blackface for the first and only time in his career. But it is the three dance duets that make this film not merely special but sublime – what Arlene Croce has called 'the true miracle film of the series'.[11] The first of the three, 'Pick Yourself Up', which, as we have seen, plays a vital part in the dramatic action, forms the sensational climax of a seamless seven-minute sequence of dialogue, song and dance that is absolutely classic Fred and Ginger, a delight from beginning to end ('Sheer heaven', as proprietor Blore aptly observes of the duet). The second, the 'Waltz in Swing Time', is breathtaking in its expression of romantic ecstasy; while the third, 'Never Gonna Dance', is almost unbearably moving, a powerful piece of drama that has no counterpart in the series, taking the normally carefree Fred and Ginger into dark new territory. *Swing Time* may be ridiculous in parts, but it is the sublime that leaves the lasting, indelible impression; as Croce justly asserts, 'There never was . . . a greater dance musical.'[12]

Shall We Dance, almost inevitably, comes as something of a disappointment after this high point, and despite a memorable score by George Gershwin it is as a musical that the film most conspicuously falls short of its predecessor. There are several fine numbers, including the jaunty 'Beginner's Luck' and 'Walking the Dog' – the first a lighthearted love song, the second an instrumental accompaniment to an unusual piece of courtship; and the lyrical romantic ballad 'They Can't Take That Away From Me', which is the equal of Kern or Berlin at their best. Crucially, however, the film's first big dance duet, 'They All Laughed', is also its last, and though it is in many respects as brilliant as its counterpart in *Swing Time*, 'Pick Yourself Up', it cannot compensate for the lack of a fully fledged romantic duet for Astaire and Rogers. What we get instead is a big production number, 'Shall We Dance', in which Astaire, most frustratingly, partners not Rogers but the ballet dancer and contortionist Harriet Hoctor (who also occupies precious screen time with a truly awful solo performance). Only a minute before the end of the film does Rogers finally join him, for the briefest of all their duets – an exquisite display but all too short to satisfy. Equally unsatisfying, though for different reasons, is the couple's second duet in the film, 'Let's Call the Whole Thing Off', a dance on roller skates which is novel but not exactly electrifying. The only other musical number is Astaire's solo routine, 'Slap That Bass', set in the engine room of the *Queen Anne* en route for New York, and though it is inventive it does not count as one of his finest achievements.

In terms of the overall quality of its dances, then, *Shall We Dance*, despite its promising title, is no match for *Swing Time*, or indeed for any of the other four films considered so far. But if its search for innovative ideas leads to some disappointing results on the musical front, *Shall*

We Dance is considerably more successful in other respects, not least in its comedy. Under Sandrich's fast-paced direction it may be a much less affecting film than *Swing Time*, and much more superficial in its characterisation, but it is not short on general entertainment value and (*pace* Mueller, who remarks that in *Shall We Dance* 'familiar formulas are overworked until they become cheerless and pat'[13]) certainly cannot be accused of a lack of originality.[14]

The plot is as implausibly contrived as any in the series, and depends on a whole series of deceptions. Astaire, who as a famous ballet dancer has adopted the stage name Petrov, not only conceals his tap-dancing ability from Rogers in 'They All Laughed' but also impulsively pretends to be Russian at their first meeting, in one of the funniest scenes of the film. Rogers also has a stage name, and it is typical of the superficiality surrounding her starry existence that she should forget what it is when she introduces herself to him. She discovers his true identity when they meet on board ship on the way back to New York from Paris, but their blossoming romantic relationship is cut short by a newspaper report claiming that they are married – this arising from another piece of deception, on the part of Astaire's manager, Edward Everett Horton. Horton, here reprising almost exactly his role in *Top Hat*, with equally hilarious results, only makes matters worse when Astaire insists that he explain the truth to Rogers, but thereafter the role of deceiver is taken over by Rogers' manager, the suave, sophisticated Jerome Cowan (seen in **2.5**, p. 68). Cowan's imagination is considerably more fertile than Horton's, and deception and absurdity both reach their peak when, in the interests of keeping Rogers and Astaire together (as a money-spinning team), he plants a dummy of her in Astaire's bed and releases a photograph of this scene to the press as conclusive proof of their marriage.

Cowan's role is one of the film's many innovations: not only is he Rogers' sole male confidant in the series, but, unlike his female counterparts, he plots behind her back for his own ends. He also joins forces with Astaire to punish Horton for deliberately lying to Rogers, in a gloriously comic scene that sees Horton, believing that the ship is on fire, rushing on deck half-dressed (minus his trousers but wearing a top hat), carrying an assortment of unlikely objects from a tennis racket to a basket of fruit, and shouting his head off – all in full view of passengers and crew. This tour de force is matched by Eric Blore's phone call to Horton from jail (Blore too has to pay the price for attempting to deceive), which creates pure comedy, equally irrelevant to the plot and equally enjoyable, out of a minor but persistent communication problem.

Virtually the only character in *Shall We Dance* who does not deliberately set out to deceive anyone else is Rogers – though she does engage in a little game of disguise in the film's closing moments. But her role is far removed from that of the sweet, natural, girl-next-door she portrayed in *Swing Time*, and indeed from any of her other roles in the series. A glamorous star, she is jaded and discontented with her life when we first see her; though she does not lose her appeal there is at times a trace of hardness in her manner that has never appeared before, and this is reflected in the very tight, artificial hairstyles and sharply tailored clothes she wears in some scenes (such as the first 'Walking the Dog' sequence, seen in **2.8**, p. 74). There is also a slightly unpleasant edge, with no trace of the usual teasing humour, to her contemptuous dismissal of Astaire's pseudo-Russian antics at their second meeting. And, for the greater part of the film (during which she is very frequently annoyed or angry with somebody or other – with good reason), her emotions are purely superficial: she is engaged to someone, but almost forgets the fact, and is clearly not in love with him; and though she eventually succumbs to Astaire's charms she is not hurt, only furious, when it appears that he has used her to other ends. Most remarkably of all, she suggests that they get married – but only so that they can then get divorced and prove to the world that they are *not* married.

But about half an hour from the end of the film, when she and Astaire (uniquely in the series) are husband and wife, Rogers undergoes a change of heart. The brief marriage ceremony, and Astaire's eloquent singing, in the swirling fog on the ferry to Manhattan, of 'They Can't Take That Away From Me', in which he declares that he will never forget her even though they may never meet again, induces a new, more serious and wistful mood. But her change of heart comes just as he, perversely, decides to play hard to get. She is genuinely hurt, first by his apparent indifference, then to discover him alone with another woman, and at last she attracts our wholehearted sympathy, just as she did in *Swing Time* when she discovered him with his fiancée. Unlike *Swing Time*, however, these deeper emotions are not explored in dance, and Rogers promptly disappears from the screen until just a few minutes before the end, to be finally reunited with Astaire at the climax of the closing production number.

It is not difficult to see why *Shall We Dance*, despite its many strengths, was the least successful film of the series to date at the box office. The next, and final, appearance of Fred and Ginger was even less successful than *Shall We Dance* in financial terms,[15] but in every other respect it would prove to be entirely worthy of its position as the last of the series.

Carefree

Carefree was released nearly sixteen months after the appearance of *Shall We Dance*, a much longer interval than had elapsed between any of the previous six films (for once there was no rush for a follow-up after the somewhat disappointing reception given to *Shall We Dance*[16]), and it stands apart from them in many ways. As already noted, it is by far the shortest of the series, with the fewest musical numbers – just four, all of which serve a dramatic function and none of which involve performers other than Astaire and Rogers (unless we count the crowd at the Medwick Country Club who join in the fun in their second dance duet, 'The Yam'). It also marks a significant change in the role played by Astaire – for once not a professional dancer (past or present), or even an entertainer of any sort, but a psychiatrist (who does, however, play the mouth-organ and admit to having wanted to be a dancer before psychoanalysis showed him the error of his ways). Rogers is in more familiar territory as a singer for a local radio station, but in the film's most daring innovation she falls in love with Astaire before he does with her, and actively pursues him – unsuccessfully – for a good quarter of the running time. Her romantic feelings are first aroused by a dream in which she dances with him, and then abruptly terminated by a session of hypnosis – both highly artificial devices, quite unlike anything we have seen before in this series, and the results of which allow Rogers to take an unusually dominant role.

Things get off to a more conventional start, however, with the usual (or rather, a variation on the usual) acrimonious first meeting between the pair, this time in Astaire's consulting room, where, to oblige Rogers' fiancé, a friend of his, he attempts to establish why she has broken off her engagement to him for the third time. This first consultation is a complete failure, Astaire having unwittingly aroused his patient's

hostility before it even begins, but later she relents and allows him to
treat her – by analysing her dreams. Unable to tell him what she has
really dreamt of, she invents a preposterous yarn, which he swallows
whole; he then administers an anaesthetic to release her inhibitions and
enable him to treat the 'mass of the most horrible neuroses' that he now
believes her to be suffering from, but before he can start the treatment
her fiancé drags her off – still under the influence of the drug – to fulfil
an engagement at the radio station. So begins an enjoyably screwball
sequence in which the now completely uninhibited Rogers runs riot,
knocking down an innocent bystander, hurling a policeman's trun-
cheon through a sheet of plate glass, offending her radio sponsors and
generally causing mayhem, all with great glee (**1.4**). She is, indeed,
responsible for a very large part of the film's comedy, while Astaire plays
a more restrained role (as befits his professional calling), and she clearly

1.4 In this novel scene from *Carefree* Rogers, under the influence of an inhibition-
releasing anaesthetic, behaves in a most unprofessional manner at the start of a
live radio broadcast. The show's announcer (Harold Minjur) is not amused.

revels in the experience. Her character, and her appearance, is altogether brighter and fresher than that of the jaded star in *Shall We Dance*, and she wisely refrains from forcing her hair into unnatural styles, leaving it a flatteringly loose shoulder length; she is at her most attractive throughout this film, and it is a wonder that Astaire resists her beauty and her charms for as long as he does. Only some twenty minutes before the end does he finally realise what he has been missing – by which time he has unfortunately hypnotised Rogers into thinking him 'a horrible monster', but this damage is, of course, happily undone in the film's closing moments.

Improbable though it is, the plot of *Carefree* is at least as well controlled as that of *Top Hat*, and the screenplay, as Mueller notes, is eminently lucid and coherent, the only one of the series to contain 'no incidental set pieces, no awkward insertions or jolts, no unmotivated lurches in direction, no scenes devoid of matter or point'.[17] (*Carefree* certainly gives good value for its eighty-odd minutes of running time.) And despite the artificiality of the dream and hypnosis devices it does allow both Astaire and (especially) Rogers to express genuine emotions, touchingly so in the scene where he endeavours to persuade her that she doesn't really love him.

The supporting cast, a strong quartet of entirely new players (three of whom are seen in **2.13**, p. 88), plays a very full role in the proceedings, and makes a substantial contribution to the comedy.[18] Luella Gear, as Rogers' aunt, is reminiscent of Helen Broderick at her best, with Clarence Kolb, an elderly judge and friend of the family, serving as the principal butt of her wit ('Joe, you know I don't dance at your age'). Ralph Bellamy, as Rogers' fiancé and Astaire's friend, is a rather dull character (in the Randolph Scott of *Roberta* mould), but he does have some good lines, especially when suffering from a hangover in the opening scene – 'If you run into my stomach on the way down, kindly have it sent up,' he tells the lift boy after a lightning ascent to the eighteenth floor of the Medical Foundation. Jack Carson, as Astaire's strapping young assistant, whom Luella Gear rather fancies, is for the most part amusing in a dry, understated sort of way, but towards the end of the film he lets rip with an improbably high-pitched impersonation (on the telephone) of one 'Miss Satsuma Naguchi', of the Honolulu *Daily Bugle*, as whom he attempts to keep Bellamy at bay while Astaire pursues Rogers – comedy turning quickly to drama as he draws her into the last of their three dance duets.

Carefree may be short on musical content in comparison with the rest of the series, and Irving Berlin's score is not quite in the same league as those of *Top Hat* and *Follow the Fleet*, but the four numbers, well spaced throughout the film, are all of high quality, and set new standards of innovation while being exceptionally well integrated into the plot. The first, Astaire's 'Golf Solo', performed (to a 'Scottish' melody) in an attempt to impress a sceptical Rogers, is an entertaining mixture of dance and impeccably timed golf, with a nice bit of harmonica-playing thrown in. The second, 'I Used to Be Color Blind', sees Astaire and Rogers dance – in her dreams – in slow motion; while in the third, 'The Yam', Rogers for once takes the initiative and leads Astaire (and a crowd of onlookers) on a merry caper around the Medwick Country Club.

For their last duet of the series Berlin supplied 'Change Partners', as fine a song as any he wrote, and the dance, eloquently demonstrating the power of hypnosis, is more than worthy of it. Like the first two numbers in the film, it is performed out of doors; *Carefree* has an unusually high proportion of outdoor, countrified scenes, which (given that the weather is invariably fine) contribute to its general freshness. It may have been the case, when Stanley Green was writing in 1973, that '*Carefree* holds the dubious distinction of being the one [of the ten Astaire–Rogers films] most people have forgotten',[19] but today it seems anything but forgettable. Fred and Ginger made their final appearance in style, ending the series on a gratifyingly high note.

2

THE ASTAIRE–ROGERS ACTING PARTNERSHIP

The Astaire–Rogers acting partnership is the core of the Fred and Ginger films, and the foundation of the musical numbers that the pair perform together. Astaire and Rogers act all the way through these films, in song and dance as well as in dialogue, and the song and dance are immeasurably enhanced by their acting skills. Their purely non-musical partnership does, however, occupy by far the greater proportion of the running time of each of the seven films, and is responsible in large measure for their enduring appeal.

As suggested in the Introduction, the essence of the Astaire–Rogers partnership, and the first defining element of the Fred and Ginger series, is the remarkable rapport between the pair and the emotional richness of their on-screen relationship – what Arlene Croce calls (in the context of their dancing together) their 'complementarity'. While this complementarity, this perfect match and understanding between two very different performers, reaches its highest expression in dance, it is no less apparent in the non-musical scenes that Astaire and Rogers play together.

Their strongly contrasting but equally appealing personas as Fred and Ginger are established from the very start of the series, in *The Gay Divorcee*, and Astaire and Rogers are indeed a perfect match in these roles: Astaire all breezy, insouciant charm and self-assurance, full of youthful ardour and falling for Rogers almost the instant they meet; Rogers spirited but more vulnerable and uncertain, determinedly resisting Astaire's advances at first, but gradually succumbing to his ardour and charm.[1] Astaire's persona is essentially unaltered in the first six films; though in *Roberta* and *Follow the Fleet* the love-at-first-sight element is replaced by a genial camaraderie, the charm and self-assurance are still very much in evidence, and he still wins Rogers' hand in the end. *Carefree*, the last of the series, sees a distinct shift as he departs from the role of happy-go-lucky song-and-dance man and, as Rogers' rather serious psychiatrist, doesn't fall for her at all until three-quarters of the way through the film; but he is charming enough for Rogers to fall for *him*, and apart from the brief scene in which he realises the error of his ways, is no more afflicted by self-doubt than he has been in previous roles. Despite the initial reversal of the usual pattern of events, Rogers herself betrays as much vulnerability and uncertainty in *Carefree* as she does earlier in the series (again excepting *Roberta* and *Follow the Fleet*, where her camaraderie with Astaire makes for a more robust, though equally engaging, relationship). This touching element of fragility and variability in her persona renders many an implausibility of plot believable; her sad, confused demeanour in the face of Astaire's apparent duplicity in *Top Hat* is a case in point. (Her fragility in this film is highlighted when Erik Rhodes tenderly remarks to his new bride after their impulsive – and happily invalid – marriage that she is 'like a flower I am afraid to crush'.) Rogers' ability to project softer qualities beneath her spirited and often haughty or downright hostile exterior is one of her most appealing attributes as an actress, and one of the most important ingredients of the Astaire–Rogers acting partnership; her occasional failure to soften her manner in *Shall We Dance* is conspicuous, and one of the factors in that film's relative lack of success.

An equally important ingredient of the partnership (and the second defining element of the series) is humour. Fred and Ginger love to tease each other, and – though Ginger is more often on the receiving end of Fred's teasing than he is of hers – they have an equally mischievous sense of fun. Nowhere is this more apparent than in *Roberta*, where there are scarcely any of the usual clashes and romantic entanglements between the pair, and their relationship proceeds almost exclusively by mutual teasing.

The sense of fun goes hand in hand with a refreshing lack of affectation; for – in comic and serious vein alike – Astaire and Rogers are both eminently natural performers, economical and restrained in expression. Neither of them is given to obvious displays of emotion, and in the romantic partnership between Fred and Ginger (the third defining element) sentimentality is firmly kept at bay at all times, as are the conventional trappings of romance. Only at the end of the series, in *Carefree*, is the viewer allowed to witness a truly romantic kiss between the pair, or something approaching a conventional declaration of love – and, as we shall see, even these come with a twist.

Such an attractive mix of ingredients could hardly fail to produce winning results, and the Astaire–Rogers acting partnership remains fresh today, decades after the first appearance of Fred and Ginger on screen. Each of the seven films in the series offers rich illustration of the qualities that make the partnership so enduringly appealing, and there is no better place to start than with the first meetings between the pair, consistently among the most enjoyable scenes in the respective films.

Contrast, complementarity and comedy: first meetings

Humour is the dominant feature of all these encounters, the majority of which involve a clash between Fred and Ginger, and all of which establish within a few short minutes their contrasting but complementary characters, creating intriguing expectations of how the course of their relationship will proceed.

While each of the first meetings is individual and reveals a different aspect of the Astaire–Rogers acting partnership, the seven examples fall into three main groups – or rather two main groups and one 'other'. In the most common scenario, featured in *The Gay Divorcee*, *Top Hat* and *Swing Time*, Astaire inadvertently incurs Rogers' hostility before or just after he meets her, is instantly or almost instantly attracted to her, and attempts to win her favour before their encounter ends, with varying degrees of success. The meetings in *Roberta* and *Follow the Fleet*, by contrast, take the form of a reunion between old friends, with no hostility on Rogers' part but much teasing on both sides, and especially from Astaire. Hostility returns in the last two films of the series, *Shall We Dance* and *Carefree*, both of which, however, turn the familiar pattern on its head, in very different ways.

It is not surprising that the formula established in *The Gay Divorcee* proved successful enough to be used again in two subsequent films, for a clash between the spirited Rogers and the charmingly mischievous Astaire is exceptionally fertile ground for comedy. The three scenes do, however, vary considerably in situation and outcome, and that in *Swing Time* stands apart from the previous two in a number of respects.

In all three films Astaire appears on screen some time before Rogers (as he does in the rest of the series), and is already established in his role, whereas little or nothing is known about Rogers at the time of their meeting. In *The Gay Divorcee* he comes upon her in the customs hall of an English seaport, where she is standing, trapped, a corner of her dress caught in a locked trunk thanks to the carelessness of her aunt, fruitlessly calling for a porter. Instead of fetching her aunt as she sweetly asks him to do, Astaire, captivated by his new acquaintance, tries to free her dress himself, and succeeds only in tearing it rather badly. His contrite apologies, the loan of his coat to cover up her ruined dress, and his hopes of seeing her again to retrieve it meet with a cold response. There has certainly been no attraction on *her* side.

Astaire in this scene is exactly the cheekily charming, carefree and self-assured character that he would portray in subsequent films, and he is responsible for most of the humour. In the face of Rogers' evident embarrassment he prevaricates with small talk, and on failing to call her aunt leans casually on the trunk, declaring brazenly 'You know, a third party might spoil this' (**2.1**), after which he teasingly mimics her renewed call for a porter. Rogers herself (looking very fetching in a rakish beret, a trim jacket and what remains visible of her dress – which reveals rather more of her shapely legs than she would wish) is convincing and appealing, showing spirit as well as a touch of humour in her response to Astaire's attempt to draw her into conversation. If she seems at this early stage less confident and at ease with Astaire than he is with her, not giving quite as good as she gets, this is at least partly attributable to the script and the situation in which she is placed; significantly, she makes her exit not with haughty dignity but in a fluster, letting fall Astaire's coat and being obliged to turn back to pick it up.

Both script and situation in *Top Hat* allow Rogers much more scope for humorous interplay with Astaire, and the outcome of the scene is very different. The sequence begins in impresario Edward Everett Horton's London hotel suite, late one evening. His conversation with Astaire having turned to marriage, Horton advises his young star to find himself a wife, whereupon Astaire spontaneously breaks into song, rejoicing – ironically, in view of what will shortly transpire – in his bachelor state ('No strings, no connections, / No ties to my affections, / I'm fancy free . . . '). Song leads quickly to dance, and Astaire gets quite carried away, tapping noisily and irrepressibly around the room. The camera pans to Rogers, rudely woken from sleep in the room below,

2.1 'You know, a third party might spoil this,' declares Astaire to an embarrassed Rogers on their first meeting in *The Gay Divorcee*. Before becoming trapped in the trunk her dress extended decorously to her ankles.

and 'rising from her satin pillows like an angry naiad from the foam', in Arlene Croce's memorable phrase.[2] Furious (her single raised eyebrow speaks volumes, leaving no doubt that this time she *will* give as good

2.2 Rogers, rudely woken from sleep, confronts Astaire in mid-dance. He is apologetic, and instantly charmed, in this their first meeting in *Top Hat*; she is altogether more in control of the situation than she was in *The Gay Divorcee* (**2.1**).

as she gets), she phones the hotel manager to complain, and he in turn phones Horton, who leaves the room to pursue the matter. But when a piece of plaster crashes down from the ceiling Rogers stalks upstairs, in her satin dressing gown, to confront the offender herself.

Astaire is making so much noise that he doesn't hear her knock; she lets herself in – and he is instantly charmed. Rogers, somewhat disarmed to find him dancing with a small statue that has just fallen from its pedestal into his arms (**2.2**), civilly explains the purpose of her call, and Astaire is suitably apologetic. But then, impishly, he explains that he has no control over his urge to dance – it's an affliction which only strikes him at this time of night, and 'As a matter of fact, I really shouldn't be left alone.' Rogers responds sarcastically but not unpleasantly, and as she turns to leave she favours the viewer, if not Astaire, with a smile. He follows her out; his 'affliction' strikes again, and he claims that there's only one thing that will stop him – 'My nurses always put their arms around me.' 'Well,' responds Rogers crisply, 'I'll call the house detective and tell him to put *his* arms around you.'

As she walks off, Astaire lights a cigarette, throwing the match into a nearby sandbin – which gives him an idea. There follows a truly charming scene in which, watched by Horton, who has returned from his fruitless errand, he sprinkles sand over the floor of their room and begins dancing again, but softly, to a much slower and quieter version of the same music. Rogers, who had gone back to bed still smiling, now happily drops off to sleep to the sound of the gently shuffling steps above her. Her sandman also succeeds in sending Horton and himself to sleep, yawning widely as he gradually winds down in a beautifully relaxed and tranquil ending to the scene.

This classic example of the first meeting shows Astaire and Rogers in the full bloom of their partnership, the honours evenly divided as they progress in the space of a few moments from complete strangers to a couple clearly ripe for courtship. Though Astaire once again initiates most of the humour, Rogers, unlike in *The Gay Divorcee*, meets him on equal terms, responding in kind instead of being merely annoyed with him, and leaves the scene decisively with the last word. Her haughtiness tempered by her secret smile, she plainly finds her noisy neighbour most attractive, and in the privacy of her own room she conveys undisguised pleasure in their encounter. This time there has been true rapport between the pair.

The formula established in *The Gay Divorcee* and developed in *Top Hat* reaches its apogee in *Swing Time*, where by the end of their initially hostile first meeting Fred and Ginger are not merely ripe for courtship but well on their way to romance. The sequence that begins with an acrimonious encounter on the street and ends, under a quarter of an hour later, with the pair united in dance (the only instance in the series of the first meeting leading directly to the first piece of courtship) includes what is perhaps the single most memorable scene of the series, and certainly one of *the* great scenes of the Hollywood musical.

The sequence involves substantial contributions from supporting players, namely Victor Moore as Astaire's sidekick, Eric Blore as Rogers' employer, and Helen Broderick, her friend and colleague (who enacts a sort of parallel first meeting with Moore, culminating in a humorously clumsy attempt to emulate the principal couple in their climactic dance duet). It is Moore, in fact, who sets the whole thing off, Astaire for once being blameless when he incurs Rogers' hostility.

Astaire has arrived with Moore in New York, after a hasty departure from his home town, dressed in the morning suit he was wearing for his aborted wedding and with only a quarter of a dollar in his pocket. He asks Rogers for change for a cigarette machine after she buys a packet from it herself in her first appearance in the film; she obliges, and the machine produces a jackpot of packets and coins. Urged by Moore, Astaire chases after her to ask for his 'lucky' quarter back, but she assumes he is getting fresh and gives him short shrift. Just then, some-one rushes past, knocking her handbag and shopping to the ground, and Moore takes advantage of the confusion to help himself to the quarter from her purse. Discovering the theft, Rogers assumes that Astaire is responsible, and calls a policeman, who takes one look at the elegantly dressed Astaire, every inch the gentleman, and threatens her with dire consequences unless she runs along (2.3). She storms off; Moore shows the dismayed Astaire the coin he has filched, and he chases after her again, having observed her enter Gordon's Dancing Academy. At the

2.3 At their first meeting in *Swing Time*, Rogers accuses Astaire of stealing a quarter of a dollar from her purse. The policeman she has summoned (Edgar Dearing) is more inclined to believe the elegantly dressed Astaire. An uncomfortable-looking Victor Moore (the real thief) tries to pull his friend away.

entrance he pauses, reading the sign which proclaims 'To know how to dance is to know how to control oneself.' The desire to explain himself is now clearly joined by other, more diverting ideas, reinforced by a glamorous picture of Rogers which he sees displayed in the foyer.

The broad outline of what follows will already be familiar. Astaire contrives to receive a dancing lesson from the very hostile Rogers, concealing his true skill, and tries unsuccessfully to set the record straight. Convinced of his apparent inability to perform even the simplest of steps, Rogers admits candidly that she can't teach him anything and advises him to save his money, thereby earning her instant dismissal from Blore. Now Astaire shows him, to Rogers' astonishment, that he has in fact learned a great deal from his teacher, and both Blore and Rogers are completely won over by the brilliant duet that follows.

It is a scene rich in comic and dramatic potential, an ideal vehicle for Astaire and Rogers, and they make the most of it. At first Rogers does not trouble to conceal her hostility, putting Astaire in his place with a firm 'Miss Carroll' when (encouraged by Blore) he addresses her by her first name. When Blore tells her that their visitor is very anxious to learn how to dance she responds with an acid 'Oh, so you won't always be stepping on other people's toes?', drawing a look of pained astonishment from her employer. Astaire meanwhile remains unfailingly affable, and when Blore attempts to establish what kind of dancing he would like to learn first (for he has shamelessly asked for 'a little of each') he says with a disarming smile 'Well, whichever takes the longest'. Now Blore instructs Rogers to begin the lesson, which she does with no very good grace but with at least the appearance of civility. There follows some delightful interplay between the mischievous, ever-charming, unruffled Astaire and the outwardly sweet, inwardly seething Rogers, obliged to be polite to her pupil under Blore's watchful eye but making her true feelings abundantly clear to him under her breath. When Astaire tries to explain what really happened earlier she mutters 'If you don't get out of here I'm going to lose my temper', to which he responds coolly 'If you talk like that I'm going to have to call a policeman', mimicking her appeal on the street ('Officer!') – just as he had mimicked her call for a porter in *The Gay Divorcee* – before quoting, even more teasingly, from the placard in the foyer: 'Our young ladies are sweet tempered, patient and understanding.'

Rogers appears to take the hint, for as the lesson progresses, and Blore leaves them, her hostility subsides under the demands of coping with her pupil's clumsiness. Soon, however, he lands on the floor, and in response to her disgruntled 'I can't teach you anything' he breaks into song (still sitting on the floor), pleading winningly 'Please teacher, teach me something.' 'I'm as awkward as a camel,' he admits, but 'I'm going to learn to dance or burst.' Rogers, mollified by this disarming behaviour, responds sweetly with the next verse, declaring 'Nothing's impossible', and exhorting him to 'Pick yourself up, / Dust yourself off, / Start all over again.' He does exactly that, but this time brings them both toppling to the floor, prompting her fateful advice to save his money.

We are now well into the first stage of courtship, and dance is about to take over, bringing the scene to its stunning and deeply satisfying conclusion. The sequence as a whole, skilfully intercutting the Astaire–Rogers and the Moore–Broderick storylines, is a little masterpiece of comedy and drama, and Astaire and Rogers' share in it is the purest delight. It is a truly magical example of their acting partnership at work.

The first meetings between Fred and Ginger in *Roberta* and *Follow the Fleet*, though quite different in kind from the three considered so far, and lacking some of their most entertaining elements (no hostility on Rogers' part, no instant attraction on Astaire's, no attempt to win her over by the exercise of insouciant charm) are nonetheless memorable, and reveal a new aspect of complementarity and (especially in *Roberta*) of comedy in the partnership.

The scene in *Roberta* is indeed a real treat – one of the most enjoyable examples of mutual teasing in the series. In an astonishingly rapid progression from *The Gay Divorcee*, the players engage in delightfully mischievous banter with such perfect rapport and timing, such confidence and ease, that one might think they had been acting together for years. In the presence of his buddy (Randolph Scott) and Madame Roberta herself, Astaire, newly arrived in Paris, is introduced to the elegantly clad Countess Scharwenka, who can apparently secure a job for his band (the improbably named Wabash Indianians). Rogers, who has earlier been seen throwing a tantrum in Roberta's salon, then turning on her charm for the hulky Scott, recovers from her initial surprise to greet

Astaire in suitably aristocratic fashion (and in mangled French), and interrupts him just as he is about to give away her true identity as his old friend Lizzie Gatz. He plays along, kissing her hand with mock gallantry (later, wickedly, he bites it), emulating her accent, and introducing himself as the 'Marquis de Indiana', a player of 'feelthy piano'. Their dialogue proceeds with exaggerated politeness for the benefit of their audience, with a cheeky aside from Astaire as to his true origins ('Non, non, madame la comtesse – just west of Pittsburgh, babe!') (**2.4**), which Rogers, clearly revelling in her role and her extravagant accent, counters with gusto. In retaliation for his final 'Pouf, eet eez nuzzing – toots! Pouf!' she puffs cigarette smoke in his face before asking to be left alone with him, whereupon Scott leads the bemused Madame Roberta out of the room, allowing the pair to drop their pretence – though Astaire takes delight in continuing it a little longer. Rogers, explaining that her title

2.4 'Just west of Pittsburgh, babe!' Astaire, who has just introduced himself as the 'Marquis de Indiana' to Rogers (in the guise of the Countess Scharwenka) on their first meeting in *Roberta*, drops his exaggeratedly polite façade for a moment to tease his old friend.

is essential for her stage career, promises to get Astaire's band a job if he won't tell on her, and the scene ends, after some more banter, with a good-natured (if somewhat shaky) pact between the pair.

The depth of rapport and easy friendship (as well as the teasing humour) demonstrated in this scene are again very much in evidence in *Follow the Fleet*, but the distinctive appeal of the first meeting in this film lies in the simple affection that Astaire, and especially Rogers, show for each other in their unexpected reunion in the Paradise Ballroom, where Rogers (in sailor costume, complete with rakish peaked cap) has just concluded her lively rendition of 'Let Yourself Go'. Astaire's performance in this scene is marred by his gum-chewing, but Rogers is beautifully unaffected, and the warmth of her 'Gosh, I'm glad to see you', as she embraces him, tears in her eyes, quite overcome with delight at meeting her old dancing partner and sweetheart again, is truly touching. Astaire, clearly glad to see her too, but less demonstrative, quickly moves into teasing mode ('I've missed you too – a little bit'), and as they go over the events of the past couple of years – Rogers wistfully regretting her decision not to marry him – their conversation is flavoured with genial banter as to the progress each has made in the other's absence (Astaire: 'If you'd have married me you wouldn't be working in a chop-suey joint like this.' Rogers: 'Well, I don't see any Admiral's stripes on *you*.'). Eventually they call a truce, shaking hands to seal their friendship, and the scene ends with a typical piece of non-kissing – of which more later.

It is in keeping with their generally innovative spirit that *Shall We Dance* and *Carefree* both depart from the familiar pattern of the first meeting – quite radically so in the case of *Shall We Dance*, in which Astaire reveals a hitherto unsuspected talent for extravagant exhibitionism, while in *Carefree* Rogers makes the most of her rare opportunity to initiate the comedy and turn the tables on her partner. Exceptionally, the whole point of both scenes is the *lack* of complementarity between Fred and Ginger at this early stage, but the comedy is of a novel sort and certainly makes for entertaining viewing.

In *Shall We Dance* Astaire arrives at the door of Rogers' hotel suite armed with a gift of flowers for the woman he has fallen in love with merely from the sight of her picture. She is in a very bad mood, her dancing partner having had the effrontery to kiss her after the last-act curtain of their Paris show, and has been venting her fury on her suave, unperturbed manager (Jerome Cowan). Announced by the maid as 'Petrov', whom Cowan recognises as 'the Russian Ballet's greatest dancer', Astaire overhears Rogers' unflattering retort: 'That's all I need to make things perfect – a simpering toe-dancer. Get rid of him – he probably only wants to say he's seen a picture of me and can't live without me.' In a rapid change of strategy Astaire discards the flowers and bursts into the room, swooping about in grandiose balletic style before coming to a rest in front of a stunned Rogers and introducing himself in a thick Russian accent (**2.5**). 'I understand you want to dance wiz me,' he declares imperiously. 'Of course, I cannot blame you, but I will not permit it.' Scorning Rogers' emphatic denial, he instructs her to 'tweest' for him, demonstrating an elegant little pirouette for her to emulate. Reluctantly she complies – and crashes into the piano. Having completely wrong-footed her in every sense, Astaire, in jocular mood, makes his exit, swooping out as extravagantly as he had swooped in.

With typical restraint, Rogers does nothing in this scene to steal the limelight from Astaire's bravura performance, and in allowing herself to be meekly cowed into submission by him she attracts a measure of sympathy which her untypically jaded and disgruntled demeanour beforehand had failed to do.

She gets her own back in *Carefree*, in a scene that could not be a greater contrast. Here Rogers is at her brightest, Astaire, as her psychiatrist, unusually sober, and it is he who is (comprehensively) wrong-footed by her. The setting is his consulting room, where, at the request of her fiancé, he has an appointment with Rogers to establish why she keeps breaking off her engagement. Expecting to find 'another one of those dizzy, silly, maladjusted females who can't make up her mind' (as he confides to a colleague on the office intercom before showing her in), he is taken aback to find how attractive she is (Rogers, smiling brightly, looking her best in a wide-brimmed hat with a big bow, pale blond hair loosely framing her face, the very picture of sweetness and light). He greets her warmly, she responds in kind, and he leaves her for a few moments to see his colleague – unaware that his unflattering remarks have been recorded on the dictating machine he was using for another case.

Rogers, still smiling brightly, takes a turn around the office, and inadvertently sets off the recording. Her initial amusement abruptly turns to anger as she hears Astaire's assessment of her; she makes to leave but retreats as he returns. When he invites her cordially to sit down she promptly takes his own chair. 'Are you always this nervous?'

2.5 Astaire, in the person of 'the Russian ballet's greatest dancer', and having
discarded his gift of flowers at the door, introduces himself to the woman he has
determined to marry in this early scene from *Shall We Dance*. Rogers here looks
distinctly more composed and haughty than she appears on screen at this point.
Her manager, the suave Jerome Cowan, looks on impassively.

she asks, coolly observing his unease after he has tried unsuccessfully to
persuade her to move. 'No, only I usually sit in *that* chair,' he answers
lamely. 'Well I won't be here very long and then you can sit in it,' she
spits. Bemused by her sudden change of mood, he endeavours to begin

the consultation, but to his every statement or question she responds in curt monosyllables or with a sarcastic comment, always cool and composed and quietly relishing his discomfort. Finally, in exasperation, he exclaims 'I wish you'd please understand that I'm only trying to help you find yourself!' (**2.6**). 'Well, if I ever get lost I'll call on you,' she says briskly, sailing out of the room as she fires this parting shot.

Rogers is on top form throughout this enjoyable encounter – confident, relaxed, throwing Astaire off balance with the greatest economy of gesture and expression, and tempering her hostility with more than a hint of amusement at his discomfort. She has come a long way since her flustered exit in *The Gay Divorcee*, and will indulge in some more humorously sarcastic baiting of Astaire before she relents.

2.6 An exasperated Astaire tries to persuade a coolly composed Rogers that she should let him psychoanalyse her. Their first meeting in *Carefree* is about to come to a most unsatisfactory conclusion (for him) as she sails out of his consulting room.

Romance Fred and Ginger style

Language and other anti-romantic elements

Fred and Ginger express their love for each other in song and, especially, in dance. In dance, they can be as tender and loving, as intimate and passionate, as the most romantic courting couple on the cinema screen. In song, Fred can speak the language of romance: he can declare to Ginger that his longing for her follows him wherever he goes ('Night and Day'); that he's in heaven when they're dancing together ('Cheek to Cheek'); that he feels a glow just thinking of how lovely she is ('The Way You Look Tonight'). But when dialogue takes over, the language of romance disappears from the scene. Given the eloquence of the dance and the song, the expression of love in speech would be at best redundant and at worst an anticlimax. Moreover Astaire hated what he called 'mushy' love scenes,[3] and anything of the kind would be incongruous in the world of Fred and Ginger, with its teasing humour and robust camaraderie, the very antithesis of romantic sentimentality. Other characters in the films (Randolph Scott and Irene Dunne in *Roberta*) say 'I love you' (whether in French or English), and outside the series, in *The Story of Vernon and Irene Castle*, Astaire and Rogers themselves declare very conventionally that they are in love with each other. But on the rare occasions when the word 'love', or other romantic language, is spoken between Fred and Ginger it comes with some sort of a twist, humorous or otherwise, deflating its romantic significance and ensuring that sentimentality plays no part in the scene.

Thus in *Top Hat* when Astaire first learns that Rogers loves him, his pleasure in her declaration is not exactly unalloyed. They have just danced together 'cheek to cheek', Rogers completely surrendering to his seduction in one of the most romantic of all their duets, and, impulsively, he has asked her to marry him. Convinced that he is firmly married to her best friend, Rogers turns on him, appalled. 'How could I have fallen in love with someone as low as you!' she exclaims, slapping his face with a vengeance before she storms off the screen. When in *Carefree* she confesses that she is in love with him, it is to explain an awkward situation: after persuading Astaire to dance with her in 'The Yam' she has attempted to tell her fiancé that it is Astaire she loves, not him, but he has misunderstood her and joyfully announced to the assembled gathering that they are to be married. Astaire is unmoved by her confession, except inasmuch as it affects her and her fiancé; he appeared delighted at the announce-

ment and clearly does not reciprocate her feelings – indeed his idea of
remedying the situation is to hypnotise Rogers into thinking him a 'horrible monster'. Later in the same film he comes closer than ever before
to a conventional declaration, but it's not that close: the words 'Amanda
darling, repeat after me: Tony loves Amanda' are spoken to a Rogers who
has just been knocked unconscious in the course of a last-ditch attempt
to enable her misguided psychiatrist to unhypnotise her.

In *Roberta*, when reminiscing about the past soon after their reunion
(**2.7**), the pair cheerfully admit that they used to be in love with each
other, but there is no suggestion that either of them still holds these
sentiments, and Astaire, who punctuates their conversation with playful bursts of tap, deflates any lingering romantic notions with a typi-

2.7 The newly reunited friends reminisce about their past friendship in *Roberta*. In
this posed still, Astaire looks rather less cheerful than he does on screen, where
he is in playful mood. The setting is the Café Russe, where Rogers has just given
a gleeful performance of 'I'll Be Hard to Handle', and in a few moments the pair
will slide into a dance duet to the same music.

cally mischievous account of how he rigged a beauty contest that Rogers won ('we got a lot of votes from the farmers with a picture of a prize heifer').

Occasionally both Astaire and Rogers speak the clichéd language of romance, but they do so knowingly, tongue in cheek, or with exaggerated expression, in a deliberate parody of such talk. The scene in *Top Hat* when Rogers tries to compromise Astaire with her trumped-up recollections of an affair in Paris sees her embrace him with a gushing 'Oh my darling!' and ask coyly 'Have you forgotten what we've been to each other?' (A few moments earlier he himself had responded to her phone call to ascertain whether he was alone with a blithely parodic 'Completely and desolately!') When he calls her bluff and matches her recollections with his, he observes ungallantly 'You've put on a little weight, haven't you.' After their dance in 'Cheek to Cheek', Rogers, having told him that she knows who he really is (or rather, who she *thinks* he is), waits expectantly for a response, then prompts him: 'Aren't you now supposed to say "We should think only of what we mean to each other", that "we're entitled to live our own lives"?' – all in extravagantly dramatic style. When she has abruptly departed after her barbed admission that she has fallen in love with him, Astaire, nursing his sore cheek, puts on a silly grin as he reflects that 'She loves me!'

In *The Gay Divorcee*, when he is moping because Rogers has not phoned after their more promising second meeting, and he explains to Edward Everett Horton why she is so special, his half-serious 'She's music, she's the buzzing of the bees in clover, she's the rustle of the leaves in the trees, she's water lapping on the shore' is duly ridiculed: 'She sounds like a series of strange noises to me,' responds Horton, unimpressed. And when he does meet her again, by chance, in the seaside hotel chosen for the assignation with her co-respondent, and she asks him in surprise what he is doing there, Astaire replies 'I came down here looking for pieces of my heart' – then laughingly denies such sentimental nonsense in the next breath.

It is not only romantic language that is deflated: any potentially romantic gestures receive the same treatment. After their first meeting in *The Gay Divorcee*, Astaire drives through the streets of London searching for Rogers until he finally comes upon her, and then chases her out into the country, bringing her to a halt by means of his own speedily erected 'Road Closed' sign – at which point he produces a well-stocked picnic basket (**2.11**, p. 82). But there is to be no romantic picnic under the trees: after she has torn up his proffered phone number, then reluctantly kept it, she drives off with the basket still on the running board of her car, bringing it crashing to the ground.

Four times Astaire buys flowers for Rogers. In *Top Hat*, immediately after he has successfully wooed her in song and dance for the first time, he extravagantly orders a whole roomful, but he somewhat diminishes his romantic credentials by charging them to Horton. In *Follow the Fleet* he is accompanied by his little pet monkey when he arrives at Rogers' apartment with a bunch of roses, after inadvertently ruining her audition for a job. But he doesn't actually give them to her: first he lets the monkey present them, and when Rogers subsequently throws them to the floor in disgust on spotting him he just sticks them in a vase while her back is turned, concluding his gesture with a casual 'I don't often try to apologise because I seldom make any mistakes.' In *Shall We Dance*, as we have seen, he discards his gift of flowers (nicely packaged in a transparent box) before he even meets Rogers, embarking instead on his impersonation of a Russian ballet dancer, and going out of his way to behave unromantically ('Don't be a silly horse,' he says, when Rogers denies that she wants to dance with him). Finally, much later in the same film, he buys her a small corsage from a flower-seller on board the ferry to Manhattan, and presents it to her in a conventional manner; but the episode follows their low-key marriage, which Rogers has instigated purely so that they can get divorced, so it hardly counts as romantic.

Astaire's determinedly unromantic behaviour towards Rogers at their first meeting in *Shall We Dance* continues into the first stage of their courtship, on board the *Queen Anne* on the voyage home to New York. No longer masquerading as a Russian (Rogers having overheard him speaking in an unmistakably American accent soon after their arrival on the ship), he tries out another novel ploy. In a sequence enacted without dialogue but to a jaunty musical accompaniment, he observes Rogers walking her little pet dog on deck, bribes a crew member to let him walk the large hound he has charge of, and greets Rogers as their paths cross. She ignores him; he joins her; she walks faster and faster to evade him, until finally she picks up her dog (who has long since given up trying to keep up with her) and goes to stand at the guard rail. The dumb show over, they have a brief conversation in which Rogers (wearing her tightest, most artificial hairstyle and sharpest of clothes) is unimpressed

by Astaire's more conventional attempt to pursue her acquaintance
(**2.8**), though as she leaves him we see the hint of a smile on her face.
The following day, in a reprisal of the dumb show, he appears on deck
with at least half a dozen dogs of assorted types and sizes in tow, and
deliberately ignores her as he parades ostentatiously past. Her own little
terrier scuttles after them, whereupon Rogers' face (now framed by a
much less forbidding hairstyle) finally breaks into more than a hint of
a smile. The next shot shows the couple strolling together arm in arm,
talking happily, and joined only by Rogers' long-suffering pet – Astaire
having no further need for his own canine accessories.

Deliberately unromantic behaviour on Astaire's part is one way of
avoiding clichéd convention, but he is blameless on the occasions when
a truly romantic mood induced by song and dance is shattered once
dialogue takes over. An already familiar example is the scene in *Top
Hat* when, moments after his seduction of Rogers in 'Cheek to Cheek',

2.8 The conclusion of the first 'Walking the Dog' sequence from *Shall We Dance*:
   a tightly coiffured Rogers gives Astaire no encouragement when he tries to get
   better acquainted at the guard rail of the *Queen Anne*.

she rudely slaps his face in the mistaken belief that he is the husband of her best friend. The 'Night and Day' sequence in *The Gay Divorcee* follows a similar pattern. Astaire has encountered Rogers by chance in the hotel where she is to meet her co-respondent, and after successfully wooing her in the course of their intensely romantic dance duet he unknowingly utters the password that will identify this professional accomplice; her mood of rapture turns abruptly to disgust, and she leaves him with an astoundingly businesslike instruction to be in her room at midnight. There are no such misunderstandings involved when he sings her a lyrical love song in *Swing Time* (to regain her favour after a week's estrangement provoked by his gambling proclivities), but his performance meets with an equally mood-shattering, if less alarming, conclusion. As he sings the final bars, declaring tenderly 'I love you / Just the way you look tonight', and rejoicing in the touch of her hand upon his shoulder, he looks up from the piano to find her head lovingly close to his – and covered in shampoo.[4] Seeing his change of expression, and then her reflection in the mirror, Rogers hastily runs back to the bathroom from which she had just emerged.

'A Fine Romance'

A subsequent scene in *Swing Time* is the most extended single example in the series of frustrated romantic aspirations, and, like the 'Pick Yourself Up' sequence earlier in the same film, it has a magical quality. Taking place in a seemingly enchanted snow-covered landscape (the air of enchantment heightened by the bell-like musical soundtrack of the opening few moments), it is a unique episode, bitter-sweet in mood; and though it includes a classic Jerome Kern song it is most memorable for its non-musical elements. As in 'Pick Yourself Up', Helen Broderick and Victor Moore play a substantial part in the proceedings, and, excepting only a brief exchange between Moore and Rogers, both they and Astaire are lighthearted throughout. It is Rogers who injects a more serious note, in one of her finest performances of the series.

The sequence follows on immediately from the rapturous 'Waltz in Swing Time', but the mood is now very different. The foursome have set off in Astaire's car for a trip to the country, their destination the dilapidated ruins of the 'New Amsterdam', some sort of pleasure resort which Broderick used to frequent in years gone by. Before they leave,

Rogers, disappointed at Astaire's lukewarm manner towards her, complains to her sympathetic friend that she only sees him at rehearsals or when other people are around; meanwhile Astaire himself, mindful of his engagement to a girl back home and lacking the courage to reveal the truth to Rogers, tells Moore not to leave him alone with her during their outing. She (wearing a stylish peaked hat, and managing to look both elegant and cuddly in her high-heeled shoes and three-quarter-length fur coat) makes affectionate overtures to Astaire when they arrive, snuggling up to him when they sit on a bench under a tree, but he just smokes his pipe and keeps his hands firmly in his pockets. She invites him to join her inside a romantic little arbour; he responds unenthusiastically that it's a bit draughty. She tells him sweetly that she likes 'being off alone' with him (**2.9**); he smiles, then thinks better of it. She says she's a little cold and snuggles up to him again; he nearly puts his arms around her but then moves away, advising her to flap her arms to restore circulation. He demonstrates, flapping them for her – and suddenly his arms are around her and their faces are very close. Shyly she says: 'You know, if some people saw us like this they might think that we were – that we liked each other.' This time he is more responsive, and they speak of how they have been thrown together: 'sort of like a romance, isn't it?', she volunteers hesitantly. He agrees, and again she nestles up to him – whereupon Moore calls out a discreet warning to Astaire, and his mood abruptly changes. 'You know, you ought to be wearing galoshes,' he informs her. Her face falls, not for the first time. 'I think we'd better go home,' she says dejectedly, walking away; then she turns back, leans her hand on a tree, and sings.

The lyric is humorously sarcastic – 'A fine romance, with no kisses! / A fine romance, my friend, this is! / We should be like a couple of hot tomatoes, / But you're as cold as yesterday's mashed potatoes' – but Rogers invests it with all the hurt and disappointment that she has so far conveyed by looks alone. Astaire, keeping his distance as Rogers walks restlessly about in the snow, remains unwaveringly light-hearted, and when she finishes her song he comes to her to (sort of) cheer her up. She tells him, still dejected and confused, that she can't make him out when he's aloof; to prove that he isn't, he draws her to him to kiss her – at which point a snowball, thrown by the watchful Moore, lands squarely on his hat.

Astaire of course joins in the fun, hitting Broderick in the eye as he

2.9 'I like being off alone with you,' says Rogers shyly, snuggling up to Astaire in their romantic snow-covered arbour in the 'Fine Romance' sequence from *Swing Time*. On screen, his hands remain firmly in his pockets at this moment, and his smile is short lived.

throws one back, and in the diversion Moore lets slip to Rogers (in an improbable piece of scripting) that Astaire is engaged to another girl. She sits down, stunned and speechless. Now Astaire bounds back to her, after telling Moore that he has decided to throw all restraint aside, and tries to carry on from where he had left off. But this time Rogers is the one who is aloof; when he tries to embrace her she resists, then she walks away in unhappy silence. Now, as he follows her back to the car, it is his turn to sing, but, unlike Rogers, he delivers his humorous verse without any hint of deeper emotion. The scene ends, with the song, as Rogers gets into the car and starts the engine and windscreen wipers, showering Astaire with snow.

By turns openly affectionate, sweetly shy, hopeful, disappointed, exasperated, dismayed, Rogers conveys all these changing moods and emotions with her characteristic restraint and lack of affectation – just a change of expression here, a different tone of voice there, a minimum of gesture. It is a highly touching and appealing performance, in a scene that in its expert blend of both comic and serious elements has no counterpart in the series.

The non-kissing tease

The snowball landing on Astaire's hat just as he is about to kiss Rogers is a classic example of what had by now become a trademark feature of Fred and Ginger's romantic partnership. As with expressions of love, other couples in the series kiss in conventional romantic style – Irene Dunne and Randolph Scott in *Roberta*, Harriet Hilliard and Scott in *Follow the Fleet* – and, outside the series, Astaire and Rogers themselves do so in *The Story of Vernon and Irene Castle*, as had Gene Raymond and Dolores Del Rio before them in *Flying Down to Rio*. But where Fred and Ginger are concerned, *not* kissing is the norm, and for much the same reasons that not saying 'I love you' is the norm. As John Mueller observes, 'Astaire had avoided kisses because he disliked mushy love scenes, because the Hollywood kiss was such a cliché, and because love is so eloquently expressed in his dances that using something so obvious would be tantamount to admitting choreographic failure.'[5] As it happens, the one occasion on which the couple do the conventional thing, right at the end of the series, is in the course of a dance – but the context exonerates both Astaire and Rogers from any suspicion of failure.

In fact they do kiss each other, twice, long before the end of the series, but as can be expected, there is nothing conventionally romantic about it, and on both occasions the kiss is initiated by Rogers. In *The Gay Divorcee*, when her husband turns up as planned after her night spent with the co-respondent, but inconveniently refuses to believe that he is really her lover, she calls out to Astaire, hiding in another room, and says 'I'm sorry to ask you to do this, but will you kiss me?', whereupon Astaire of course obliges. In *Top Hat* the event occurs at the beginning of the scene in which Rogers attempts to compromise Astaire about their imaginary affair in Paris; the kiss follows immediately after the gushing 'Oh my darling!' with which she greets him, and is met by an astonished 'Hello. How've you been?'

Between *The Gay Divorcee* and *Top Hat* lies the kiss-free zone of *Roberta* (the pair embrace, but go no further, at the end of their final, ecstatic dance duet), but in *Follow the Fleet* the business of not kissing becomes an obvious tease for the first time. Here, after they shake hands to call a truce on the occasion of their reunion near the beginning of the film, Astaire says hopefully 'Let's kiss and make up.' 'No,' replies Rogers, 'let's just make up. That'll give you something to work for.' Later that night, when they are saying goodbye on the steps of her apartment block, they attempt to kiss but are deterred, twice, by the presence of a policeman walking by, and part with just a resigned 'Goodnight' from Rogers.

Swing Time takes the tease a stage further, with not only the snowball incident but also an off-screen kiss that the viewer is prevented from witnessing, a probable on-screen kiss that is also obscured from view, and possibly one other non-kissing event. When Astaire looks up from the piano after his tender performance of 'The Way You Look Tonight', he and Rogers seem to be definitely heading for a kiss, but the sight of her shampooed head puts paid to any such idea. Right at the end of the film, after they have celebrated their union by singing that same song and 'A Fine Romance' in harmonious counterpoint, they embrace and almost certainly kiss, but not before Astaire has swung round so that his back is to the camera – as a result of which we can only surmise what happens next. The off-screen kiss, occurring shortly after the 'Fine Romance' sequence, is the biggest tease of all, and, like the only two actual kisses in the series so far, is initiated by Rogers. Disillusioned and claiming that she is no longer interested in Astaire, she is encouraged by Broderick (on the grounds that he has given up gambling and so can't want to go back to his fiancée) to 'go up and give him a great big kiss', and when she demurs Broderick taunts her that she hasn't got the nerve to do it. Off Rogers marches to Astaire's dressing room, beautifully gowned in preparation for a dance, to prove her wrong. She knocks, he calls out 'Come in' and she enters; she makes to kiss him (twice) (**2.10**), he retreats, taken aback (twice); she asks awkwardly 'How d'you like my dress?', he admires it; she rushes off, he stops her; he admires the dress some more, and, having talked himself gradually into the right mood, pins her against the wall by the door and is on the point of kissing her when the nightclub owner walks in. The opening door hides the lovers from both our view and his, and he is about to leave when he hears them breathing rather fast – whereupon they are revealed, beaming idiotically, Astaire with a great smudge of lipstick on his face.

Shall We Dance is another kiss-free zone, the lovers, and indeed the husband and wife, not even coming close to a clinch, but *Carefree* makes up for it with what Astaire jokingly calls 'the kiss of the century'.[6] The catch is that it takes place only in Rogers' dreams, as the climax of a very dream-like dance performed (as is the kiss) in slow motion. And even

2.10 Emboldened by Helen Broderick's taunts, Rogers, beautifully gowned (beneath the shimmering cape is the dress she will wear for 'Never Gonna Dance'), attempts to give Astaire a 'great big kiss' in this teasing scene from *Swing Time*.

here it defies convention: as Mueller notes in his interestingly detailed analysis of this unique event, Astaire 'has taken on that most hoary of Hollywood clichés and revitalized it with a fresh eroticism'. Though the lovers end up in 'the classic Hollywood-kiss pose', with Rogers lying 'surrenderingly in his arms as he leans over her', it is she who consummates the kiss: 'In languorous slow motion, she reaches upward, wraps her arms around his neck, and then gradually pulls her body up until her face meets his.'[7]

Rogers wakes to disappointing reality, and the closest she gets to kissing the man of her dreams in real life is when she is lying on the couch in his surgery under the influence of a hypnotic drug. After administering it Astaire instructs her temptingly to 'act wholly on the impulse of the moment' – which she instantly complies with by reaching up to kiss him, a blissful smile on her face. He pushes her back, and leaves her for the drug to take full effect, at which point her fiancé finds her and gets mistakenly kissed in his stead. Later, Astaire finally begins to doubt the wisdom of a strategy which involves implanting monstrous thoughts about himself into her mind, and has an illuminating conversation with his subconscious self in the mirror. 'Kiss her, you dope!' exhorts his alter ego, after advising him to remove those damaging thoughts, but, typically, no such kiss materialises on screen.

Marriage

When Astaire and Rogers first kiss each other in *The Story of Vernon and Irene Castle*, Astaire has just proposed marriage and Rogers has accepted him, in wholly conventional style. Fred and Ginger, of course, do things rather differently. Though all the films in the series end in their marriage (or, in the case of *Shall We Dance*, their reconciliation), nowhere is there a scene in which Astaire proposes to Rogers and she accepts. Only on two occasions does he propose to her at all – impulsively, at a relatively early stage, and she rejects him, implicitly or explicitly. Elsewhere she (sort of) proposes to him; or she announces to others that they are to be married; or she suggests that they marry purely so that they can then get divorced; or there is no mention of marriage at all, and we simply see the pair walking to the altar in the closing moments. Usually a celebratory song or dance rounds off the proceedings, after a minimum of dialogue. In four of the seven films Rogers is either married (actually or supposedly) or engaged to someone else when she and Astaire finally cement their union (in the case of *Shall We Dance* she is on the point of divorcing him), but husbands or fiancés are dispatched without ceremony as plot complications are happily resolved.

The Gay Divorcee sets the tone for the series in an early scene, Astaire's second meeting with Rogers, when he has finally caught up with her after chasing her car into the country outside London. Having blocked her exit with his 'Road Closed' sign, and opened his picnic basket, he asks blithely what he can offer her: 'Frosted chocolate, Cointreau, Benedictine, marriage . . . ?' (**2.11**). Naturally, she doesn't take his casual proposal seriously, and the subject is not mentioned again until the closing scene, when her husband turns up at the prescribed time to find her improbably ensconced with her co-respondent. After Astaire has kissed her as requested, convincing the husband that they are lovers, Rogers announces

2.11 'Frosted chocolate, Cointreau, Benedictine, marriage . . . ?' offers Astaire, opening his well-stocked picnic basket. Not surprisingly, Rogers does not accept his proposal at what is only their second meeting in *The Gay Divorcee*, but he does succeed in getting her to keep his phone number – and in learning her name as she drives off, bringing the basket crashing to the ground.

that 'After the divorce we're going to be married.' (Presumably the matter has been settled between them in the course of the night spent as a companionable threesome.) The husband maliciously responds that there will be no divorce as he is going to forgive her, but he is then conveniently unmasked as a philanderer by the hotel waiter, and makes a hasty exit. 'Meet the future Mrs Holden,' says Astaire with great satisfaction, when Rogers' lawyer and aunt turn up to ask whether the plan worked, and the couple express their elation in a joyful dance over tables and chairs in the closing scene.

In *Top Hat*, Astaire decides to ask Rogers to marry him immediately after the 'Paris' scene, reluctantly promises Horton that he will wait until he (Horton) has found out more about her, then, as we have seen, casts his promise aside and impulsively proposes to her shortly after they have danced together in 'Cheek to Cheek', only to have his face slapped. Sad and confused, Rogers, equally impulsively, agrees to marry her dress designer and protector, Erik Rhodes, who now seems the only person she can turn to. In a neat reprise of their first meeting, Astaire, who has finally learned of Rogers' misunderstanding as to his identity, taps noisily on the floor of the room above the bridal suite to engineer another meeting with her, during which he explains (off screen) who he really is. Their marriage can now be taken for granted, the only specific reference being a typically oblique 'Not till I've asked Mr Beddini for his wife's hand', when Broderick advises Astaire to take the first plane back to London. It remains only for Eric Blore to reveal that it was he, disguised as a clergyman, who married Rogers and Rhodes (**2.12**), and the stage is set for the couple to dance their way happily off the screen.

Rogers' readiness to throw away her future on the most wildly improbable of suitors again creates a last-minute obstacle in *Swing Time*, though here, exceptionally, it is the sudden arrival on the scene of Astaire's fiancée that prompts her foolish decision to marry bandleader Georges Metaxa. She clearly takes no pleasure in the prospect, and, with Astaire equally unhappy in his own situation, honour bound to marry a woman he does not love, the mood is unusually serious as the lovers meet for what they believe is the last time. But comedy soon takes over, the fiancée's surprise announcement that she is in fact marrying someone else triggering gales of hysterical laughter all round – except for Rogers, who in the absence of any overture from Astaire remains glumly committed to her own imminent wedding. Not until a few moments before the event is due to take

place, when she sees Metaxa emerge from his dressing room wearing a pair of trousers several sizes too large (thanks to a trick played on him by Astaire and Moore, reflecting the ruse by which Astaire missed his own wedding at the start of the film), does she finally join in the laughter, and inform the vicar delightedly that 'There isn't going to be any wedding!' To spare the helplessly hysterical Astaire the trouble of proposing, the angry, humiliated Metaxa then, quite unbelievably, comes over all magnanimous, and observes to Rogers 'Oh, then you're going to marry *him*?' 'Yes, I guess so,' replies Rogers, still laughing like mad, and with her ex-fiancé cheerfully serenading them the pair walk off arm in arm, ending the film in perfect harmony as they blend in counterpoint a verse from two of its most memorable songs.

The subject of marriage between Fred and Ginger, supposed or actual, occupies an unusually large proportion of the running time of *Shall We Dance*, the only film of the series in which the couple become husband and wife in the course of the action rather than at its conclusion. It is also the only film in which Astaire declares his intention to marry Rogers before he so much as sets eyes on her: 'I haven't even met her,' he tells Horton at a very early stage, after admiring her image in a flip-picture book of her dancing, 'but I'd kinda like to marry her.' 'Think I will,' he adds casually as he walks out on his horrified manager. But before he has the chance to ask her, their burgeoning romance on board the *Queen Anne* is stymied by a newspaper report claiming that they have been secretly married for years, and then, by a little stretch of the imagination, that 'a blessed event is imminent'. In her fury at Astaire, whom she mistakenly believes to be responsible for the reports, Rogers decides to marry her fiancé (another remarkably foolish choice), but as one embarrassing report leads to another, and she is (by devious means) pictured in her nightgown on Astaire's bed, the fiancé backs off in alarm. Sitting on the grass in New York's Central Park, where she and Astaire have fled to escape the reporters besieging their hotel, she reflects that if only they could get a divorce it would put a stop to all the false reports – and then hits on the idea of asking him to marry her so that she can start proceedings in the morning. This novel episode is given

2.12 The denouement of *Top Hat*: Erik Rhodes (right) glowers on discovering that his marriage to Rogers is invalid, while (from left) Edward Everett Horton, Helen Broderick and Eric Blore (the fake clergyman) observe the happy couple approvingly. The scene is staged in a (relatively) small corner of the lavishly vast bridal suite of their Venice hotel.

an additional humorous twist by the appearance of a policeman who
happens to be walking by, and overhears her attempting to persuade an
apparently reluctant Astaire (who is mischievously prevaricating): 'You
got me into all this – the very least you can do is marry me,' she declares,
and the shocked policeman draws the obvious conclusion.

The next scene shows them in the New Jersey registry office, under-
going a low-key ceremony, after which they take the ferry back to a
foggy Manhattan, and have an equally low-key exchange about how
they will now go their separate ways. 'I didn't know getting married was
so depressing,' a wistful Rogers remarks, 'I'm sorry now I asked you.'
Astaire, who appears remarkably unperturbed at the prospect of losing
her, assures her, in the film's greatest song, that 'Our romance won't end
on a sorrowful note', and that he will always remember the way she looks
and acts, the way she's changed his life. 'They can't take that away from
me,' he sings with feeling, as they leave the ferry in subdued mood, with
Rogers seemingly close to tears. Back at their hotel, her depression deep-
ens as, casually declaring 'Well, I guess the honeymoon's over', Astaire
rejects her friendly overtures and retires to his own room. His misguided
attempt to play hard to get misfires badly when the woman who was
responsible for starting the rumours of their marriage in the first place
reappears on the scene, leading Rogers to believe that they are having an
affair. She abruptly leaves the hotel just as he finally decides to make his
true feelings known, and next appears some days later, accompanied by
her former fiancé, a summons for divorce in her hand. Astaire is dancing
in a Broadway show produced by Rogers' manager, and his performance
leads to their swift reconciliation, a brief dance and song obviating the
need for any dialogue and bringing the film to its joyful close.

There are no such elaborate complications in *Carefree*, where Astaire
spends the greater part of the time attempting to persuade Rogers to
marry someone else. When he finally sees sense he is thwarted, first by
the effectiveness of his own treatment and then by a court order obtained
by Rogers' fiancé (Ralph Bellamy), forbidding him to see her again.
With the help of her aunt (Luella Gear) and his assistant (Jack Carson)
he almost succeeds, through dance, in reversing the unfortunate effects
of his hypnosis, but he is thwarted once again by Bellamy. Matters are,
naturally, resolved at the last minute, but in the most extraordinary fashion. Prompted by Carson and aided by Gear, Astaire gains entrance to
the room where Rogers is being dressed for her wedding, with the inten-

tion of knocking her out so that he can get to her unconscious mind. As he prepares to strike the blow his courage fails, at which point Bellamy bursts in (**2.13**) and inadvertently does the job for him, Astaire ducking instinctively just as he throws a hefty punch. While Carson and Gear hold the hapless Bellamy down, Astaire speedily rehypnotises the bride-to-be, and they are next seen walking arm in arm to the altar, Rogers blissfully unconcerned about her black eye.

In the two remaining films, *Roberta* and *Follow the Fleet*, the question of marriage is both raised and settled in the teasing style that is typical of Fred and Ginger's more comradely relationship. In *Roberta*, though the pair admit early on that they used to be in love with each other, there is no suggestion of marriage, or indeed romance, until over three-quarters of the way through the film, when they are trying to persuade Irene Dunne that Randolph Scott really loves her, despite the fact that they are always quarrelling. In a delicious piece of dialogue, Astaire remarks: 'That's nothing – people in love are always quarrelling with each other. Now you take Liz and myself, for instance.' Rogers, in Polish-countess mode, turns on him with an emphatic 'Leez? Who eez theez Leez?', to which he responds: 'Oh, a little country girl from back home that I'm thinking of marrying – you know, big feet, dumb, simple, oh, very simple.' With such a beginning, it's hardly surprising that it is left to Rogers to clinch matters at the end, which she does after they have danced together, in exquisitely romantic style, in 'Smoke Gets in Your Eyes', the climax of a musical fashion show. Backstage, and with Astaire paying her only half his attention, she casually declares her willingness to give in to him. 'Me? I didn't say anything,' he responds. 'But I thought you were about to want to marry me,' she persists, and, still dividing his attention between her and the stage, he agrees. 'Well, I accept,' says Rogers graciously. He thanks her in friendly fashion and they shake hands as if concluding a business deal, before returning to the stage for an exuberant final dance of celebration.

Rogers also finds herself proposing to Astaire at the end of *Follow the Fleet*, though less graciously. Earlier in the film, at the time of their original reunion, the once-rejected Astaire has told her that his enlistment in the navy ends in the spring, and 'we'll pick up where we left off, only this time you'll ask *me* to marry *you*'. True enough, after their stunning performance of 'Let's Face the Music and Dance', when they are offered a job by an important producer, Astaire makes it a condition of their

acceptance 'that Miss Martin asks me to marry her'. Rogers complies with a terse 'Well, will you?', to which he mischievously responds 'You'll have to ask father!' Miraculously, this brief epilogue succeeds in bringing the film to a satisfying conclusion without any sense of anticlimax after the glamour and virtuosity of their romance in dance.

In serious vein

We have already seen that the scripts of the Fred and Ginger films occasionally touch a serious note, or at least allow Astaire and Rogers to portray more serious emotions. Usually, as in the 'Fine Romance' sequence, it is Rogers who suffers a change of mood from the prevailing lightheartedness, while Astaire remains cheerfully unaware of (or insensitive to) the hurt or disappointment he is causing her. Thus in *Top Hat*, after she has slapped his face in outrage at his impulsive proposal, she is seen to be miserably confused by his apparently deceitful behaviour; and in *Shall We Dance*, while he remains remarkably composed at the prospect of their imminent separation after their hasty marriage, she clearly feels it keenly, and is hurt by his offhand behaviour when they return to their hotel.

In *Carefree* it is again Rogers who suffers while Astaire, though in a more sombre frame of mind, clinically dissects her feelings for him after she has confessed that she is in love with him. In his consulting room he first establishes, while she replies in gentle monosyllables ('No, Tony', 'Yes, Tony'), that she thought she loved him purely because she dreamed about him. He then gives her a lengthy lecture, explaining that 'very often the dream fantasy makes things seem true to the dreamer when in reality they have no basis in fact', that she had merely mistaken her temporary dependence on him for love, and would have fallen in love with any doctor. As Rogers brushes away a tear and remains silent, he asks her (with an amazing lack of perception) what's wrong, and when she replies, in quiet despair for her own prospects, that she is just worried about her fiancé, he sets about remedying that situation. With Rogers meekly compliant, he hypnotises her into believing that she loves her fiancé, not her doctor, and that he doesn't love her. 'Tony doesn't love me,' she repeats obedi-

2.13 Rogers, in her bridal dress, little realises that she is about to be dealt a knock-out blow by the groom (Ralph Bellamy, second left). Co-conspirators Luella Gear and Jack Carson (yelling out a warning to Astaire) will keep Bellamy out of action while Astaire speedily works on Rogers' unconscious mind in this penultimate scene from *Carefree*.

ently – but three times, each with a sadder, more despairing inflection. At last Astaire realises that maybe he is missing something, a suspicion that is promptly confirmed by his subconscious mind in a lighthearted exchange in the next room.

In this scene, as in the 'Fine Romance' sequence and the other brief examples, Rogers' performance is notable for its restraint and economy of expression, more affecting than any conspicuous display of emotion. That Astaire can be equally affecting when he too is in despair is demonstrated, briefly, later in the same film, when his attempt to undo the effects of his disastrous hypnosis through dance is thwarted at the critical moment. It is demonstrated more fully in the only scene of the series in which the mood on both sides is intensely serious, Astaire and Rogers each suffering equally in an unhappy situation which compels them to part despite their love for each other. Here, for once, their predicament does not arise from devices such as mistaken identity, false reports of marriage, or dreams, but is entirely credible. It is a most moving scene, and, like the two other outstanding sequences discussed earlier, it occurs in that miracle film, *Swing Time*.

Astaire's fiancée has turned up unexpectedly, to his dismay as well as Rogers', who, after rushing out of his dressing room almost in tears, decides to marry the other man in her life, smarmy bandleader Georges Metaxa. Astaire interrupts the newly engaged couple as they stand together in the otherwise deserted ballroom where he and Rogers were due to perform a dance (but now cannot because of a separate plot twist that only adds to their dismay), and asks to speak to her. Metaxa leaves at her request, and in the ensuing dialogue the pair exchange sad, awkward apologies while Rogers nervously clasps her hands together, fingering her ring. As Mueller notes, 'The words are sparse and tentative, the logic elusive and essentially irrelevant.'[8] She tells Astaire, who has been trying to 'figure this thing out', of her engagement, that 'it's all decided now', and, dropping her hands, walks off without a word when he says a sombre 'Goodbye'. He calls her back to wish her good luck, and there is another awkward, inconclusive exchange before Rogers, as if she can't help herself, asks him 'Does she dance very beautifully?' 'Who?' asks Astaire. 'The girl you're in love with.' 'Yes,' he says, intensely, looking into her eyes, 'very'. Registering his meaning, she adds 'The girl you're engaged to – the girl you're going to marry.' 'Oh, I don't know,' he says dejectedly, still fixing his eyes on hers, 'I've danced with you. I'm never going

2.14 'I've danced with you. I'm never going to dance again,' says Astaire dejectedly to an unhappy Rogers, fingering her engagement ring. This unusually serious scene from *Swing Time* shows both performers at their most affecting.

to dance again' (**2.14**). For the second time she turns and walks away, very slowly, but this time he stops her with a song, a strange, yearning song, that ends with the sad refrain 'Never gonna dance. / Never gonna dance. / Only gonna love you. / Never gonna dance.' The mood is now set for the dance of despair that concludes the scene, the most powerfully moving piece of work that Astaire and Rogers ever performed together.

Three years later, in *The Story of Vernon and Irene Castle*, a story that ends tragically, their skills as serious actors would be exploited more fully, but Astaire and Rogers were never more affecting in serious vein than in this late scene from *Swing Time*.

3

THE MUSICAL NUMBERS

The Fred and Ginger series attracted the talents of some of the most distinguished composers of the day. Cole Porter's 'Night and Day' (from *The Gay Divorcee*) and most of Jerome Kern's music for *Roberta* were borrowed from earlier stage shows, but the scores of the five films beginning with *Top Hat* are all original. Irving Berlin contributed both words and music to *Top Hat*, *Follow the Fleet* and *Carefree*; Jerome Kern was responsible (in addition to *Roberta*) for *Swing Time* (with lyrics by Dorothy Fields); and George Gershwin for *Shall We Dance* (with lyrics by his brother, Ira Gershwin). The score of *The Gay Divorcee*, being the work of several different hands, is somewhat variable, and overall less impressive than its one star song, but the remainder are of consistently and often outstandingly high quality.

Astaire and Rogers were extremely fortunate to be dancing together at a time when these great composers were working, and the importance of their contribution to the series cannot be overstated. Their music not only enriched the films with a succession of superb songs – the series gave birth to at least a dozen classics (six Oscar winners or nominees among them), and only a handful of the more than three dozen featured are less than memorable – but provided Astaire and Rogers with the ideal inspiration for their dances. It is scarcely possible to imagine the films without these musical scores, and one is even tempted to speculate as to whether the Astaire–Rogers dancing partnership would have reached quite such dizzy heights without the contribution of composers of the calibre of Porter, Kern, Gershwin and Berlin. Berlin in particular was at the peak of his powers during this period and much in demand in Hollywood, where he enjoyed great stature (remarkably for a composer he was used as a selling point in trailers for *Top Hat*, shown playing the piano), and we can only be grateful that RKO was able to secure his services for as many as three films in the series.

Most of the songs appear in several guises, not only as dance but also as background music, in expert and often very beautiful arrangements; these are the work of the various musical directors, orchestrators and arrangers involved in the series – Max Steiner and Robert Russell Bennett are the most prominent among them – and of Astaire's rehearsal pianist, Hal Borne, all of whom contributed enormously to the impact and appeal of the musical numbers.

Of the thirty-eight individual songs in the series, about half a dozen feature in purely vocal form while the great majority also form the basis of a dance (or in one case part of a dance) at some stage in the film, usually immediately following the song. Nine songs are given to various 'other' performers, although two of the nine are also sung by Astaire and/or Rogers. Of the remainder, by far the greater number are solos for Astaire, including eight performed independently of Rogers (most of which involve a chorus or other performers) and ten sung directly to her; six are solos for Rogers; and six are duets, though Rogers makes only a minor contribution to one of them. One further song ('Bojangles of Harlem') is, uniquely, sung only by a female chorus while Astaire performs a dance routine, solo and in partnership with them. There are also three instrumental compositions, all involving Rogers in some capacity, two of which feature in dance form and the third as the accompaniment to a silent, non-dancing sequence.[1]

Numbers for performers other than Astaire and Rogers

The first of this group, and the first musical number of the series, makes an early appearance, right at the beginning of *The Gay Divorcee*. 'Don't Let It Bother You' is hardly the most memorable of songs, but it is harmless enough and serves a purpose. Sung by a group of French chorus girls on the revolving stage of a Paris nightclub, who manipulate little finger dolls as they sing, it leads to a shot of Astaire and Edward Everett Horton, sitting at one of the restaurant tables (and likewise engaged with finger dolls). The two men find themselves without their wallets when the time comes to pay the bill, and Astaire reluctantly agrees to

The musical numbers

Numbers that feature as both song and dance are grouped below according to their performance as *song* (excepting 'Bojangles of Harlem', which is an Astaire dance but sung only by a chorus). For example, 'Night and Day' is listed as an Astaire solo, even though it also features as a dance duet. The appendix gives an analysis of the different guises in which the numbers appear.

	For other performers	Instrumental	Solos for Astaire Independent of Rogers	In partnership with Rogers	Solos for Rogers	Duets
The Gay Divorcee	Don't Let It Bother You Let's K-nock K-neez The Continental		A Needle in a Haystack	Night and Day	The Continental	
Roberta	Russian Song Yesterdays Smoke Gets in Your Eyes Lovely to Look At		Let's Begin		I'll Be Hard to Handle	I Won't Dance Lovely to Look At
Top Hat			No Strings Top Hat, White Tie and Tails	Isn't This a Lovely Day (To Be Caught in the Rain) Cheek to Cheek	The Piccolino	
Follow the Fleet	Get Thee Behind Me, Satan But Where Are You?		We Saw the Sea I'd Rather Lead a Band	Let's Face the Music and Dance	Let Yourself Go	I'm Putting All My Eggs in One Basket
Swing Time		Waltz in Swing Time	Bojangles of Harlem	The Way You Look Tonight Never Gonna Dance		Pick Yourself Up A Fine Romance
Shall We Dance		Walking the Dog	Slap That Bass Shall We Dance	Beginner's Luck They Can't Take That Away From Me	They All Laughed	Let's Call the Whole Thing Off
Carefree		Golf Solo		I Used to Be Color Blind Change Partners	The Yam	

perform in order to prove that he is the famous dancer that Horton says he is. His short display of tap to a lively arrangement of the song naturally has the desired effect, and, more importantly, establishes who and what he is before he meets Rogers.

The less said about the second number in this film given to other performers the better. 'Let's K-nock K-neez' (the title is an accurate reflection of the content), staged in the English seaside hotel where the majority of the action takes place, is entirely dispensable. Notable only for the appearance of a young Betty Grable, who makes overtures to (of all people) Horton, most uninvitingly clad in shorts and a vest, it is the only number combining both song and dance that does not feature either Astaire or Rogers. As John Mueller observes, 'The best moment is at the end, when Astaire enters in the background, quietly watching. Standing still, he commands more attention than all the frantic performers in the foreground.'[2]

'The Continental', a big production number which involves most of the cast at some point, as well as a chorus of dancers, is by far the lengthiest, and most tedious, musical event in *The Gay Divorcee* (and indeed the series), although the song itself won an Oscar in 1934 for its composers Con Conrad and Herb Magidson.[3] Erik Rhodes puts his heart and soul into his rendition of the song, complete with accordion accompaniment, but it is as superfluous as the subsequent turn by another singer (Lillian Miles), who makes her first and last appearance in the film with a rather loud performance, first on screen and then in voiceover as the dancing chorus continue to dominate the proceedings. The number only justifies its existence in the opportunity it gives Astaire and Rogers to dance together on two separate occasions, beginning and ending the event in style.

There are no extraneous performers in *Roberta*, and the four lyrical Jerome Kern songs that belong to this group are all given to the film's official star, Irene Dunne. She sings the first two, the 'Russian Song' and 'Yesterdays', with a guitar accompaniment provided by the doorman (Dunne's cousin and, like her, a member of the Russian royalty), to Madame Roberta as she takes a rest on her sofa. 'Yesterdays' ends, in tastefully understated style, in the death of the old lady, one arm dropping lifelessly to her side after the performers, with Randolph Scott and Astaire in attendance, have quietly left the darkened room. 'Yesterdays' is a memorably beautiful ballad, the 'Russian Song' (based

on a folksong) less memorable but an appropriately gentle lullaby, and Dunne sings them both with attractive simplicity and feeling, if not the most mellow of voices. She brings the same qualities to the film's best-known song, the classic 'Smoke Gets in Your Eyes', which she performs, dressed in regal fashion complete with tiara, to an appreciative private audience in the Café Russe (**3.1**). The number is well integrated into the action, beginning in impromptu fashion as Dunne hums the tune strummed by a band of balalaika players. Halfway through she spots Scott and breaks off; he is angry with her for selling his girlfriend a dress he disapproves of, and they exchange some harsh words before she resumes singing, finally breaking down in tears on the last phrase of the song. Later in the film Astaire and Rogers will perform one of their loveliest dance duets to the same music, this time in a very slow orchestral arrangement.

The music of Dunne's final song, the Oscar-nominated 'Lovely to Look At',[4] does sterling service in the latter part of the film, when it is first heard as an orchestral accompaniment to the lengthy musical fashion show staged to showcase Roberta's new designs. Beautifully gowned again, Dunne begins the song (in her by now familiar style) as she makes her entrance at the top of the stairs; the orchestra rises to its feet in admiration and doubles as a male chorus as she descends, watched by an entranced Scott. Part of the lyric – 'You're lovely to look at, delightful to know and heaven to kiss' – is more appropriately sung by a man, and Astaire duly takes it over when Rogers enters later in the proceedings.

Harriet Hilliard does not have Dunne's star quality, or a voice of any distinction, and she gives insipid performances of the two songs allotted her in *Follow the Fleet* (not among Irving Berlin's best). The first, 'Get Thee Behind Me, Satan', was apparently originally intended for Rogers in *Top Hat*,[5] but it seems an unlikely song for her, quite different in style from the lively, upbeat numbers she does perform. To make an impression it needs a singer with a more arresting voice and considerably more personality than Hilliard possesses. Having gone out of her way to attract Scott's attentions, and succeeding, she now reflects, somewhat improbably, that she might be unwisely succumbing to temptation. Later, when he rebuffs her at a party given

3.1 Irene Dunne, regally dressed, gives an impromptu performance of 'Smoke Gets in Your Eyes' in the Café Russe. She has not yet spotted Randolph Scott, who will cause her to break down at the end of the song. Seated on her right is her cousin (Victor Varconi), emigré Russian prince turned doorman and guitar-player.

by the woman he has now taken up with, she gives an appropriately tearful account of 'But Where Are You?' – a public performance, ostensibly in Rogers' stead (Rogers being slightly indisposed after an unfortunate experience with some bicarbonate of soda earlier in the day), but again this rather mooning ballad is not at all Rogers' type of song. It would suit Dunne better, and one can imagine her injecting more spirit into it, and attracting more sympathy in the process.

Instrumental numbers

The three purely instrumental numbers in the series could not be more unlike each other, both as pieces of music and in the use to which they are put. The first, the 'Waltz in Swing Time', does in fact appear briefly in vocal form, sung by a chorus over the opening credits of *Swing Time*, but its main appearance is as the music for a dance duet, performed as an exhibition piece by Astaire and Rogers about halfway through the film, in the full bloom of their romance. It has no real dramatic purpose but is one of the outstanding highlights of the film and the series. It is also briefly reprised later, in the very different context of the 'Never Gonna Dance' sequence. The music was composed, largely by Robert Russell Bennett, at Astaire's request;[6] he wanted a waltz that would swing, and that is certainly what he got. It is an exhilarating piece, bold, brash, rhythmically complex and full of verve, yet with quieter, more lyrical moments – the perfect complement to a dance that is both brilliantly virtuosic and raptly intimate.

There is no dance to 'Walking the Dog', but the two episodes in *Shall We Dance* that it accompanies, during which Astaire gradually breaks down Rogers' resistance on board the *Queen Anne* by cheekily imitating and then upstaging her as she walks her little pet terrier on deck, are as effective a piece of courtship as any of the Astaire–Rogers dance duets. George Gershwin's music, imaginatively scored by the composer himself for a chamber ensemble including piano and saxophone, instead of the usual large orchestra, is both enjoyable in its own right (it was later published separately as *Promenade*) and ideally suited to the occasion, its catchy theme setting a sprightly walking pace and lending a cheery, jovial air to the proceedings. *Shall We Dance* may be lamentably short of full-scale dance duets for Astaire and Rogers, but it is certainly not short of high-quality music.

Astaire's 'Golf Solo' in *Carefree* is a dance of sorts, but, as the title suggests, it is notable more for his wizardry with a golf club than for dance as such. Like 'Walking the Dog', it plays an important role in the development of his relationship with Rogers, though this time (as can be expected from *Carefree*) the number ends with a far from conclusive victory for Astaire. He is practising his drives on a stretch of grass in the grounds of the Medwick Country Club when he catches sight of Rogers, just arrived on the scene and observing him from a small bridge a few feet away. Last seen leaving his consulting room after turning the tables on him in their disastrous first meeting, she laughs mockingly when Astaire misses his next two shots, and taunts him with his theories about the mind ('Maybe you were hitting it with your subconscious mind – you know, the one that dreams?'). Then she asks him what happened to his theory of coordination – 'doing several things at the same time' – and Astaire immediately takes up the challenge, instructing his Scots golfing coach to 'set 'em up'.

Now the music begins, Astaire taking out his harmonica (much to Rogers' surprise, though the viewer has seen him playing it in the opening sequence with Ralph Bellamy) to demonstrate, with an appropriately Scottish melody (Berlin's 'Since They Turned "Loch Lomond" into Swing', never identified by its title), that he can play it and tap dance at the same time. Rogers settles down to watch him with an amused smile, and he looks up at her in self-satisfied fashion more than once in the course of the number, though in the interests of avoiding any distracting intercutting there are no further reaction shots. After a brief turn on the harmonica he abandons it for golf clubs, first doing a Scottish 'sword' dance over two clubs crossed diagonally on the ground (a comic episode, involving what Mueller accurately describes as 'the delicate leg-shake-while-fluttering-flaps-of-sweater step'[7]); then hits a few balls with one of the clubs while continuing to dance; then with the side of his right foot deftly kicks five more, neatly lined up in a row, despatching a sixth with his club; and finally, as the music reaches its climax, drives another five, powerfully and with stunning timing and accuracy, into the far distance.[8] Ending his tour de force with a flourish of dance, he looks up expectantly, justifiably pleased with himself – only to discover that Rogers has left the scene.

Her appearance out of nowhere at the start of the sequence is slightly contrived (though it is credible enough as she too frequents the country club), but the ensuing dialogue is cleverly linked to her first meeting with Astaire, and his amazingly well-coordinated display follows legitimately from it. She is evidently impressed, for when they next meet, in a bicycle-riding sequence, and she enlightens him as to why she was initially so hostile, her manner turns much more cordial, and she is positively solicitous when he suffers an undignified tumble into a bush after his brakes fail.

Solos for Astaire

Solos performed independently of Rogers

The nine numbers in this category are a diverse group, demonstrating Astaire's extraordinary versatility as singer and dancer. They range from the simplicity of 'A Needle in a Haystack' (*The Gay Divorcee*) to the elaborate staging, with special effects, of 'Bojangles of Harlem' (*Swing Time*); from the ultra-elegance and refinement of 'Top Hat, White Tie and Tails' (*Top Hat*) to the informal jamming of 'Slap That Bass' (*Shall We Dance*). With the exception of 'A Needle in a Haystack' and 'No Strings' (*Top Hat*), which share a broadly common structure and style, no two numbers are alike; and with the exception of 'Slap That Bass' all of them have a legitimate place in the action of the films. Though none are performed (knowingly) for Rogers' benefit, or in her presence (as are all the songs in the next group), four of them have an important connection with her.

The first of these, Con Conrad and Herb Magidson's 'A Needle in a Haystack', the first full-scale solo for Astaire in *The Gay Divorcee*, for all its (apparent) simplicity sets a standard that is never really surpassed later in the series, despite the greater complexity and inventiveness of some of the other numbers. The sequence, which takes place in the living room of Astaire's London home, follows almost immediately on his first meeting with Rogers. She has returned the coat he lent her after tearing her dress on their first meeting, and, disappointed that she has not included any note, or her address, in the parcel, he declares to Horton that he is going to start looking for her. 'Well, it shouldn't be difficult,' responds Horton, on his way out, 'After all, there are only three million women in London.' Whereupon Astaire, sitting on his sofa in his dressing gown, starts to sing, with a lyric that begins as naturally as speech, and could not be more appropriate to the situation: 'It's just like looking for a needle in a haystack, / Searching for a moonbeam in the blue, / Still I've got to find you.' It is a fine song, easily the best in the film after 'Night and Day', its lilting, gently descending melody perfectly expressing Astaire's yearning, and its rising, more upbeat middle section his determination, to find the woman he has so hopelessly fallen for: 'I'll roam the town in hopes that we'll meet, / Look at each face I pass on the street' – which is exactly what he does at the conclusion of his performance.

The dance that gradually comes into being with the second verse is an Astaire classic. His valet enters with a selection of ties, and Astaire, still singing, casually throws off his dressing gown, chooses a tie, leans pensively on the mantelpiece as the verse ends, and, as the music takes on a more insistent beat, starts tapping. Unstoppable, he dances his way effortlessly round the room as he completes his dress, finally leaving as the valet tosses him his hat and umbrella. The music ends with the dance, but resumes immediately as he roams the streets, apparently for days on end, until he finally (and quite literally) bumps into Rogers in her car.

Only one other Astaire solo in this group is more seamlessly integrated into the action of the film: 'No Strings', from *Top Hat*, which directly precipitates his first meeting with Rogers. Here Astaire breaks spontaneously into song on Horton's suggesting that he should find himself a wife, but this time the song emerges from dialogue with no perceptible break. One moment he is speaking – 'In me you see a youth who's completely on the loose – no yens, no yearnings, no strings, no connections' – and the next he is singing: 'no ties to my affections, / I'm fancy free . . . '. (The last four words of dialogue are in fact the first words of the song, heightening the organic relationship between the two.) The dance begins just as spontaneously, and, like 'A Needle in a Haystack', involves tapping in an improvisatory fashion around the room (with Horton instead of Astaire's valet for an audience). But the tapping this time is rather more vigorous; and the dance is brought to an untimely conclusion by Rogers' appearance at the door to confront the perpetrator of the noise that has disturbed her sleep.

The song itself is a typically catchy, upbeat Berlin number, but more important for our purposes is the manner and quality of Astaire's singing. He gives exceptionally fine performances throughout the series, and though 'No Strings' is not the most outstanding example it does dem-

onstrate very clearly why Astaire was such a first-rate singer in his field. Berlin himself summed it up neatly when he said: 'I'd rather have Fred Astaire introduce one of my songs than any singer I know – not because he has a great voice, but because his delivery and diction are so good that he can put over a song like nobody else.'[9] The pianist and actor Oscar Levant went even further, declaring (in 1965) that 'Fred Astaire is the best singer of songs the movie world has ever known';[10] and Rick Altman, in *The American Film Musical*, gives one of the reasons why, pointing out that Astaire's natural, untrained singing style – a seamless extension of his speaking ('song as speech with pitch') – was perfectly suited to musicals, where 'singing is not a learned art . . . but a natural expression of a character's emotions'.[11] That Astaire also brought a great musicality, feeling and eloquence to his singing is demonstrated most clearly by the group of lyrical love songs with which he woos Rogers.

Like 'No Strings', his first solo in *Roberta* also precipitates his first meeting with Rogers, though not quite so seamlessly. 'Let's Begin' is a comic number, performed by Astaire's band as an impromptu audition piece for the benefit of the Countess Scharwenka in the hope of securing a job. Rogers, newly charmed by 'big, beautiful American' Randolph Scott and readily agreeing to hear what his friends sound like, is seen tapping her feet in time to the infectiously cheery music, gradually dancing her way onto the balcony overlooking the players. Astaire, in the middle of a routine in which he has been singing and generally cavorting about with members of the band (including a man with a falsetto voice and a woman's wig), spots her and interrupts his performance, whereupon Rogers recognises him in turn and hastily disappears inside. The band continues to play while Astaire rushes after her, running into Scott on his way up, and the music comes to a natural end just before their meeting takes place – with Astaire unaware that his old friend and the Polish countess that Scott is so eager to introduce him to are one and the same person.

The last of the songs in this group that have a connection with Rogers occurs near the end of the lengthy, elaborate production number that concludes *Shall We Dance*, performed by Astaire with (variously) a corps de ballet, a solo ballerina and a chorus of Rogers lookalikes. The lively title song (**3.2**) introduces the most enjoyable section of the number, after the rather ghastly ballet sequences, and occupies a unique posi-

3.2 Astaire, fronting a chorus of Rogers lookalikes, sings the lively title song from *Shall We Dance* – unaware that his estranged wife is shortly to join him on stage.

tion. Astaire sings it unaware that Rogers, from whom he is estranged, has been sitting in the audience watching him, and he performs the brief solo dance that follows equally unaware that she is about to join him on stage as one of the chorus – a ploy that of course ends in their reconciliation. The number is thus intimately related to the plot, and its dramatic purpose is served before the pair actually begin their final dance duet. After the smoothest of transitions they conclude their performance with a brief reprise of the song that led to the film's other dance of reconciliation, 'They All Laughed', gleefully declaiming 'They all said we'd never get together, / They laughed at us and how, / But ho ho ho! Who's got the last laugh now?' – the (slightly revised) lyric fitting the new situation to perfection.

The remaining numbers in this group, having no connection with Rogers, have no real function in the plot. But most of them are at least superficially integrated into their surrounding material and have a legitimate place in the proceedings, whether in setting the scene and establishing the tone of the film (as in the first number from *Follow the Fleet*) or, more frequently, in simply showing Astaire in performance in his screen role. The first, 'Top Hat, White Tie and Tails', the title number from *Top Hat*, falls into the latter category; one of Astaire's most celebrated routines, it epitomises the elegance and sophistication that are synonymous with his name. Performed with a male chorus, all dressed in the manner prescribed (**3.3**), it forms part of the London show, produced by impresario Horton, in which Astaire stars, and which is referred to several times in the early scenes. Astaire's winning delivery of Berlin's masterly song (both melodically memorable and rhythmically complex) is as immaculate as the dance that follows, in which – to mention just one notable feature – he makes endlessly inventive use of his cane, finally 'shooting' each member of the chorus with it as if with a rifle. To quote the lyric, Astaire's performance 'simply reeks with class'. The sequence is the last of the film's London scenes, and we next see Astaire in Venice, where he has flown with Horton in pursuit of Rogers – a move hastily determined in the last few seconds before he goes on stage.

Both 'We Saw the Sea' and 'I'd Rather Lead a Band' could be removed from *Follow the Fleet* without detriment to the plot, but the film would be the poorer. 'We Saw the Sea', the opening number (following some brief scene-setting shots of ships and sailors), establishes

3.3 'Top Hat, White Tie and Tails': the Astaire elegance and sophistication personified in this celebrated routine. Astaire's cane is an essential feature of his solo dance and doubles as a rifle in the number's concluding sequence.

the carefree, nautical theme with a cheerful tune and some diverting rhymes, as Astaire, leading a band of sailors on deck, complains of the dullness of navy life ('Instead of a girl or two in a taxi / We were compelled to look at the Black Sea'). The number ends with Astaire doing a mock collapse after the last line – 'We're never seasick / But we are awful sick of sea'; and the action begins as Randolph Scott announces that they have shore leave – 'to give the girls in 'Frisco their big break'.

'I'd Rather Lead a Band', with another very catchy tune, simply reinforces Astaire's credentials as a song-and-dance man, leader of the ship's unofficial band. Staged three-quarters of an hour into the film, after the shore leave has been abruptly terminated (leaving both Rogers and Harriet Hilliard in the lurch), it is integrated into a wholly superfluous scene in which Astaire, the band and a non-singing chorus of sailors, all in dress whites, mount an impromptu performance for some visiting dignitaries. Astaire conducts, sings (with some quite outrageous rhymes – 'If Josephine had left Napoleon and climbed in my lap, / I'd say "Go back to Nap", / I'd rather lead a band'), taps, inspects the chorus and generally has a good time – as does his enthusiastic audience.

Astaire's next solo number, 'Bojangles of Harlem', from *Swing Time*, is his most adventurous yet, though equally irrelevant to the plot. It is staged immediately after the teasing off-screen kiss in his dressing room: after Rogers leaves he bounds onto the chair in front of the mirror to apply his makeup, elatedly singing the opening phrase of the song to himself, which leads neatly into the performance. That's all the singing he does, the female chorus taking over the vocals on stage. In an ostentatious, sporty costume and blackface (reflecting the subject of the song, the black tap dancer Bill 'Bojangles' Robinson),[12] Astaire makes an extraordinary entrance behind a gigantic pair of outstretched legs, and in the second part of this action-packed number dances against a back projection of three giant shadows of himself – his first use of special effects in the series. When he takes his bow (after an infectiously rhythmical solo display of tap) he spots his fiancée in the audience, to his dismay, and the number leads smoothly into the next stage of the action, the fiancée leaving her seat to follow him to his dressing room.

There is no such transition either before or after 'Slap That Bass', from *Shall We Dance*, the one wholly gratuitous number in this group, and the least successful in every respect. Staged in the 'spacious, shiny, immaculately white, and preposterously unreal'[13] engine room of the

Queen Anne shortly after Astaire and Rogers have boarded it for their voyage back to New York, it begins with Astaire watching appreciatively as an all-black jazz band have a jamming session. He takes up the song after one of the band has sung a verse, and then begins to dance around the large space at his disposal. In one episode giant pistons start moving, very rhythmically, forming a shadowy backdrop against which he imitates their movements.[14] It's all very novel, but the dance lacks coherence, and given the absence of any dramatic motivation or even the slightest link with the plot, fails to justify its inclusion in the film.

Solos performed in partnership with Rogers

No such criticism can be levelled against the ten songs in this group, all of which are at the very least convincingly motivated and well integrated into their respective films.[15] Seven of the songs form the prelude to a dance duet; one of these, 'Let's Face the Music and Dance' (from *Follow the Fleet*) is extraneous to the main action of the film but integral to the staged drama in which it is incorporated, while the remainder play an essential part in the development of the plot. They also exhibit two defining elements of the series that are not to be found in Astaire's solos performed independently of Rogers: complementarity and romance; for all the songs either reflect or precipitate a development in the romantic relationship between the pair.

The group contains some of the finest, most memorable songs of the series, and they find in Astaire the perfect interpreter. He excels in the lyrical love songs with which he woos Rogers, while she, listening with varying degrees of pleasure, sorrow, acquiescence or resistance, quietly contributes to the impact of each number. Many of the songs are in fact not just songs but mini-dramas, in which Rogers does a lot more than listen, and Astaire a lot more than sing; the importance of Rogers' contribution is reflected in the heading of this section. They both act their way through all the numbers they perform together (both solos and duets), and just how much their acting skills contribute to their musical performances can be judged by listening to the soundtrack of the songs: half the impact is lost when the visual element is missing.

The first of these mini-dramas is the first romantic song of the series, Cole Porter's 'Night and Day' from *The Gay Divorcee*. The music of 'A Needle in a Haystack' strikes up dramatically (taking over from the nonchalant 'Don't Let It Bother You') when, some time after their second meeting, with its aborted picnic, Astaire and Rogers spot each other by chance in the hotel where she is to meet her co-respondent – she (wearing a white ballgown) sitting at a table with her aunt, he on a balcony overlooking the restaurant. Astaire of course knows nothing of the planned assignation, and Rogers, embarrassed by the whole affair, does not want him to find out about it. She rushes off; he chases after her, and as the music leads into the theme of 'Night and Day' he catches up with her in a romantically deserted dance area looking out onto the sea at night. They have a brief conversation, she wondering what he is doing in the hotel, he declaring that he has been 'thinking of you, longing for you, waiting to hear from you'. She reveals that she tried to phone him but was told that he had left London, and, delighted, he presses her to stay; she asks him not to, but when he complies her face falls. 'Don't go,' he says (and she smiles happily), 'I've so many things to say to you'; and so the song begins. Rogers keeps her smile as he sings the first few lines, with their insistently repeated notes, 'Like the beat, beat, beat of the tom-tom . . . like the tick, tick, tock of the stately clock . . . like the drip, drip, drip of the raindrops', but as he reaches the point – 'a voice within me keeps repeating you, you, you' – her expression changes and she turns and walks away. (Throughout the rest of the song, and the ensuing dance, her actions and expression reveal her conflicting emotions – not wanting to leave but not daring to stay.) He follows her, singing Porter's beautiful chromatic melody with heartfelt yearning and ardour, the lyric expressing precisely, but more eloquently and passionately, the state of mind he has already admitted to her – 'this longing for you follows wherever I go . . . / In the silence of my lonely room / I think of you night and day . . . ' She has been sitting, facing him, but on those words she walks away again; each time she moves off he stops her, up to and beyond the triumphantly upbeat ending of the song, until finally he draws her into dance – and conquers her remaining resistance.

Completely different in mood, but similar in pattern, is the first of Astaire's two songs of seduction in *Top Hat*, 'Isn't This a Lovely Day (To Be Caught in the Rain)'. A delightfully playful number, it occurs at an early stage in the film, before Rogers has had the chance to mistake Astaire's identity. Following up their promising first meeting, he has purloined a hansom cab in order to drive her to the nearby riding stables, and has mischievously revealed his presence by some rhythmic tapping as she sits inside – prompting a secret smile from her. We next see Rogers riding up to a bandstand in the park, where she takes shelter from a thunderstorm. Astaire draws up in his cab and offers to rescue her, but she firmly resists all his friendly overtures; then, frightened by a sudden clap of thunder, she rushes instinctively into his arms, retreating in embarrassment a moment later. She sits on a small bench, and Astaire sets about enlightening her as to the causes of thunder, taking the opportunity to move closer and closer to her as he demonstrates the physical processes involved. 'When a clumsy cloud from here meets a fluffy little cloud from there, he billows towards her' (he approaches accordingly, and Rogers retreats); 'She scurries away and he scuds right up to her' (he sits down, and she moves to the end of the bench); 'She cries a little, and there you have your shower' (her back to Astaire, she is now smiling); 'He comforts her, they spark – that's the lightning. They kiss' (she turns on him, shocked at the implication) '– Thunder.' On cue, a drumroll provides the thunderclap; she is startled but then relaxes as Astaire, with a satisfied smile, launches into the jauntily tuneful, eminently appropriate song – 'The weather is frightening; / The thunder and lightning / Seem to be having their way. / But as far as I'm concerned it's a lovely day.'

Rogers, riding crop in hand, gets up, but her smile to the camera reveals that she has no thought of escaping him; he follows her as she moves to another bench and sits down again, and from then on she listens with not even a semblance of resistance. With, for the most part, her back to Astaire and her face to the camera, she provides an expressive silent commentary on his singing (an amused smile, a glance in his direction or up at the sky), making it quite clear to the viewer that she does not find his intimations of a cosy togetherness away from the stormy weather at all disagreeable (**3.4**). His performance is, indeed, highly engaging, and he gives both words and music their full worth, combining lightheartedness with ardour. 'Let the rain pitter patter / But it really doesn't matter / If the skies are gray. / Long as I can be with you it's a lovely day,' he sings finally; then getting up, and whistling the tune, he casually initiates the next stage of the number, a playful dance that will end with the pair joyfully and unequivocally united.

By the time they next meet in dance Rogers is unhappily convinced that Astaire is the husband of her best friend (Helen Broderick). The action has moved from London to the Lido in Venice, where Broderick

3.4 'Isn't This a Lovely Day (To Be Caught in the Rain)': Taking shelter in a bandstand, Rogers is clearly not displeased to hear Astaire declare that the inclement weather has done him a favour by bringing them together.

has been taking the sea air for her health, and Rogers has tried, without success, to compromise Astaire with a fabricated tale of an affair in Paris. Aware that she believes her husband to have flirted with her, but unaware that Astaire is the man in question, Broderick is looking forward to introducing her two young friends (with matrimony in mind), only to be robbed of the pleasure – and the chance to clear up the misunderstanding – when Astaire greets Rogers by name as he joins them for dinner in their hotel. Around them, couples are dancing (to the music of 'Cheek to Cheek'), and to Rogers' embarrassment and confusion Broderick encourages the pair to 'run along and dance and don't give me another thought'. Reluctantly, Rogers complies, and Broderick adds to her confusion by egging her on with significant winks and gestures. Finally Rogers gives in, declaring 'Well if Madge doesn't care I certainly don't', to which Astaire, blithely unaware of her misapprehension, replies 'Neither do I. All I know is that it's – ' (and here the song begins) 'Heaven, I'm in heaven, / And my heart beats so that I can hardly speak; / And I seem to find the happiness I seek / When we're out together dancing cheek to cheek.'

Rogers listens happily, her eyes fixed warmly on Astaire, a smile of pleasure on her face (**3.5**). She looks lovely, in an elegant white feathered dress and a most becoming hairstyle, a single plait framing her face to give her a very pure, chaste appearance; and her manner is equally chaste, for she does nothing to draw attention to herself. Astaire for his part gives a truly wonderful performance of Berlin's beautiful song, negotiating an ever-rising melodic line with extraordinary delicacy and ease,[16] and, as the music modulates briefly to the darker minor key, declaiming passionately 'Dance with me / I want my arm about you'. Throughout, he fits his actions precisely to the words; he is always 'cheek to cheek' with Rogers when the lyric demands it. The song ended, the orchestral music builds up dramatically, and they move away from the other couples to a secluded area where their purely social dancing will lead without pause into one of their most celebrated duets.

If integration within the plot had been the overriding consideration in their next film, *Follow the Fleet*, there would have been no opportunity for Astaire the gum-chewing sailor to woo Rogers with a song as romantic as 'Cheek to Cheek'; but fortunately a place was found outside of the prosaic script for 'Let's Face the Music and Dance', one of the supreme musical highlights of the series. The only link with the plot is that the number is performed as part of a benefit show on board the *Connie Martin*, a ship which the foolish Harriet Hilliard has gone to great expense to salvage for the benefit of the unworthy (and unknowing) Randolph Scott. Staged right at the end of the film, the number enables Astaire and Rogers to shed their limiting on-screen roles and enact a drama that simply oozes glamour and romance. Despite being

3.5 Rogers, still convinced that Astaire is a married man, but throwing caution to the winds, listens with a smile of pleasure as he sings of how heavenly it is to be dancing cheek to cheek with her.

entirely unconnected with the main action of the film it has an internal justification and unity, and it is compelling in both musical and dramatic terms.

The sequence opens with a brief prologue which establishes (without any dialogue) the dramatic and emotional context. Snatches of the song's themes are heard in the scene-setting orchestral accompaniment as Astaire, at first surrounded by attentive young women, loses all his money at the gambling table and is subsequently shunned by them. As they parade past, ostentatiously turning away from him in disdain (the scene has changed to a shiny, glamorous and typically unrealistic black and white set overlooking the sea at night), the melody of Berlin's superb song is heard for the first time in its true colours, sumptuously played on low strings. The music then changes to a dramatic, transitional phase as Astaire stubs out his cigarette and takes out his gun. He is about to shoot himself when he catches sight of Rogers, elegantly gowned, and also on the point of suicide, climbing onto a balustrade to throw herself into the sea. He pulls her back and, with a smile, shows her his gun, as if to say 'Me too'; she tries to snatch it, whereupon he flings it away and she moves off, slowly, to stand helplessly with her hands clasped. He shows her his empty wallet, and she leans in despair against a wall. With a smile he flings the wallet away – and then the melody returns as, gently, tenderly, he abandons gesture for song: 'There may be trouble ahead, / But while there's moonlight and music, / And love and romance, / Let's face the music and dance.' On the word 'romance' Rogers closes her eyes in silent misery and turns her face to the wall. As Astaire completes the first verse she turns and walks away, but dreamily, not as if to escape him; he follows her and she makes no resistance as he puts his arm in hers, and when he sings the words 'love and romance' for the second time her expression is less despairing.

Astaire's performance is, as ever, immaculate, his singing lyrical and expressive while at the same time light and airy, the perfect complement to the deeper, richer orchestral accompaniment. Rogers, wonderfully convincing in her entirely unaccustomed role as a tragic, heartbroken figure, demonstrates again that she can convey a world of meaning with nuances of expression. She scarcely looks at Astaire until the last few bars of the song, but on his final, emphatic exhortation to face the music and dance she meets his eyes with something like acceptance. She is ready now to be drawn into that dance, the glorious duet that concludes the number.

Drama and glamour give way to the uncomplicated expression of love in the next song Astaire sings to Rogers, Jerome Kern's Oscar-winning 'The Way You Look Tonight' from *Swing Time*. Unlike the ones considered so far, it does not lead to a dance, and it does not emerge quite so seamlessly from the preceding dialogue or action, but it is convincingly enough integrated into the scene. A week has elapsed since the pair's first meeting, and their triumphant demonstration of dancing prowess in 'Pick Yourself Up', but Rogers is annoyed with Astaire because of his penchant for gambling (which has caused them to miss an audition at a prestigious nightclub) and refuses to see him. Helen Broderick, who has benefited handsomely from his winnings, argues that he was not to blame, and that Rogers is being foolishly stubborn in missing the rescheduled audition. Reluctantly Rogers agrees to let him see her, but she then goes off to the bathroom to wash her hair. Astaire enters, but Rogers (from inside the bathroom) gives him a hostile reception. He agrees to leave, but first acknowledges that 'maybe I was wrong the other night'. She relents, confessing that maybe *she* was wrong; they argue; he says goodbye and pretends to leave; she calls him back – whereupon he walks over to the piano, plays an introductory few bars, and sings a tender love song.

Mueller observes that 'since the Astaire–Rogers romance has not yet progressed that far, the song is delivered as a randomly selected ballad Astaire happens to have on the tip of his larynx at the moment.'[17] But he sings it with heartfelt sincerity, and Rogers, interrupting her hair-washing to listen, is clearly touched. 'Some day, when I'm awfully low, / And the world is cold, / I will feel a glow just thinking of you / And the way you look tonight,' he sings (and by now his piano accompaniment is supported by an orchestra), in the only song of the series that he addresses to Rogers *without* looking at her. Quietly she opens the bathroom door and stands there, in her dressing gown, a towel round her neck and her hair covered in shampoo, watching him; then she slowly walks over to him and puts her hand, very tenderly, on his shoulder. As he finishes the song he looks up, in a state of bliss, but this mood of exquisite romantic togetherness is shattered when he sees the way she actually looks.

The scene ends with Rogers rushing back to the bathroom in dismay, but the music is immediately reprised in the next scene, which shows Georges Metaxa conducting his band and singing the last few bars of the song, addressing them to Rogers as she dances with Astaire among other couples in the nightclub. His brief performance, horribly smarmy and suggestive, is quite excruciating, and if the viewer has not already been convinced of the superiority of Astaire's beautifully simple, unaffected delivery the comparison with Metaxa will be illuminating.

Though the song as performed by Astaire does not (for obvious reasons) lead directly to a dance duet, the music is again reprised, in a ravishing orchestral arrangement, in the 'Never Gonna Dance' sequence towards the end of the film. Here, unusually, it takes over from the theme of 'Never Gonna Dance' itself as Astaire finishes the song, the last note of the refrain doubling seamlessly as the first note of the reprise. The circumstances in which he sings this rather odd song will be familiar from chapter 2: a despairing last meeting between the lovers before (as they suppose) they part for good, each to marry someone they do not love. Astaire, having declared that now he has danced with Rogers he's never going to dance again, halts her with the song as she turns to leave, walking slowly up one side of a curving double staircase to the exit. The camera shows him from above throughout his performance, though not from Rogers' viewpoint. The melody is not as immediately memorable as Kern's other songs for this film (though the refrain is haunting), and the lyric is very strange, with some puzzling references (one Major Edward Bowes[18] and the Marx Brothers among them). It is certainly not a conventional love song – 'Though I'm left without a penny / The wolf was discreet, he left me my feet and / So I put them down on anything / But the la belle, la perfectly swell romance' (the last line a reference to the dialogue in the 'Fine Romance' sequence earlier in the film) – although it includes an unambiguous expression of love: 'And to heaven, I give a vow / To adore you . . . ' But, puzzling though it is, Astaire sings it with such yearning and conviction, and Rogers listens with such wistful, unquestioning attention, that it seems entirely appropriate. On the last iteration of the mournful refrain Astaire moves towards her and she to him; he looks down in despair, then, to the beautiful theme of 'The Way You Look Tonight', turns to watch her as she carries on walking down the stairs and away from him. He follows her, and gradually it becomes apparent that the moment of their inevitable parting will not come until they have danced together for one last time. In the course of their duet, which features a reprise not only of 'The Way You Look Tonight' but also of the 'Waltz in Swing Time', the 'Never Gonna Dance' theme itself is transformed from a mournful lament into a resounding blast for full orchestra, reaching a furious climax in the last few moments of the dance.

Dance is conspicuous by its absence at key moments in the film that had the difficult task of following *Swing Time*, and neither of the two songs that Astaire sings to Rogers in *Shall We Dance* leads to a duet with her at any point. In the case of 'Beginner's Luck' it is no great loss: this cheerful Gershwin ditty (which makes its first appearance, in instrumental form, very early in the film, as Astaire the ballet dancer indulges in a little illicit tap in the privacy of his own room) amply fulfils its function in the space of just over a minute allocated to it after the second 'Walking the Dog' sequence. Having successfully wooed Rogers on board ship by the end of this novel episode, Astaire walks over to the guard rail with her, and they have a brief, lighthearted conversation. 'Look how lucky I am,' he declares happily. 'The first time I find myself on a boat with somebody like you, it turns out to be – you!' The song, celebrating his beginner's luck, follows without pause, and Rogers, her little pet dog in her arms, listens with a contented smile on her face. In typically anti-romantic style, Astaire's declaration in the song's closing line – 'the first time that I'm in love I'm in love with you' – is greeted by a cacophony of barking from the dogs in the adjacent kennels.

'They Can't Take That Away From Me', which comes at a much less promising stage in their relationship, is in an altogether different class. The film's greatest song, and one of the very finest of the series,[19] it is ideal material for a romantic Astaire–Rogers dance duet, but the opportunity is sadly missed. Like 'Beginner's Luck', Astaire sings it on board ship, but this time it is the ferry to Manhattan, where he and Rogers are returning after their hasty marriage in the New Jersey registry office. The theme of the song is heard as he buys her a corsage from a flower-seller on deck; they get out of their car and (again like 'Beginner's Luck') stand at the guard rail. But instead of celebrating their new union they speak only of how their relationship will shortly end, Astaire with apparent equanimity, Rogers unable to disguise her regret. Astaire, however, makes up for his seemingly casual acceptance of their imminent separation with a wonderfully warm and expressive performance of Gershwin's great ballad, in which he declares that he will never forget her. The lyric avoids sentimentality with its light references to the homely and everyday; among the things about her that he will always remember are 'the way you sip your tea . . . the way you sing off key'. Rogers, fingering her corsage, smiles, but her face takes on a more serious expression when he comes to 'the way you haunt my dreams', and on 'the way you've changed my life' a close-up shows her eyes filled with tears. At the end she looks down, then walks pensively back to the car as the music comes to a gentle stop.

The setting of this scene is, as Mueller observes, not ideal for a romantic dance,[20] and the way the pair are dressed – Rogers in a fur coat and pillbox hat, Astaire in a smart suit and trilby – is equally unsuitable. But nowhere in *Shall We Dance* is the *mood* more ripe, and the film's greatest flaw is its failure to provide a romantic duet for Astaire and Rogers, at this or any other point, to the music of its one outstanding and truly romantic song. The melody reappears many times as background music, in exquisite arrangements, but when a dance finally materialises it is a travesty of what might have been – a duet between Astaire and the ballerina Harriet Hoctor that has nothing romantic about it and serves only to reinforce the enormity of the missed opportunity.[21] When Astaire and Rogers, well past her prime, finally did dance a duet to 'They Can't Take That Away From Me', in *The Barkleys of Broadway*, it unfortunately fell far short of their performances at the height of their partnership, and did nothing to compensate for the omission from *Shall We Dance*.

There is no such problem with Astaire's two solos in *Carefree*, both of which are highly romantic and lead, either directly or shortly afterwards, to a dance duet. They are, however, completely different from each other in style and mood. The first, 'I Used to Be Color Blind', is the song with which Astaire serenades Rogers in her dreams, after she has, on his prescription, eaten a meal of dream-provoking foods. Given the choice of dishes – seafood cocktail with whipped cream, a 'largeish' Welsh rarebit ('and double up on the cheese,' says Rogers), lobster 'with gobs of mayonnaise', cucumbers and buttermilk, and strawberry shortcake – it's a wonder she doesn't have a nightmare; but the meal over, and the rest of the party feeling decidedly queasy, Rogers claims she 'never felt better'. Though she denies being sleepy, she is next seen stretched out on her bed, fully dressed, with a smile on her face; and to the sound of dreamy, indeterminate music, mingled with snatches of dialogue ('cucumbers and buttermilk', 'strawberry shortcake'), the dream sequence begins. Typically, in this film that sees so many reversals of their usual roles, it is Rogers who leads Astaire onto her dream landscape (a suitably unreal sort of tropical affair), but once in place he takes the lead in properly romantic style.

The sequence was originally intended to be shot in colour, and Berlin composed the lyric with this in mind.[22] Thus Astaire sings of 'how a dreary world can suddenly change'; 'I used to be color blind,' he tells Rogers, 'but I met you and now I find / There's green in the grass, / There's gold in the moon, / There's blue in the skies.' The song is short and, though not one of Berlin's greatest, is melodious and fits the purpose well. There is, fortunately, nothing dreamlike about Astaire's singing, which is as unaffectedly lyrical as we have come to expect, and Rogers receives his flattering declaration with a smile of pleasure. First she sits on a bank to listen; then he takes her by the hand and leads

her about the landscape (**3.6**); and finally, inevitably, their steps turn to dance, with a seamless shift into dreamy slow motion.

Many twists and turns of the plot later, Rogers has been hypnotised by Astaire into hating him and loving Ralph Bellamy, who has obtained a court order forbidding Astaire to see or even speak to her again. Astaire, meanwhile, has seen the error of his ways, and with the connivance of Rogers' aunt (Luella Gear) tries to get to Rogers to undo the effects of his hypnosis. Her engagement to Bellamy is being celebrated in the Medwick Country Club, and they and their guests are dancing to the music of 'Change Partners' when Astaire enters with his assistant and co-conspirator, Jack Carson. He asks Gear to dance, and, ignoring his prohibition, manoeuvres his way into the path of Bellamy and Rogers to ask *her* to dance. Bellamy refuses on her behalf, prompting Gear to remark 'You'd better forget it for a while. If you can't talk you can't tell her.' So Astaire resorts to song instead, a song that fits the situation so perfectly it is difficult to believe that Berlin had written it years beforehand, in anticipation of a change of dancing partner at some point in Astaire's career.[23] 'Must you dance ev'ry dance with the same fortunate man?' he sings, very invitingly, while Gear, enjoying her role as decoy, smiles; 'You have danced with him since the music began. / Won't you change partners and dance with me?' Rogers remains impassive, but Bellamy, cheek to cheek with her, glares at Astaire when he continues: 'Must you dance quite so close with your lips touching his face?' Then, preparing the viewer for what is to transpire: 'Ask him to sit this one out and while you're alone / I'll tell the waiter to tell him he's wanted on the telephone.' The song, and the dance, over, the obtuse Bellamy is duly lured away to take a call from Miss Satsuma Naguchi (Carson in an amusingly improbable comic turn), while Astaire follows Rogers out into the fresh air to bring his plan to fruition, in a beautifully eloquent dance duet, the last of the series.

None of the numbers in this group is more flawlessly woven into the plot and script, and Astaire's delivery of Berlin's classic song – light, restrained, not so much singing as musical speech – is perfectly attuned to the context. 'Change Partners' is as fine an example as any of Astaire's art as a performer of songs in the film musical.

3.6 'I Used to Be Color Blind': Astaire serenades Rogers in her dreams, describing how she has suddenly brought colour into his dreary world. At this stage in the number the closer screen shot does not include the fairy-tale castle in the background, but it comes into view as the pair cross over onto the giant water-lily leaf on the left and begin their slow-motion dance.

Solos for Rogers

The six songs in this group all involve Astaire to some degree. Four are sung by Rogers largely or entirely for his benefit, and he is in her audience for all or part of the other two. All six form the basis of a dance duet, though in most cases the dance comes a little later in the proceedings. The music of one song, 'Let Yourself Go' (from *Follow the Fleet*), also features in the only solo dance given to Rogers in the series.[24] The songs are all convincingly motivated and well integrated into the dramatic action, though they are not quite so organically related to their surrounding material as are Astaire's solos; most are performed as set pieces, in front of an audience or in rehearsal.

Not surprisingly, none of Rogers' solos are love songs; all are light-hearted and none have a direct bearing on her relationship with Astaire, though she sings one of them ('The Yam', from *Carefree*) in a ploy to entice him into dance. The one song she sings that does have a most intimate bearing on their relationship, 'A Fine Romance' (from *Swing Time*), is shared with Astaire, and as such is grouped with the duets in the next section.

Like Astaire, Rogers did not have an outstanding voice, but she certainly knew how to deliver a song and gives enjoyable performances of all her numbers. Unlike Astaire, who is as fine a singing actor at the start of the series as he is at its close, she demonstrates a marked development, gaining considerably in confidence and poise after *The Gay Divorcee*. (She was, of course, already an experienced performer, but not quite in the style called for in this film.) Here, in 'The Continental', her performance is sweet and animated, but it seems a little dated now. She and Astaire are leaning on a balcony overlooking the dance floor in their hotel; he has just enlightened her as to his true identity, and co-respondent Erik Rhodes is keeping them prisoner until he has fulfilled his commission. The music strikes up, and Astaire, looking at the dancing couples below, remarks that it's 'not a bad tune'. 'It's the newest thing over here,' says Rogers, and when he asks her if she knows the words she nods and starts to sing. 'The Continental' is a song about a song and a dance, the lyric describing the romantic nature of the chore-ography – 'You kiss while you're dancing . . . You stroll together arm in arm, / You nonchalantly glide along with grace and charm' – and thus preparing the way for the duet that will eventually follow. Rogers' singing is fine, but her facial expressions and eye movements are perhaps a little overdone, and her rather unflattering makeup and hairstyle (with girlish fringe) heighten the dated effect. Astaire for his part makes an appreciative and responsive listener – smiling, whistling a few bars, tapping impulsively and clapping his hands on 'A certain rhythm that you can't control'. Finally, unable to resist the temptation any longer, he takes her in his arms and whirls her around the limited space at their disposal. Shortly he will think up a ploy to fool Rhodes so that they can escape to join the couples on the dance floor, in a duet that more than fulfils the expectations generated by the song. The music is later reprised for the brief celebratory 'Table Dance' that rounds off the film.

'The Piccolino', from *Top Hat*, is also a song about a song, and it fulfils much the same function as 'The Continental', occurring at the same stage in the plot. Rogers has finally learnt who Astaire really is, and they are dining in the restaurant of their hotel (it is carnival night in the film's extravagantly unreal version of Venice) while Horton, Broderick and Rhodes are out of the way, thanks to the resourceful Blore. Neither of them knows yet that Rogers' very recent marriage to Rhodes is invalid, and while she feels guilty Astaire declares 'Let's eat, drink and be merry, for tomorrow we have to face him.' The music of 'The Piccolino' is heard, gondolas sail by and the dancing chorus (shown in **5.3**, p. 164) enter. Their display leads without pause into the song, which Rogers sings to Astaire (again an appreciative listener) as they sit at their table. It is a thoroughly appealing performance, lively and expressive without any suspicion of exaggeration, and the song itself is a delight, with a more than usually inventive Berlin lyric on an appropriately Venetian theme. 'By the Adriatic waters / Venetian sons and daughters / Are strumming a new tune upon their guitars,' it begins, and it goes on to describe the composition of the tune in question, 'written by a Latin, / A gondolier who sat in / His home out in Brooklyn and gazed at the stars'. Rogers duly mimes the strumming and the gazing; but on the last line, 'And dance to the strains of that new melody', it is the chorus who take up the invitation for another elaborate display, including a rendition of the song. Finally it is the turn of Astaire and Rogers themselves to take to the floor, as the chorus retreat into the background. As with 'The Continental', the music is reprised in a brief celebratory tag at the end of the film, which also borrows from the choreography of the main duet.

If Rogers was guilty of slight overemphasis in 'The Continental', she deliberately pulls out all the stops for 'I'll Be Hard to Handle' (from *Roberta*), her second solo of the series and very far removed from her first. The sweet young thing who sang demurely to Astaire in *The Gay Divorcee* is transformed into a seasoned performer, brimming over with confidence and mischief as she gleefully describes how difficult she can be to control. 'In a temper I'm terrific, / I throw chairs and tables and I never miss,' warns Rogers, clearly in her element, making the most of her 'Polish' accent ('I'll be ch-hard to ch-handle') and supplementing her vocal antics with gestures to match. The number, featuring shortly after her first meeting with Astaire, is performed to the accompaniment of his band in an informal rehearsal at the nightclub where Rogers is the resident singer. Uniquely, it follows immediately, without any intervening dialogue, and only the sign 'Café Russe' to set the scene, after Irene Dunne's 'Russian Song'. A cut near the beginning shows us Astaire enjoying the performance from his vantage point on the central staircase, and at the song's conclusion Rogers joins him for some light-hearted reminiscing about their past, which leads very spontaneously into their playful duet to the same music.

Rogers is also the resident singer at the Paradise Ballroom in *Follow the Fleet*, and we first see her in her dressing room, a few minutes into the film, as she is getting ready to entertain the audience of newly arrived sailors. While she puts the finishing touches to her sailor's costume she gives her dowdy sister (Harriet Hilliard) some good-natured tips on how she might make herself more attractive to men, and asks one of the girls (a young Lucille Ball) to 'fix her up'. Then, with her peaked cap at a jaunty angle, she goes out on stage, and gives a lovely performance of Berlin's 'Let Yourself Go', with a chorus of three backing singers (including another young star in the making, Betty Grable). The lyric, appropriately enough, recommends dance as a means to relax and forget one's troubles – 'Let the dance floor feel your leather, / Step as lightly as a feather, / Let yourself go' – and Rogers delivers it with great verve, loosening up convincingly herself on the word 'Relax', and singing out fearlessly when the music shifts up a key, to exhilarating effect. Towards the end of the song there is a cut to Astaire entering the ballroom, busily chewing gum; he quickly spots Rogers, and as she finishes her performance he rushes backstage after her, attracting her attention by playing a little fanfare on a pipe he happens to be carrying. It is obviously familiar to her,[25] for she responds with an instinctive burst of tap before turning round – and so begins their affectionate reunion. A short time later they will join the other couples on the dance floor, and gradually be drawn into a spectacular display of their prowess.

Rogers' solo tap routine to the same music later in the film, performed quite independently of Astaire as an audition piece for a new job, is another very engaging piece of work; but though her audience is impressed she doesn't get the job, for the dance is followed by an ill-fated reprise of the song, unwittingly sabotaged by Astaire's misguided efforts to be helpful.

Her two remaining solos in the series are both, like 'Let Yourself Go', very public performances (with Rogers again in the role of professional, though not resident, singer), and they show her in excellent form, beautifully relaxed and confident. Astaire is present in the audience for both of them, and both are followed almost immediately by a dance duet, but the circumstances are very different.

For 'They All Laughed', from *Shall We Dance*, the setting is the rooftop nightclub of Rogers' New York hotel, shortly after her return to the city, and she is a star guest. The band is playing 'Slap That Bass', and she is dancing with her fiancé among the other couples when Astaire, accompanied by Horton, enters the ballroom. Furious with him for (as she believes) spreading the rumour that they are married, she gives him an unfriendly look and carries on dancing. At this point her manager (Jerome Cowan), who has clearly arranged their meeting, sends a note to the bandleader, who nods conspiratorially. The music stops, the couples resume their seats and the lights dim. A spotlight falls on Rogers, the band strikes up again (this time with the music of 'They All Laughed', first heard much earlier in the film on board the *Queen Anne*), she stands up to acknowledge the applause, then walks on stage to sing, to a jazzy, very enjoyable arrangement of Gershwin's song.

The lyric dwells at first on the lessons of history – how people originally laughed at pioneers such as Columbus, Edison, the Wright brothers and Marconi but then changed their tune. As Mueller observes, it 'does not reveal its true subject – love – until halfway into the chorus',[26] and when it does, Rogers' fiancé (William Brisbane) basks in the reflected glory. On the closing lines – 'They all said we never would be happy, / Darling let's take a bow, / But ho ho ho! / Who's got the last laugh now?'[27] – he sits beaming with empty-headed self-congratulation (amply fulfilling Cowan's earlier description of him as 'a Park Avenue cluck with the longest yacht and the shortest chin ever christened') while Astaire looks miserable, only joining in the applause after several seconds of glum silence. Rogers, however, does not invest the lyric with any significant overtones, and does not appear to glance in either man's direction in the course of the song,[28] which she delivers with an appealing freshness and directness, making economical but effective use of gesture on lines such as 'How many many times the worm had turned' and 'When he said the world was round'. Her performance over, she makes to leave the stage, but finds herself trapped into dancing with Astaire, in the film's one and only full-scale duet and its major musical highlight. As we saw earlier, the pair briefly reprise the closing lines of the song at the end of the film, the lyric now happily celebrating their final reconciliation.

'The Yam', from *Carefree*, is also performed in the presence of the two men in Rogers' life, her psychiatrist (Astaire) and her fiancé (Ralph Bellamy), but this time it is all Rogers' idea and, in a reversal of the scenario in 'They All Laughed', a ploy to engineer a dance with Astaire. The setting is the Medwick Country Club, where Rogers has just informed her aunt (Luella Gear) that she is in love with her doctor. She has recently run amok in the city streets while under the influence of an anaesthetic administered by Astaire, and he has been admonished by a judge and friend of the family (Clarence Kolb), who warns Astaire that he will hold him responsible for her actions. The party are to dine together, but before they sit down Rogers tells her psychiatrist that she'd like to dance with him, 'right now'. He suggests that she should dance with her fiancé first, whereupon in a taster of the mischief she will cause if he doesn't comply, she picks up a bread roll and hurls it at the judge. Astaire gives in gracefully, and they start to dance, but the music comes to an end almost immediately. Disappointed, Rogers asks the bandleader to play another number, and he agrees on condition that she sing it.

So begins Berlin's delightfully absurd song, all about a trader in sweet potatoes, and 'The little step that you see him do / With ev'ry yam that he sells to you'.[29] Rogers, obviously enjoying herself, performs it in style, demonstrating the step as she sings, and also fitting her actions to the words on 'Raise your hand and sway / Like you hold a tray' (her evening bag serving the purpose). She moves about a lot during this song, and

3.7 'The Yam': Rogers, on top form, gives an impromptu performance of the song to an audience of diners at the Medwick Country Club in a ploy to persuade Astaire to dance with her. The evening bag she holds in her right hand doubles as a tray at the appropriate point in the lyric.

uses her dress to good effect, holding up one of its filmy layers in her left hand as she sings (**3.7**). Finally, having urged her audience to 'Come on, shake your depression / And let's have a yam session', she persuades Astaire to join her, and a good time is had by all as the onlookers are gradually drawn into the merry dance that follows. Halfway through it Rogers resumes singing, in a sort of coda to the main song that mentions various other dance steps (including the Charleston and the Black Bottom), and allows her yet more scope for descriptive gesture.

'The Yam' shows Rogers at her peak as a solo singing actress, a dashing, captivating performance that exploits to the full every opportunity presented by the song without any suggestion of striving for effect. She has matured almost beyond recognition since that first, demure appearance on the balcony in *The Gay Divorcee*.

Duets

Four of the six songs in this group are fully fledged duets, in which
Astaire and Rogers play an equal part; in 'Lovely to Look At' (from
Roberta), Rogers makes a minor contribution to what is primarily an
Astaire solo; while in 'A Fine Romance' (from *Swing Time*) Astaire sings
his shorter share of the lyric after Rogers has performed the song as a
solo and dialogue has intervened. Only 'A Fine Romance' and the other
duet from *Swing Time*, 'Pick Yourself Up', have any important dramatic
function, but the remainder are at least credibly integrated into their
respective films. As can be expected, the duets exhibit the first defining
element of the series, complementarity, with humour and (in most cases)
at least a dash of romance in addition. All except 'A Fine Romance' lead
to a dance (of sorts); in the case of 'I Won't Dance' (from *Roberta*) it is
an Astaire solo, while the dance duet to this music comes much later,
and indeed follows not long after 'Lovely to Look At'. 'A Fine Romance'
is also exceptional in that it is the only one of the six songs which is not
entirely lighthearted in tone.

The 'I Won't Dance' sequence begins with the great treat of Astaire
playing the piano, a very upbeat arrangement of Jerome Kern's lively
song.[30] It is his band's opening night at the Café Russe, with the
Countess Scharwenka topping the bill, and everyone is there, including Randolph Scott, who sends his unpleasant girlfriend packing just
before Astaire starts to play. He finishes with a flourish, and proceeds
to conduct his band, at which point Rogers appears on the scene, in a
shimmering gown. A mischievous look on her face, she slinks around
him in a half-dancing sort of way; apparently unprepared for this intrusion he stops the band, but she carries on regardless. He brings her to
a halt, and asks patiently if there is anything he can do for her. She
gestures that she wants him to dance; he refuses and turns to conduct
again, whereupon she immediately breaks into song. 'Think of what
you're losing / By constantly refusing to dance with me,' she pleads (in,
of course, her Polish accent). Astaire, alternately singing and conducting, insists 'I won't dance!', his theme being that she is so lovely, 'My
heart won't let my feet do things they should do.' Rogers, pouting with
disappointment at his refusal, brightens considerably on being told the
reason for it. She persists, however, declaring (in a unique reference to
a previous incarnation) 'When you dance you're charming and you're

gentle, / 'Specially when you do the Continental' – both she and Astaire briefly assuming a pose from that duet as she sings. (Astaire's reaction to her compliment, all bashful pleasure, is one of the many delights of this duet.) But he is adamant, and on his final 'I know that music leads the way to romance, / And if I hold you in my arms – I won't dance!' she smilingly leaves the scene.

There follows some comic business with a pair of large Cossacks, standing on guard nearby, who frogmarch Astaire to the bottom of the steps and leave him to perform a romance-free tap dance on his own, to enthusiastic applause. The number leads smoothly into the subsequent action, with a cut to Scott, drunkenly taking up the refrain of the song having polished off the dozen brandies he ordered to console himself for the failure of his own romance.

The second song that Astaire and Rogers perform together in *Roberta*, 'Lovely to Look At', first sung by Irene Dunne in the course of the lengthy musical fashion show staged at the end of the film, serves also as the orchestral accompaniment to the parade of models. Last to enter is Rogers, in a gorgeous black cape and gown, and Astaire, who has been conducting the orchestra and compering the show, gives her an affectionately admiring look as he removes her cape and begins to sing. This time, the flattering lyric is appropriately divided between the pair, and Rogers, smiling with pleasure on 'You're lovely to look at, delight-ful to know and heaven to kiss, / A combination like this – ', completes the line: 'is quite my most impossible dream come true, / Imagine find-ing a boy like you.' At this, she puts her arm in his and they walk slowly over to the dance floor while Astaire continues: 'You're lovely to look at, it's thrilling to hold you terribly tight, / So we're together the moon is new / And oh it's lovely to look at you – '. 'Tonight', the final word, is left unspoken; and as the orchestra completes the phrase the music merges seamlessly into the theme of 'Smoke Gets in Your Eyes' (another song given to Dunne earlier in the film). Astaire and Rogers move just as seamlessly into dance, which sustains the mood of loving together-ness established by the song – mischief and teasing for once abandoned as the pair express the true depth of their mutual affection.

'Lovely to Look At' is one of the very few songs performed by Astaire in partnership with Rogers that does not form the basis of a dance duet at any point,[31] and when they conclude the film with a euphoric cel-ebration of their forthcoming marriage (swiftly agreed backstage), it is to a reprise of the appropriately upbeat 'I Won't Dance' – with scant regard for the contradiction.

Like the main 'I Won't Dance' sequence, 'I'm Putting All My Eggs in One Basket' (from *Follow the Fleet*) begins with Astaire's piano playing, and it is another treat. This time, however, in contrast to the dinner suit and white grand piano that befitted the Café Russe, the scene shows him in casual rehearsal clothes, a sailor's hat on his head and a cigarette hanging from his lips, sitting on a wooden barrel at a honky-tonk upright. Comically, once he has hauled one of the strings into tune and played a few casual chords, he swivels the barrel round several times, as if fine-tuning his seating position – a manifestly pointless operation.

The occasion is a rehearsal for the fundraising show in aid of the *Connie Martin*, the ship salvaged by Rogers' sister (Harriet Hilliard), and the sequence is set on its deck. When Astaire finishes his wonderfully enjoyable, jazzy rendition of Berlin's song (which is greeted by an irreverently discordant blast from his band) he has a brief conversation with Rogers, sitting on a wooden trestle a few feet away, about Hilliard's tedious problems. But 'Let's not worry about it now – we ought to run through that new number,' he says, and without much more ado he asks the band to strike up. With Rogers still seated, her back to the camera, he puts a foot on the trestle and sings. The song, an expression of mutual fidelity, is one of Berlin's most charming, and it is charmingly sung by both performers. In their duets Astaire and Rogers never sing at the same time (excepting the brief reprises that conclude *Swing Time* and *Shall We Dance*), and most commonly, as here, they simply sing alternate verses and/or a chorus. Each is clearly pleased and touched to hear the other declare, with obvious affection, 'I'm putting all my eggs in one basket, / I'm betting ev'rything I've got on you. / I'm giving all my love to one baby, / Heaven help me if my baby don't come through' (**3.8**). This is no mere rehearsal for a show but the most tender moment in the entire film, each partner equally warm and sincere in their delivery. They move around during the song, allowing Rogers to face the camera for her verse, but they remain companionably close; at its finish they get up and, without pause, begin their rehearsal of the dance portion of the number – an excuse for a piece of pure comedy.

The theme of 'Pick Yourself Up', the next duet in the series, is initially heard as Rogers approaches the cigarette machine at which she first

3.8 The most tender moment in *Follow the Fleet*: Rogers delivers her verse of 'I'm Putting All My Eggs in One Basket', matching the warm affection Astaire displayed in his own share of the duet.

meets Astaire in *Swing Time*. The circumstances in which they sing this classic Jerome Kern song – the memorable dancing lesson at Gordon's Academy – will be familiar from chapter 2: Astaire has just fallen over in his very convincing simulation of clumsiness, and Rogers, disgruntled and dishevelled by her fruitless attempts, declares that she can't teach him anything. She sits down; he remains on the floor, and the song begins, a musical extension of their dialogue – but, as always, Astaire is more successful at winning Rogers over in song than he is in speech. His disarming admission of awkwardness coupled with his determination to do better – 'My two feet haven't met yet, / But I'll be teacher's pet yet, / 'Cause I'm going to learn to dance or burst' – has the desired effect, and Rogers, her hair (miraculously) now as unruffled as her temper, responds in kind. The lyric is as catchy as the tune ('Don't lose your confidence if you slip, / Be grateful for a pleasant trip'), and Astaire listens with a happy smile to his teacher's encouragement. On 'Work like a soul inspired' she stands up to emphasise the point, but he remains on the floor until she exorts him to 'Take a deep breath, / Pick yourself up, / Dust yourself off' – with a musical pause between each phrase that allows him to effect the appropriate actions – and 'Start all over again', at which point he enters with a new verse.

Their relationship has by now progressed to such a degree that she makes no protest when he matches his actions to the words on 'To feel the strength I want to, / I must hang on to your hand'; and the song is so embedded in the scene that they do not even reach the end of it before Rogers resumes the lesson: Astaire's last phrase, 'Maybe by the time I'm fifty / I'll get up and do a nifty', is left hanging in the air, with no final cadence, when Rogers declares with a smile 'All right, I'll show you again.' Her pupil shows no sign of improvement, however, and the 'three steps to the left, three steps to the right' that she once more attempts to teach him end very rapidly with both of them on the floor. Now Astaire completes the song, mischievously giving Rogers her own advice with a final 'Pick yourself up, / Dust yourself off, / Start all over again', but her patience has run out and she is not amused. Her employer (Eric Blore), his attention attracted by the disturbance, overhears her tell Astaire that he is a hopeless case – and, as we know, Blore's severe reaction leads to a stunning demonstration of just how much Rogers has taught their new recruit.

'A Fine Romance', the second number sung by Astaire and Rogers in *Swing Time*, does not lead to a dance, but, as Arlene Croce observes, 'Both the song and the scene that leads up to it . . . are as knowingly and tenderly staged, directed and performed as any dance.'[32] Again, the scene in question will be familiar from chapter 2 – an ill-fated outing to the country, in the snow, during which Rogers is disappointed and hurt by Astaire's coolness towards her and learns to her dismay of his engagement to another girl. Rogers' and Astaire's individual contributions, separated by a stretch of dialogue, are as convincingly integrated into the sequence as any number in the series.

The theme of the song has already been played as background music earlier in the film, but it does not make its first appearance in this scene until the dialogue explicitly turns to romance. As Astaire, having resisted Rogers' affectionate overtures and told her to flap her arms to get warm, suddenly finds himself holding her in what looks suspiciously like an embrace, the strains of 'The Way You Look Tonight' establish a more romantic mood; and as Rogers shyly suggests that their experience, all that has happened to them since their first meeting, is 'sort of like a romance', the theme of the song to come is tenderly played on strings. 'Yes,' agrees Astaire; 'As we say in French, "la belle romance"', to which Rogers replies happily 'La *swell* romance'. Here Victor Moore, Astaire's watchful friend, discreetly suggests that things have gone far enough, and Astaire unceremoniously breaks the romantic mood. In the falling snow the dejected Rogers leaves him to walk back to the car, but before she has gone very far she turns back to face him, and so the song begins.

Rogers' delivery of the humorously sarcastic lyric ('We should be like a couple of hot tomatoes, / But you're as cold as yesterday's mashed potatoes') is touching rather than amusing, as she gives vent to all the hurt and disappointment Astaire has caused her. The staging of her performance, with Astaire following her as she moves off, restlessly, to sit on a tree stump, and then a snow-covered bench, reflects the emotional distance between them. He remains several feet away from her, and while he is, as always, a responsive listener, his expressions and gestures are all playful in kind, in keeping with his mood throughout the sequence. (On 'You're calmer than the seals in the Arctic Ocean, / At least they flap their fins to express emotion' he duly flaps his arms, a smile on his face.) Only when Rogers comes despairingly to the end of her two verses does he join her, and attempt to convince her that he is not as aloof as he seems; but here again Moore disrupts the proceedings, and by the time Astaire joins her again she has, unknown to him, heard the shattering news of his engagement. Again he follows her as she walks off, and when she resists his advances he responds with the third verse of the song, its lyric paralleling that of the first two ('You never give the orchids I send a glance! / No, you like cactus plants, / This is a fine romance!'). But for once his singing, unlike hers entirely untroubled in tone, fails to win her over; she carries on walking away from him, back to the car, and doesn't even wait for him to finish before she starts the engine.

The song makes its final appearance (with a completely new lyric) in much happier circumstances, right at the end of the film, when Astaire has been relieved of his engagement and his rival Georges Metaxa has been relieved of his trousers, just moments before his scheduled marriage to Rogers. Accepting the loss of his bride with astonishing good humour, Metaxa breaks into song, and is (briefly) joined in turn by Moore and Helen Broderick, each doing their bit to add to the jollity as the young lovers walk off arm in arm. Astaire himself sings a whole new verse, in which he bids a conclusive goodbye to his gambling past, while Rogers, in harmonious counterpoint, reprises (almost unchanged) the last verse of 'The Way You Look Tonight' – an inspired stroke.

Whereas in 'A Fine Romance' Rogers invests a humorous lyric with true feeling, in 'Let's Call the Whole Thing Off', her final full-scale duet with Astaire, she treats references to broken hearts in a manner untouched by any serious emotion. The Gershwin song is, admittedly, lighthearted in tone, but it is typical of the rather superficial quality of Rogers' relationship with Astaire throughout the greater part of *Shall We Dance* that she does not really mean what she says when she declares 'But oh! If we call the whole thing off / Then we must part. / And oh! If we ever part, / Then that might break my heart!' Nor, it must be said, does Astaire appear to be any more serious when he sings the same words, and each listens to the other with much the same degree of composure at the prospect of an imminent parting. Unlike their other duets, and the songs Astaire sings to Rogers, the lyric on this occasion does not truly reflect their situation or state of mind; after all, Rogers suggests only moments later that they should get married just so that they can then get divorced. (After their marriage, as we have seen, they both display much more genuine feeling when Astaire sings 'They Can't Take That Away From Me'.)

The setting for 'Let's Call the Whole Thing Off' is New York's Central Park, where the pair are taking refuge from reporters following the publication of incriminating photographs (supposedly) showing Rogers in her nightclothes on Astaire's bed. They have been roller-skating and stop for a rest on a seat away from the crowds, where they discuss their predicament – the difficulty of denying that they are married in the face of the photographs. 'I don't know what to do,' says Rogers. 'I don't eyether,' replies Astaire. 'The word is eether,' says Rogers, and after a similar exchange about the pronunciation of 'neither' Astaire abandons speech for song. 'Things have come to a pretty pass. / Our romance is growing flat,' he sings, while Rogers listens calmly, half a smile on her face. The lyric amusingly details all the other words they pronounce differently, evidence that 'we two will never be one', but concludes that they can't call the whole thing off – 'For we know we need each other, so we / Better call the calling off off.' Having settled the question, and with nothing more to be said but with the infectious music still playing, it's obviously time they took to their feet for a dance on roller skates – in which novel fashion the number concludes.

4

THE DANCE DUETS

Introduction

The twenty-two dance duets that begin with 'Night and Day' in *The Gay Divorcee* and end with 'Change Partners' in *Carefree* exhibit, as a group, all five defining elements of the Fred and Ginger series, and as such represent the culmination of the Astaire–Rogers partnership. The first three of these elements – complementarity, or the rapport and emotional richness of the relationship between Fred and Ginger; humour; and romance – are not specific to dance; they are central both to the non-musical scenes and to the songs that Astaire and Rogers perform together. The fourth element, drama in dance, is closely related to romance, for romance is at the heart of all the dance duets in which a drama is played out, whatever the mood or the circumstances. And at the heart of virtually every duet of the series lies the fifth and final defining element, intimately related to the first: the manifestation in dance of the complementarity between Fred and Ginger, the expression in dance of the emotional richness of their relationship. These final two elements distinguish the dance duets of the Fred and Ginger series from the solo dances performed by Astaire and from virtually all the duets performed by Astaire and Rogers in the three other films they made together.

Astaire's solo dances in the series are often rich in humour ('No Strings' is one of many such), always inventive and technically brilliant ('Top Hat, White Tie and Tails' and 'Bojangles of Harlem' are two outstanding examples) – but that, so to speak, is all. None of his solos has any intrinsic dramatic content, any real emotional significance or, inevitably, any romantic element. ('Top Hat, White Tie and Tails' involves some dramatic action, in which Astaire systematically 'shoots' each member of his chorus with his cane, but the action neither tells a story in itself nor is related in any way to the plot of the film.) Where his solos do have a dramatic function the drama stems from factors external to the dance itself – the noise of his tapping wakes Rogers from sleep in *Top Hat* ('No Strings'), she recognises him in the course of his band's informal audition piece in *Roberta* ('Let's Begin'), she is impressed by his amazing performance with a golf club in *Carefree* ('Golf Solo'); while on the emotional front numbers such as these reveal nothing more than that Fred is a character full of high spirits and good humour. Without Ginger the vital element of complementarity is missing; to return to Arlene Croce's observation quoted at the beginning of this book, 'When Fred dances alone, he's . . . simply Astaire . . . self-defined.'

The Astaire–Rogers duets outside the series are equally limited in dramatic, romantic and emotional respects, though there is a humorous element in at least one or two of them. The very first meeting in dance of Astaire and Rogers, 'The Carioca', from *Flying Down to Rio*, ends in delightfully humorous style as the pair stumble about the stage after bumping their heads together; and 'Bouncin' the Blues', from *The Barkleys of Broadway*, is playful in mood throughout. The element of mutual teasing, so characteristic of Fred and Ginger, is, however, missing from both these numbers, as it is from the films as a whole. In *Flying Down to Rio* the pair are only casual friends, and in *The Barkleys of Broadway* they are a married couple given more to bickering and fighting than to teasing. For the same reasons romance, and hence drama, is entirely absent from their scenes together in *Flying Down to Rio*; and in *The Barkleys of Broadway* the one attempt at a romantic duet (a long-delayed reprise of 'They Can't Take That Away From Me') sadly fails because Rogers is no longer the dancer, or the actress, she was in the 1930s.

There is still much evidence, even in *The Barkleys of Broadway*, of an emotional bond between Astaire and Rogers, and this complementarity is at the heart of their much fresher, more youthful relationship in *The Story of Vernon and Irene Castle*. But the majority of the duets in this film are exhibition pieces of ballroom dancing, quite different in character from those in the Fred and Ginger series, with no emotional, dramatic or romantic significance. Only in 'The Last Waltz', performed after a lengthy separation between the pair, does their loving relationship truly receive expression in dance, but the mood is not sustained throughout the number, a rather fragmented medley of three different waltzes.

Distinguished as they are by the defining elements, the dance duets of the Fred and Ginger series are distinguished by other qualities, too, most notably technical brilliance combined with an appearance of spontaneity – qualities which are by no means unique to the series (or to the duets) but which had not been seen on the cinema screen before the advent of Astaire and Rogers. Many of the duets, in particular the predominantly serious, romantic numbers, exhibit yet another outstanding quality: a visual beauty that set a new aesthetic standard for dance in the Hollywood musical. In duets such as these Astaire and Rogers attain a level of artistic achievement that transcends the bounds of musical comedy, yet is so firmly rooted in its context that it never seems incongruous. And in duets such as these they explore a range of dramatic and emotional expression, from ecstatic joy to the deepest despair, that transcends the limitations of the predominantly light-hearted, even-toned scripts, achieving vividly and eloquently in dance what dialogue and even song can only prepare the way for.

From conception to screen

With the exception of 'Night and Day' and the 'Table Dance', both borrowed and adapted from the stage version of *The Gay Divorcee*, all the dance duets in the Fred and Ginger series were created specifically for the films and specifically for the Astaire–Rogers partnership. Astaire was largely responsible for the choreography of the duets, as well as his own solos. Working with dance director Hermes Pan (who also choreographed the chorus dancing in the production numbers), and pianist and arranger Hal Borne, he would start to prepare them months in advance. As Rogers was always involved in making other films during the period of the series, Pan would play her part in her absence, and then teach her the steps before she started an intensive six-week period of rehearsals with Astaire. Astaire, a perfectionist to his fingertips, was a tireless rehearser, and Rogers equally so;[1] moreover she made a significant creative contribution to the duets (as did Pan). As Mark Sandrich, the director of five of the seven films, has said:

> You would be surprised how much [Rogers] adds to the number. Fred arranges them, and then when they get to rehearsing, Ginger puts in her own suggestions. And they're sensible ones. Fred discusses every one with her at length, and a good many of them are used.[2]

Rogers herself remarks that she 'had plenty of input' in their routines, and lays claim to a number of memorable ideas, including the 'shadowing' in 'Isn't This a Lovely Day', the 'getting stuck on one step' in 'I'm Putting All My Eggs in One Basket', the leaps over the tables at the end of 'The Yam', and the hypnotism in 'Change Partners'.[3]

(Rogers also reveals, somewhat amazingly, that she practised in low heels and only switched to higher ones when filming began.[4] Dancing in high heels could be a hazardous business on the hard, shiny Bakelite floors used in most of the numbers, part of the extravagant art deco sets that were a trademark feature of the series.[5] And the danger of slipping was not the only hazard: in one famous example Rogers' feet were bleeding after the forty-seven takes required for the finale of 'Never Gonna Dance' – the perfectionism apparent in rehearsals extending to the filming of each dance.)

Astaire's creative contribution to the dance duets was not limited to the choreography; as Arlene Croce notes, he also tightly controlled the use of music, from start to finish of the development of a number, and possibly even influenced the composing in some instances.[6] Arrangements were worked out with Hal Borne at the piano, and not only were the steps often adapted to suit the music but the music was sometimes adapted to suit the steps.[7]

Camera work

Astaire's first solo dance in *The Gay Divorcee*, 'Don't Let It Bother You', the duet 'Night and Day' and (especially) the chorus work in 'The Continental' from the same film show the sort of disfiguring, distracting camera work that was typical in musicals of the time (including *Flying Down to Rio*) – close-up shots of the dancer's feet and lower legs, shots from odd angles and through obstructions (under a table, through a venetian blind), rapid cutting on every bar of the music. Once Astaire was able to take full control of the filming of his dances, from *Roberta* onwards, he outlawed such effects, insisting on showing the dancers in full figure throughout, with the minimum of editing or shots from different angles. As John Mueller observes, 'His guiding principle was to let the dance speak for itself and to keep the camera work observant but unobtrusive.'[8] Astaire believed that, in all types of dancing, 'the movement of the upper part of the body is as important as that of the legs',[9] and indeed both he and Rogers use their arms and hands a great deal, and to great effect, in their duets. In both 'Pick Yourself Up' and 'They All Laughed', for example, arm movements are a very specific feature of the choreography, and in 'Change Partners' they take on a dramatic significance, as Astaire hypnotises Rogers with his hands, and she raises and lowers her arms at his command.

The Astaire–Rogers dance duets are intensely *intimate* events, the absolute antithesis of the huge spectacles that Busby Berkeley brought to the cinema screen in the early 1930s, spectacles that were viewed to best advantage from a roving camera mounted high above the dancers. In a typical Berkeley number the dancers themselves (massed ranks of anonymous chorus girls) were merely a means to an end – the creation of spectacular and ever-changing visual effects; the less the dancers were identifiable as individual human beings the more spectacular were the effects. In the Astaire–Rogers duets the dancers themselves, and the relationship between them, are the whole point of the dance, and the unobtrusive camera work allows the two dancers to take centre stage throughout. Even those duets performed in front of an audience (such as 'Smoke Gets in Your Eyes' and the 'Waltz in Swing Time') or in the midst of a large chorus (such as the second 'Continental' duet) are intimate events, in which Astaire and Rogers dance purely for each other and pay no heed at all to the chorus or (with few exceptions) to the audience. (By contrast, in Astaire's solo numbers the chorus is an integral part of the routine, and in 'Bojangles of Harlem' he even dances briefly with individual chorus girls.) Occasionally, as in 'They All Laughed', they acknowledge the applause at the end, but only in 'Let Yourself Go', where they deliberately set out to impress their spectators and fellow competitors in a dance contest, and 'Pick Yourself Up', where they are equally concerned to impress Rogers' employer, do they acknowledge the presence of their audience in the course of their performance; and only in 'The Yam' do they involve others in their dance – but then 'The Yam' is exceptional in more than one respect.

In both 'Let Yourself Go' and 'Pick Yourself Up' the camera, quite legitimately, cuts to one or two reaction shots of the audience, but though the technique is legitimate the effect is distracting, and we lose a precious few moments of the dance itself. Likewise there are two brief cuts to the duped Erik Rhodes shortly after the start of the second 'Continental' duet. Reaction shots (which, much less legitimately, also disfigure the couple's very first duet, 'The Carioca' in *Flying Down to Rio*) are never otherwise used while a dance is in progress. Some of the duets are shown in one continuous shot – 'I'll Be Hard to Handle', 'Let's Face the Music and Dance' and the 'Waltz in Swing Time' are notable examples; and in most there are no more than one or two cuts, all unobtrusive and designed to show the dancers from the most advantageous angle, or to give a closer view, as they move about the stage. 'Cheek to Cheek' is a rare example, at this stage in the series, of more obtrusive camera work, whereby the dancers are rather distant on occasion, seen from a viewpoint impeded by the elaborate set; elsewhere the camera's faithful concentration on the figures of the dancers themselves adds immeasurably to the impact and aesthetic appeal of their performance. In just two or three cases Astaire allows an exception to the 'full figure' rule, with a cut to an upper-body shot at a particularly intimate moment of the dance serving to heighten the closeness of the relationship between the dancers ('The Continental' and 'Change Partners'), or a similar shot focusing attention on the activity of the moment, as when Rogers takes time out of dancing to experiment with moving her left arm in 'I'm Putting All My Eggs in One Basket'. As Mueller points out, by the time 'Change Partners' was filmed Astaire had come up with a technique that minimised the disruptive effect of such a cut, the camera *tracking* instead of cutting back to a full-figure perspective.[10] This technique is also used on the one occasion that the dancers' feet and lower legs are shown in close-up, at the beginning of 'The Piccolino', which Mueller interprets as 'a happy in-joke' (the joke extending to the title sequence of *Top Hat*, which, as he notes, shows the dancers *only* from the waist down).[11]

Whether or not there is a cut, almost all the dances were filmed in one continuous take, with generally three cameras recording simultaneously from slightly different angles – centre, left and right. Even the change to slow motion in 'I Used to Be Color Blind' is, astonishingly, accomplished within a single take (and without a cut). Two exceptions are 'Never Gonna Dance', which takes place on two separate levels of the set, linked by a curving double staircase, and which was filmed in two sections, with a cut as the dancers reached the upper level; and 'The Yam', which travels extensively through the Medwick Country Club (and was apparently, and unbelievably, filmed in a hundred takes over two days[12]).

Integration and dramatic relevance

Astaire made few claims for his dances, but one of them was that 'they had a reason . . . they told a part of the story . . . they belonged in the plot'.[13] This is true of many of his solos and his duets with other partners, but most especially of his duets with Rogers. All these dances were conceived as an integral part of the films in which they appear; all 'had a reason', and the great majority 'told a part of the story', whether in advancing the plot or in simply marking a phase in the emotional relationship between Fred and Ginger. With very few exceptions the dances 'belonged in the plot': they sprang directly from their dramatic or emotional context and could not have been created in isolation from it. Of the twenty-two duets in the series only three have no truly integral relationship with their context: 'I'm Putting All My Eggs in One Basket' and 'Let's Face the Music and Dance' (both from *Follow the Fleet*), the one a piece of pure comedy, the other an emotionally charged drama staged as part of a show; and 'Let's Call the Whole Thing Off' (from *Shall We Dance*), a novelty dance on roller skates with no real dramatic or emotional content or relevance. Even these three duets, however, can be said to 'have a reason', in that they are at least superficially integrated into their surrounding material. Both the numbers from *Follow the Fleet* are presented – one in rehearsal, the other in performance – as part of the fundraising effort in aid of Harriet Hilliard's ship-salvaging project; and the dance on roller skates follows very naturally from a song which itself springs convincingly from the preceding dialogue.

'Let's Call the Whole Thing Off' is just one of many numbers in which dance follows not only naturally but quite seamlessly from dialogue and song (or, in the case of 'Smoke Gets in Your Eyes', from song alone); other examples include 'Night and Day', 'Isn't This a Lovely Day', 'Cheek to Cheek' and 'Never Gonna Dance'. In some numbers the transition from song to dance is effected by means of some intervening dialogue, and the dance springs just as seamlessly, and just as convincingly, from that dialogue; notable examples are 'I'll Be Hard to Handle', 'Pick Yourself Up' and 'Change Partners'. Several of these numbers, such as 'Pick Yourself Up', are not only convincingly integrated and dramatically relevant but fulfil in themselves a vital dramatic function, so much so that if they were removed from the film the plot would not make sense. (Conversely, however, these duets, mini-dramas in their own right like some of the songs that precede them, make perfect sense even when divorced from their context.) Others, such as 'Smoke Gets in Your Eyes', simply express in dance the emotional bond between Fred and Ginger – as does the 'Waltz in Swing Time', a rare example of a dance that does not spring from either dialogue or song, but is nevertheless prepared for in the script.

In performance

Though they share a common purpose, 'Smoke Gets in Your Eyes' and the 'Waltz in Swing Time' are poles apart in choreographic terms, the one a creation of the utmost simplicity, the other the most complex of all the duets in the series. Both nonetheless give an impression of effortless skill and spontaneous expression – qualities that are typical of all the duets in performance.

Complexity and simplicity

The complexity of the 'Waltz in Swing Time' only becomes apparent on repeated viewing and study; neither this duet nor any of the others gives an impression of being difficult or complicated. All but one of them last no more than three minutes, and in that short space of time they convey their humorous, dramatic or emotional point with the greatest clarity and directness – a clarity that is achieved through a deceptive economy of means. As Mueller observes, Astaire's dances are economically choreographed, with no 'grab bag of effects', but 'they are in no sense simple. Beneath the uncluttered texture lurks an amazing and endlessly revisitable world of nuance and subtle complexity.' He goes on to note that 'In preparing a ballet tribute to Astaire in 1983, [choreographer] Jerome Robbins, together with two New York City Ballet dancers, spent twelve hours analyzing one Astaire dance [with a view to duplicating it] – and still felt they had not grasped all the detail.'[14] The dance in question was one of Astaire's duets with Rita Hayworth, 'I'm Old Fashioned', from *You Were Never Lovelier* (1942); it is much less complex than the 'Waltz in Swing Time', and one can well imagine that twelve hours would be not nearly enough to grasp all the detail in this astonishing work. And in all that endlessly re-viewed detail, in the 'Waltz' as in the other twenty-one duets, there is not a single superfluous or ill-judged movement or gesture; in their dancing as in their acting, both Astaire and Rogers demonstrate a faultless sense of proportion throughout the series.

The complexity of the 'Waltz' and the (apparent) simplicity of 'Smoke Gets in Your Eyes' are both means to the same end: the expression of the emotional richness of the relationship between Fred and Ginger – ecstatic joy in the one, serene togetherness in the other. There is no other purpose to either dance; neither has any dramatic function. By contrast 'Change Partners' has a very specific dramatic function, the (re)hypnosis of Rogers, and this final duet of the series demonstrates more clearly than any other how the most economical of choreographic means can achieve the most telling of dramatic effects. Yet the dance is not so simple that we ever tire of its clarity and directness; and, as always in this series, the choreography itself is only half the story. Each duet, whether complex or simple, owes its impact as much to the acting skills of Astaire and Rogers as to the steps they perform.

Perfection and spontaneity

> Just try and keep up with those feet of his sometime! Try and look graceful while thinking where your right hand should be, and how your head should be held, and which foot you end the next eight bars on, and whether you're near enough to the steps to leap up six of them backward without looking. Not to mention those Astaire rhythms. Did you ever count the different tempos he can think up in three minutes?

So spoke Ginger Rogers in a 1936 interview,[15] and it is a tribute to her skill as well as Astaire's that we never find ourselves thinking about the mechanics of a dance – whether hands, heads and feet are in the right place at the right time – or noticing how many different tempos are at work in the space of a single short duet. Their performances always seem effortless, and one movement simply flows into the next without the slightest hint of awkwardness. Those long, intensive hours of rehearsal achieved a technical perfection and degree of confidence that enabled both dancers to give an impression of casual, even improvisatory, skill. The exhaustive rehearsal of every step, every move, is never apparent on screen; on the contrary, each duet seems to be danced for the first time before our eyes, as if spontaneously.

The majority of the duets are of course 'impromptu' in character, arising from rather than imposed on the dramatic situation, and performed as if on the impulse of the moment, supposedly without any rehearsal. In these numbers the illusion of spontaneity stems in part from the casual or apparently impulsive manner in which the dance begins: the pair slide into dance from a slow walking pace ('Isn't This a Lovely Day', 'Never Gonna Dance'); they slip seamlessly from an unobtrusive piece of social dancing into a full-scale duet ('The Continental', 'Cheek to Cheek'); they begin almost in spite of themselves when one is impelled by the other into performing before an audience ('Pick Yourself Up', 'They All Laughed', 'The Yam'); or they suddenly find themselves in the middle of a dance contest ('Let Yourself Go'). Many of these dances end with an unashamed flourish, often accompanied by a burst of applause from the admiring spectators; but in some cases the illusion of spontaneity is reinforced by an ending that simply merges back into the action of the film: 'Night and Day', 'Cheek to Cheek', 'Pick Yourself Up' and 'Change Partners' are notable examples.

The most spontaneous-seeming of all the duets is 'I'll Be Hard to Handle' (from *Roberta*), whose improvisatory character stems not just from the casual, impulsive manner in which it begins and ends but to a large extent from its particular choreographic style – a playful frolic between two old friends that really seems to be made up as they go along. Towards the end of the same film comes a duet quite different in style, performed this time in front of an audience and supposedly rehearsed, but 'Smoke Gets in Your Eyes' appears to slide into being just as spontaneously as other more obviously 'impromptu' numbers, and ends in similar fashion. The same cannot be said of the 'Waltz in Swing Time', the only other duet of its kind in the series, and the most stunningly virtuosic that Astaire ever created. Like 'Smoke Gets in Your Eyes', the 'Waltz' is performed in front of an audience, but this time as an obvious exhibition piece, both beginning and ending with a flourish. Exceptionally, it is announced in advance, and there can be no doubt that it has been carefully rehearsed beforehand by Astaire and Rogers in their screen roles. It clearly could not possibly be improvised, and yet it exhibits the same remarkable quality of spontaneity that distinguishes the supposedly impromptu numbers, achieving the illusion that it is being performed for the very first time. What sustains this illusion, in the 'Waltz' as in 'I'll Be Hard to Handle', is not merely the apparently effortless skill of the performance – the technical perfection and confidence acquired in those long hours of rehearsal – but, equally if not more importantly, the *acting* skills of Astaire and Rogers: their ability to project emotion as if it is being experienced for the very first time.

In both these quite contrasting duets (as in many others) the emotion is joy – pure and ecstatic in the 'Waltz', flavoured with teasing humour in 'I'll Be Hard to Handle'; but Astaire and Rogers are equally skilful at projecting more serious emotions in dance, most notably in 'Never Gonna Dance' and in 'Change Partners', both of which are 'impromptu' numbers and sustain the illusion of spontaneity throughout.

Art and artistry

At the same time as they sustain the illusion of spontaneity, Astaire and Rogers succeed somehow in creating a feeling of inevitability; for it is impossible to imagine their duets taking shape any differently. This is a quality they share with all enduring works of art, and yet the creation of works of art could not have been further from the minds of Astaire, Rogers or anyone else involved in the series. The motivation for the films was popular entertainment and financial profit; as Astaire remarked wryly in a television documentary some years later, 'we were just trying to make a buck'.[16] In his autobiography he explicitly disavows an intentionally artistic motive, declaring 'What I think is the really dangerous approach is the "let's be artistic attitude". I know that artistry just happens.' But he goes on: 'Believe it or not, there is even an artistic way to pick up a garbage can.'[17] Astaire might not ever have picked up a garbage can in his dances (though he comes remarkably close in his brief stint as a road-sweeper in *The Belle of New York*, 1952), but in a solo such as 'A Needle in a Haystack' he certainly demonstrates that there is an artistic way to perform other commonplace actions; and in their duets he and Rogers demonstrate, for the first time on the cinema screen, that emotion can be artistically expressed in dance. John Mueller, in the opening paragraph of his monumental study of all Astaire's musical films, has no doubts as to his artistic credentials, stating:

> It is the central contention of this book that Astaire 'just happens' to have created a large body of works of the highest artistic value, that he is one of the greatest dancers and choreographers who ever lived, that he is one of the master artists of the century.

It is one of the central contentions of *this* book that Ginger Rogers was an equal partner in the realisation on screen of the greatest dance duets that this master artist created.

Ginger Rogers: Astaire's equal and best partner

While Astaire has consistently been acclaimed for his work as dancer and choreographer throughout his long career, Rogers' contribution to their partnership has not always received due credit. Rogers herself did not fail to notice this inequality of treatment; as she said (with modest understatement) in an interview in the 1980s, 'It's interesting that people refer to "the Fred Astaire pictures", but you see, I was in them too, and so I take umbrage at that.'[18] Her achievement as Astaire's dancing partner has been undervalued partly because she was not primarily a dancer, favouring straight films over musicals for the greater part of her career, and indeed only coming to prominence as a dancer as a result of their partnership; consequently she has been taken less seriously than Astaire as a performing artist. More significantly, their partnership has been seen as unequal because Astaire was the major creative force behind their duets. Some commentators have placed a rather extreme interpretation on Astaire's role, among them Jerome Delameter, in his chapter on Astaire and Rogers in *Dance in the Hollywood Musical*, who states that 'Theirs was not a true partnership of equals; it was, instead, a Pygmalion–Galatea/Svengali–Trilby relationship.'[19] Rogers refutes the notion that Astaire made her what she was, moulding her to the shape he willed: 'He was not my Svengali. A lot of people think he was, but he was not. I was my own woman.'[20] And she imprinted her own unique stamp on their duets, bringing to them qualities that owed nothing to Astaire's influence, and that are conspicuous by their absence in his duets with other women. That Astaire did play the major part in the genesis and choreography of their duets is beyond question, but Rogers' contribution *on screen* is every bit as important as his.

Like Astaire, Rogers had danced professionally in vaudeville and on the Broadway stage before her first appearance on screen, and she had danced too in some of her early films. But, unlike Astaire, her dancing was incidental and she was essentially untrained; moreover he had been performing since before she was even born. At the start of her career with Astaire, Rogers was consequently much less accomplished and technically secure than he (and some of his later partners), but as the series progressed her technique and confidence developed to an outstanding degree. She became capable of ever more complex and dazzling feats, and was fully a match for Astaire in anything she was called on to perform. The cartoonist who famously observed 'Sure he was great, but don't forget that Ginger Rogers did everything he did, backwards and in high heels'[21] might have been exaggerating the literal truth, but pardonably so. Indeed, Rogers' mastery of the increasingly demanding choreography that Astaire created is so complete and apparently effortless that it almost belies the true extent of her skill.

Unlike some of Astaire's other partners (such as Eleanor Powell) Rogers was, however, not interested in technical display for its own sake; her one solo in the series (the 'audition' dance in *Follow the Fleet*) is appealing rather than stunning. Outside of her partnership with Astaire she danced very little, and was more concerned to establish a career as a serious actress. Her technical skill as a dancer was therefore put almost entirely at the service of Astaire's creations, and it developed as his demands on her grew.

His own career at the time revolved almost exclusively around their partnership (he made only one film without Rogers in the course of the series, the not very successful *A Damsel in Distress* in 1937), and, as noted earlier, with the exception of 'Night and Day' and the 'Table Dance' all his duets with Rogers were created specifically for her. She was to prove perfectly suited to his own choreographic style: elegant and graceful, economical of gesture and unaffected; and no other woman would inspire him to create dances so rich in dramatic and emotional expression. She was also an ideal match for Astaire in purely physical terms – he, dark-haired, slender and not too tall; she, blond, slim and just the necessary few inches shorter – and they always looked unquestionably right when dancing together. Of all the beautiful women that he would partner in the course of his long career, none was more appealing in her beauty than the youthful Ginger Rogers of the 1930s,[22] and though Astaire was several years older than she (he was thirty-five to her twenty-three at the start of the series) the disparity in their ages was never apparent.

Though Rogers has received less acclaim than Astaire over the years for her contribution to their partnership, she has generally been recognised, by serious commentators and the viewing public alike, as his 'best' partner. Her qualifications for this accolade (other than her purely physical attributes) are well summed up by Mueller:

> Rogers was outstanding among Astaire's film partners not because she was superior to the others as a dancer but because, as a skilled, intuitive actress, she was cagey enough to realize that acting did not stop when

dancing began. She seemed uniquely to understand the dramatic import of the dance, and, without resorting to style-shattering emoting, she cunningly contributed her share to the choreographic impact of their numbers together.[23]

As other commentators have suggested:

> Ginger Rogers has remained in the public consciousness as the star who not only responded most naturally to the role demanded of her in the partnership but also drew out the best in Astaire.[24]

Hermes Pan, Astaire's dance director who rehearsed Rogers, agrees that she was outstanding among his partners:

> There was a certain magic between Fred Astaire and Ginger Rogers . . . there's never been the same electricity that has happened as when Fred and Ginger danced together.[25]

For Arlene Croce, Astaire's dancing with partners other than Rogers is 'a world of sun without a moon'.[26] In her essay 'Dance in film' she observes:

> Later there were other girls whose technical abilities were more developed than Ginger Rogers's – Eleanor Powell, Rita Hayworth, or Cyd Charisse – but with none of them was Astaire able to achieve the romantic intensity of his dances with Rogers.[27]

And even Astaire himself, who was resolutely unforthcoming about his partners, acknowledged that Rogers 'got so that after a while everyone else who danced with me looked wrong'.[28]

Nevertheless, the accolade of 'best partner' was bestowed by reviewers of the day on more than one of Astaire's other co-stars, and though few would share their views today it is worth examining the evidence for the light it throws on Rogers' own achievement. How do Astaire's dancing partners in the post-Rogers era measure up to her? What qualities did she bring to her partnership with Astaire that are found wanting in his duets with other women?

In the eighteen musical films, for various studios, that he made without Rogers after the last of the RKO series, Astaire had a succession of other partners, from Eleanor Powell in *Broadway Melody of 1940* (1940) to Cyd Charisse in *Silk Stockings* (1957),[29] most of whom made a single appearance with Astaire. With the exception of Lucille Bremer, who featured as his non-speaking dancing partner in two duets in the revue-format *Ziegfeld Follies* (1946) and also co-starred with him in *Yolanda and the Thief* (1945) (an absurd film that neither of them can redeem), only three leading women partnered Astaire in more than one film: Charisse, Rita Hayworth and Vera-Ellen. A projected second pairing with Judy Garland after the success of *Easter Parade* (1948) turned instead into a late revival of the Astaire–Rogers partnership, after Garland dropped out of rehearsals for *The Barkleys of Broadway*.

Garland, a superb singing actress and no mean dancer, was in a class of her own. Like Rogers, she excelled in comedy, but their styles were very different; it is difficult, for example, to imagine Rogers in the role of a tramp, which Garland assumes so successfully in 'A Couple of Swells' from *Easter Parade* (**4.1**). She did not attempt to compete with Rogers on the romantic front, and indeed her first dance with Astaire in this film amusingly parodies the typical romantic duet, in which Garland is seen as hopelessly inept.

4.1 Judy Garland, partnering Astaire in 'A Couple of Swells' from *Easter Parade* (1948), relishes her role as a better class of tramp.

Eleanor Powell, by contrast, is very much in control throughout her performance in *Broadway Melody of 1940*; already firmly established as a dancing star in her own right before her pairing with Astaire, she is a flawless, formidable tap technician, who does ballet too (much less convincingly), and makes a rather forbidding partner for him in his first film post-Rogers. Her first solo, with male chorus, is pure exhibitionism, the antithesis of Rogers' style; its very title, 'I Am the Captain', suggests an authority and masculine self-confidence that are no part of Rogers' persona (there is no sign in Powell of Rogers' attractive vulnerability), and as Edward Gallafent observes, 'From its opening (Powell slides down a ship's mast) through its subsequent high kicks, splits and the tossing of Powell between the members of the chorus, this dance has an athleticism which underlines its distance from Rogers's dance.'[30] Significantly, it is Powell who initiates her first duet with Astaire, the playful 'Jukebox Dance' – by demonstrating to him a step from her routine that he admits he can't quite get the hang of. (There could be no more telling contrast with 'Pick Yourself Up', at the height of the Astaire–Rogers partnership, in which Astaire sweeps Rogers off her feet after mischievously concealing his dancing ability.) Later Powell dons a tutu for a vacuous balletic display, after which she partners an uncomfortable-looking Astaire, dressed harlequin-style, in a sequence reminiscent of his equally uncomfortable pairing with Harriet Hoctor in *Shall We Dance*. Their final two duets, both part of the glamorously staged production number 'Begin the Beguine', with its stunning black mirrored set and white costumes, are in a different class. The first is a visually beautiful Spanish-style mixture of ballroom and tap, the second, their most famous duet, a virtuosic tap routine. Both are highly impressive display pieces, in which Powell accommodates herself well to Astaire's more restrained choreographic style – but they are no more than that. In the climactic tap routine the pair are at once dazzling and relaxed, but they dance (almost literally) at arm's length throughout the duet (**4.2**), which is devoid of emotional or dramatic interest. One would never guess that they are supposed to be in love with each other.

An even more unlikely marriage, in every respect, is that of Astaire and Betty Hutton (*Let's Dance*, 1950), who is amazingly loud and unsubtle in her musical numbers, and in one truly awful duet, 'Oh Them Dudes', in which the pair clown about the stage in cowboy costumes, succeeds in pulling Astaire down to her level. Performers such

as Marjorie Reynolds (*Holiday Inn*, 1942) and Joan Leslie (*The Sky's the Limit*, 1943) are much more appealing, as well as competent dancers. Their romantic-style duets with Astaire are attractive, but they lack the romantic intensity that Croce refers to; neither Reynolds nor Leslie sets the screen alight or has seriously been regarded as a match for Rogers. Nor has Jane Powell (*Royal Wedding*, 1951), though she is, after Garland, the most engaging of all Astaire's one-film partners. A vivacious and unaffected actress, she acquits herself well in her diverse musical numbers: she is a graceful and sympathetic partner (if a little too short for Astaire) in their romantic-style ballroom duets, and shows considerable comic flair. But her role, as his sister, is lightweight and – unlike Garland's in *Easter Parade* – does not give her scope to portray more than lightweight emotions. On the evidence of this single film, Jane Powell is very promising as an all-round successor to Rogers, but she has too much to prove, both technically and dramatically, to be considered in the same league as her.

The three women who after a successful first appearance with Astaire (as both acting and dancing partner) went on to partner him in a second film were all, like Eleanor Powell and unlike Rogers, trained dancers: Vera-Ellen and Cyd Charisse both had a background in ballet, while Rita Hayworth had been trained by her father, a Spanish vaudeville dancer, and danced professionally from a young age. Their technical skill is never in doubt, and all three were acclaimed by at least some contemporary reviewers as Astaire's best partner.[31] How do these claims stand up to scrutiny today?

Of the three, Cyd Charisse is the furthest removed from Rogers in her dancing style. When we first see her, in *The Band Wagon* (1953), she is dancing on stage as a prima ballerina,[32] doing typical prima ballerina stuff: pirouettes, leg extensions, lifts, arabesques; and this is clearly the choreographic vocabulary she is most comfortable with. In her first duet with Astaire in this film, 'Dancing in the Dark', these balletic gestures, though very much in evidence, are not overdone. The duet sets out to explore whether two performers of very different genres, and of very different ages (both on and off the screen – Astaire was twenty-two years older than Charisse) can successfully dance together, and it

4.2 Eleanor Powell and Astaire are on equally splendid form in their virtuosic display at the end of 'Begin the Beguine', the stunning finale to *Broadway Melody of 1940* (1940), but there is an emotional as well as physical distance between them.

demonstrates conclusively that they can. The pair have got off to a bad start in their relationship and in their rehearsals for the show around which the film revolves, but after a hesitant beginning, in the romantic setting of a park at night, they achieve a truly beautiful blend of their different styles, and are drawn closer together in the process. The duet is a flawless piece of work, as convincingly motivated and seamlessly integrated into the scene as the best of the Astaire–Rogers numbers, and (exceptionally in the post-Rogers era) showing a real emotional progression.

Four years later, however, in *Silk Stockings*, Charisse seems to have forgotten the power of understatement. All her dances in this film, both solos and duets, are very balletic and exhibitionist in style – 'Fated to Be Mated', an energetic duet staged on a series of vacant film sets, is a typical example (**4.3**) – and it is a style that soon becomes repetitive

4.3   Cyd Charisse in typically unrestrained mode, partnering Astaire in 'Fated to Be Mated' from *Silk Stockings* (1957). She performs wide splits such as this one several times in the course of their duet.

and predictable: we just know that every now and then she will lift one (or both) of those famously long legs high up in the air, or do a wide split, or a low fall in Astaire's arms. Astaire's duets with Rogers have no such predictability, and Rogers never imposes a particular style of her own: she simply responds to whatever the dance calls for, always complementing Astaire, never gratuitously drawing attention to herself. Charisse is an exceptionally fine dancer, with an apparently effortless technique (she is also a likeable, unaffected actress), but her tendency to exhibitionism is both out of keeping with Astaire's own style and ultimately self-defeating, becoming tiresome rather than impressive. 'Dancing in the Dark' apart, Charisse does not consistently demonstrate the self-restraint or sense of proportion that distinguish Rogers' performances. One cannot imagine her, for example, falling under Astaire's spell as the hypnotised Rogers does to such moving effect in 'Change Partners' – the temptation to kick a leg in the air would, one suspects, be too great for Charisse to resist. She is evidently quite at home as the man-killing, ultra-glamorous brunette in the elaborate 'Girl Hunt Ballet' near the end of *The Band Wagon*, where, wearing a scarlet dress slashed to the waist, and scarlet high-heeled shoes, she slinks around Astaire and partners him in fearsomely predatory and uninhibited style. It is a riveting performance, undeniably appropriate for the (highly artificial) context, but it is very far from romantic and is, indeed, rather repelling.

Vera-Ellen, who appeared with Astaire in *Three Little Words* (1950) and *The Belle of New York* (1952), is as gifted a dancer as Charisse, and a match for her partner in a variety of dancing styles, including tap and ballroom. She is also a warm and appealing actress (though not as skilled a dancing actress as Rogers, with a more limited range of expression) and has an obvious sense of fun, which is well exploited in her comic duets with Astaire. They perform some charming and very enjoyable numbers together, the best of which, such as 'Oops', staged on and around a horse-drawn tramcar (**4.4**), are to be seen in *The Belle of New York*. But, ballet-trained like Charisse, Vera-Ellen is equally given to exhibitionist display; those gratuitous high kicks, leg extensions and the like intrude every now and then, and when she is let loose to perform solo, as in 'Naughty But Nice' from the same film, in which she adopts the unlikely persona of a vamp, she does little else but kick her legs in the air in an extraordinarily tasteless manner. (It

4.4 Girl-next-door Vera-Ellen adopts a favourite balletic pose in 'Oops', a charming duet from *The Belle of New York* (1952), staged on and around a horse-drawn tramcar in early 1900s New York. Astaire does not take his brief turn of duty as the tramcar driver very seriously, hence the convenient absence of other passengers.

is instructive to compare this performance with Rogers' solo in *Follow the Fleet*, a model of decorum and infinitely more appealing.) Unlike Charisse, and, more significantly, unlike Rogers, Vera-Ellen is unconvincing in 'glamorous' mode: while Rogers, whose glamour is innate and dignified, is both girl-next-door and goddess, Vera-Ellen is just girl-next-door. She would be completely out of her depth as the aloof, doom-laden figure that Rogers portrays so memorably in 'Let's Face the Music and Dance'.

Not so Rita Hayworth, whose image as 'Love Goddess' originated in a highly glamorous photograph published by *Life* magazine shortly before the first of her two films with Astaire, *You'll Never Get Rich* (1941), was released, and who four years after the second (*You Were Never Lovelier*, 1942) personified the ultimate screen goddess in *Gilda*. Hayworth is most definitely *not* the girl-next-door; she simply exudes glamour, but the aloofness that comes with it permeates much of her performance — and not only when her role demands it. (After their first meeting in *You Were Never Lovelier* Astaire likens her personality to 'the inside of a refrigerator'.) She frequently wears a rather supercilious expression on her face, and there is little real warmth, or humour, in her relationship with Astaire in either of her films. (Admittedly, neither performer is helped by plots which set new standards of artificiality and improbability.) But her iciness melts in their dances, where she is at her best, and *You Were Never Lovelier* in particular contains two very fine duets, the romantic 'I'm Old Fashioned' and the playful 'Shorty George', both much closer in style to some of the Astaire–Rogers duets than are those with Vera-Ellen – though they do not carry any particular dramatic or emotional significance. Like Vera-Ellen, Hayworth lacks Rogers' range of facial expression, but she shows herself more than equal to the considerable technical demands that the duets pose. Despite her impressive technique and stunning looks, however, she is not as graceful as Rogers; she is more statuesque in build and lacks Rogers' exquisite lightness of movement. Frequently, too, she holds her right arm up in the air as if she's not quite sure what else to do with it (**4.5**). In 'I'm Old Fashioned' she comes closer than anyone else to the romantic Rogers – but it's not close enough.

Not even Rita Hayworth, then, can match Rogers in purely visual appeal, and in common with Cyd Charisse, Vera-Ellen and Astaire's dozen or more other dancing partners she falls short of her in at least one other vital respect. Not only did Rogers bring out the best in Astaire (there is nothing in his later films that even comes close to the three brilliantly expressive duets in *Swing Time*), she played her part with a unique sensitivity to the emotional, dramatic and choreographic demands of each and every dance they performed together. Whether mischievously playful ('Pick Yourself Up'), ecstatically romantic ('Waltz in Swing Time') or plumbing the depths of despair ('Never Gonna Dance'), Rogers never fell short: both technically and expressively, she triumphed in them all.

The three main groups of duets – the big production numbers with chorus, the predominantly fast and humorous playful duets, and the predominantly slow and more serious romantic dances – reflect a broadly common pattern or mood. They do, however, overlap to some degree, as many of the playful duets, and at least two of the production numbers, are also highly romantic; moreover one or two in the series (such as the 'Table Dance') do not strictly belong to either the playful

4.5 The ultra-glamorous Rita Hayworth, right arm extended in a characteristic pose, partners Astaire in a dance to the title song of *You Were Never Lovelier* (1942) that was actually cut from the film. But the same pose and setting, though not Hayworth's dress, feature in 'I'm Old Fashioned', the film's big romantic duet.

or the romantic category. But while the duets in each group, and across the series, have a great many features in common, no two are alike in choreographic terms, or in the image they present to the viewer. In his autobiography Astaire states 'I have always tried to carry out my steadfast rule of not repeating anything in dance that I've done before',[33] and in these twenty-two duets that rule is steadfastly unbroken.

The dance duets: by group

	Production number	Playful duet	Romantic duet
The Gay Divorcee	The Continental	Table Dance	Night and Day
Roberta		I'll Be Hard to Handle I Won't Dance	Smoke Gets in Your Eyes
Top Hat	The Piccolino	Isn't This a Lovely Day (To Be Caught in the Rain)	Cheek to Cheek
Follow the Fleet		Let Yourself Go I'm Putting All My Eggs in One Basket	Let's Face the Music and Dance
Swing Time		Pick Yourself Up	Waltz in Swing Time Never Gonna Dance
Shall We Dance	Shall We Dance	They All Laughed Let's Call the Whole Thing Off	
Carefree		The Yam	I Used to Be Color Blind Change Partners

The dance duets: chronological order and timings

	Dance duet	Min./sec.
The Gay Divorcee	Night and Day	2′ 50″
	The Continental (1)	1′ 51″
	The Continental (2)	1′ 42″
	Table Dance	1′ 10″
Roberta	I'll Be Hard to Handle	2′ 44″
	Smoke Gets in Your Eyes	2′ 13″
	I Won't Dance	0′ 50″
Top Hat	Isn't This a Lovely Day (To Be Caught in the Rain)	2′ 25″
	Cheek to Cheek	3′ 00″
	The Piccolino[a]	2′ 05″
Follow the Fleet	Let Yourself Go	2′ 47″
	I'm Putting All My Eggs in One Basket	3′ 00″
	Let's Face the Music and Dance	2′ 40″
Swing Time	Pick Yourself Up	1′ 56″
	Waltz in Swing Time	2′ 36″
	Never Gonna Dance	2′ 50″
Shall We Dance	They All Laughed	2′ 25″
	Let's Call the Whole Thing Off	2′ 02″
	Shall We Dance	0′ 45″
Carefree	I Used to Be Color Blind	1′ 53″
	The Yam	4′ 03″
	Change Partners	1′ 53″

[a] Both the music and the choreography of this duet are reprised in a 30-second tag at the very end of the film.

5

THE PRODUCTION NUMBERS

Each of the three production numbers in the series – all big, lavishly staged ensemble pieces with chorus – features at least one Astaire–Rogers dance duet, though in the case of the title number from *Shall We Dance* it occupies less than a minute at the end of a ten-minute extravaganza. 'The Continental', from *The Gay Divorcee* (an even lengthier spectacle), features two more substantial duets; and 'The Piccolino' (*Top Hat*), the only one of the three not to seriously outstay its welcome, concludes with a two-minute duet that is not much shorter than the chorus's two separate routines combined. 'The Continental' and 'The Piccolino', both direct successors to 'The Carioca' from *Flying Down to Rio*, are broadly similar in style and pattern, while 'Shall We Dance' takes a quite different direction.

The first of the three, 'The Continental', set in the seaside hotel where co-respondent Erik Rhodes is to fulfil his professional obligations to Rogers, is at once the best and the worst. Like 'The Carioca', it features a lengthy routine of chorus dancing in couples, elaborately staged, distractingly directed and edited, and intercut with material from diverse supporting players – a sequence that lasts a full seven and a half minutes, leaving less than half that time for Astaire and Rogers themselves to perform. But the two separate duets that begin and end the number are among the most beautiful of their work. For the first time in the series we see the pair dancing as lovers, all misunderstandings resolved, and it is a very special treat.

Astaire, summoned (as her supposed co-respondent) to Rogers' hotel suite at midnight, has enlightened her as to his true identity, but Rhodes, arriving shortly afterwards and taking his responsibilities very seriously, refuses to let either of them leave until the night is over.

Rogers' performance of the song puts them in the mood for dancing, and Astaire soon devises an inventive piece of subterfuge to fool their jailer, allowing them to escape the confines of the suite to join the couples on the ballroom floor below.

Rogers, having not only changed her dress but undergone an improbably rapid change of hairstyle while Astaire set up his ruse, seems to have acquired a new poise and glamour. Gone is the girl-ish fringe she had briefly adopted; now her hair is swept back in a much fuller and more flattering style, as it was for the 'Night and Day' sequence earlier in the film – but then she was tentative, unsure of herself and of Astaire. Now she glows with happiness and con-fidence, and, wearing a strikingly elegant two-tone ballgown (even in monochrome, the flame-like shading on the flared skirt seems to reflect that glow), she is as graceful and alluring as she would ever be. For his part Astaire (dressed, as in all the numbers in this group, in his trademark white tie and tails) adds a nice touch of gallantry to his usual deftness and elegance, kissing her hand in chivalrous fashion at the appropriate point in the music (**5.1**). (The lyric of the song here, 'You kiss while you're dancing', is interpreted more literally by the chorus dancers; Astaire's restraint is entirely typical.)

They begin their first duet unobtrusively, merging with the crowd as just one more couple for a piece of unremarkable social dancing, but then they try out a few more adventurous steps and are gradu-ally given the floor to themselves as the others stand back and watch them admiringly. But they dance purely for each other, absorbed in the sheer joyousness of the occasion and oblivious of the crowds around them. The choreography, closely reflecting the music, is full of contrasts ('The Continental' was described by RKO as 'a combina-tion of smooth gliding rhythms and hot breaks'[1]), but through it all Astaire and Rogers sustain a mood of romantic, even rapturous, inti-macy that in some ways anticipates that of the 'Waltz in Swing Time'. It is remarkable that, after the initial few moments of social dancing, they do not hold each other until nearly a minute into the duet; they do hold each other for a large part of the second half, but the most intimate moments come near the end, when an upper-body medium shot shows them dancing very close, face to face but without touch-ing, their arms outstretched to form a diagonal cross in the dance's most characteristic motif. Here and throughout, the warmth of the

5.1 'You kiss while you're dancing': a glowing, confident Rogers gracefully receives Astaire's gallant interpretation of the lyric of 'The Continental' in the first of their two duets to this music. She makes stylish use throughout both duets of the chiffon scarf in her left hand.

rapport between the pair is palpable, even at this early stage of their partnership.

The duet ends as Astaire spins Rogers rapidly into his arms, whereupon the onlookers applaud enthusiastically and, realising where they are, the pair rush away (for fear of being spotted by Rhodes), to be met by the chorus advancing inexorably to begin their marathon performance. Towards the end of it Rhodes discovers that he has been duped, but he can do nothing to stop the lovers as, getting up from the table at which they have been sitting, out of his sight, they give way to the urge to dance again and begin their second duet, which concludes the 'Continental' sequence. This second appearance, staged on, at the foot and at the top of the wide staircase leading up to the hotel's exit, is more deliberate in style; now Astaire and Rogers are framed by neat rows of chorus dancers (in a diamond-shaped formation) (**5.2**), but they still manage to sustain an impression of intimacy in the midst of them. Their duet includes references to various 'continental' dances:[2] they begin with a Spanish tango, move into a Hungarian czardas and then, in romantically subdued lighting, descend the staircase in a graceful Viennese waltz. Moments later, after an exhilaratingly jazzy performance on the ballroom floor (here, and throughout the two duets, Rogers uses to great effect the chiffon scarf she holds in her left hand), they rush up the stairs at a gallop, and leave the scene with as much disregard for the attendant crowd as they had entered it.

Though 'The Piccolino', the second of the three numbers in this group, has many features in common with 'The Continental', length is fortunately not one of them. The whole sequence, including the song, lasts little more than six minutes, of which less than a half is taken up by the dancing of the chorus. They are mostly seen from above, executing symmetrical formations in the manner of the Busby Berkeley numbers (**5.3**), and look nicely decorative; apart from a rather absurd shot from behind the legs of one of the female dancers at the start of their second routine there is none of the irritating direction and editing that made the earlier number so tedious.[3]

'The Piccolino' occurs at precisely the same point in the plot as 'The Continental' – when all misunderstandings have finally been resolved and Rogers, fully aware of Astaire's identity and intentions

5.2 Intimacy in the midst of the crowd: Astaire and Rogers have eyes only for each other as they dance up the staircase in their second 'Continental' duet. The pose shown here, with their arms held diagonally, actually belongs to the first duet and does not appear on screen in this one.

towards her, returns his love. (As in *The Gay Divorcee*, however, she is inconveniently married to someone else at this point – or so we are supposed to believe – having impetuously tied the knot with her ridiculous suitor, Erik Rhodes.) Like 'The Continental', the number is staged on the dance floor of a hotel, but *Top Hat* is a cut above *The Gay Divorcee* in the sets department, and the vast ballroom in which 'The Piccolino' is performed, on carnival night in Venice, comes complete with manifestly unreal canals, gondolas and bridges (some of which are seen in **5.3**). As Astaire and Rogers take their seats for a celebratory dinner, the music strikes up and the chorus duly stream over the bridges (and from other unseen corners of the set) to perform their first routine, which leads directly into Rogers' lively rendition of the song, itself followed by the chorus's second appearance. Finally they clear the stage as Astaire and Rogers leave their seats to begin their duet, which concludes the number.

For this dance of celebration Rogers wears a sparkling white dress, and the dance is equally sparkling (**5.4**); as Mueller observes, the choreography cleverly reflects not only the melody but also the bubbly accompaniment of Berlin's catchy song.[4] 'The Piccolino' is full of bouncy joy and good humour, playful in mood and fast-moving throughout, and here it parts company with 'The Continental', for 'The Piccolino' has none of the rapturous intimacy that was such a memorable feature of the first duet in that sequence. There the lovers were in their own private world; here they are clearly aware that they are performing in front of a crowd. Their entrance (like that in the second 'Continental' duet) is made in deliberate style, and they end their performance with a flourish, speeding back to their table, resuming their seats and raising their glasses in a toast with impeccable timing. In 'The Continental' the applause of the crowd as Astaire finally spun Rogers into his arms came as an intrusion, waking them up to their surroundings and causing them to flee for fear of being spotted by Rhodes. 'The Piccolino', though a delightful piece, lacks the special glow created by this aura of romantic intimacy.

The third and last of the big set pieces with chorus, the title number that concludes *Shall We Dance*, is an elaborate mixture of ballet

5.3 'The Piccolino': part of the chorus's second routine, staged in *Top Hat*'s lavishly unreal version of Venice.

5.4 Astaire and Rogers, who is finally aware of who he really is, dance a bouncy duet of celebration in anticipation of their forthcoming marriage, bringing 'The Piccolino' to a close.

and Broadway, quite different in pattern from the previous two, and, unlike them, fulfilling an important function in the plot. Astaire and Rogers are estranged (only a short while after their perfunctory marriage), Rogers having stormed out of Astaire's life on discovering him alone with another woman. His scheduled ballet at the Metropolitan, New York, has been cancelled because of the notoriety surrounding him, and Rogers' manager (who is largely responsible for the notoriety) has offered to give him a slot in his Broadway show. Disconsolate at losing Rogers, and prompted by the sight of the dummy of her that her manager used to devious purposes earlier in the film, Astaire hits on an idea for his number: if he can't dance with Rogers herself he will dance with images of her. Hence the entry of the all-female chorus in identical dresses and Rogers face masks, for the Broadway sequence of the number. Ballet and Broadway are, however, intermingled, somewhat haphazardly, and to the accompaniment of some very odd, indeterminate music, for a good part of the time, and the number is also intercut with the arrival of Rogers, armed with a summons for divorce, and some comic business from Edward Everett Horton and Eric Blore. Every now and then Harriet Hoctor makes one of her ghastly appearances, gliding around the stage vacantly, fluttering her arms and bending backwards almost double so that she can, as Croce neatly puts it, 'kick herself in the head'.[5] The beautiful melody of the film's greatest song, 'They Can't Take That Away From Me', is thrown away on a duet between Hoctor and an uncomfortable-looking Astaire, and it's an immense relief when she and the corps de ballet finally flutter off the stage and Astaire strides back on to it, looking as relieved as we are to see him, to sing the jaunty title song (**3.2**, p. 102). Meanwhile Rogers, amazed and touched at the sight of all the images of her, goes backstage – to reappear disguised as one of the chorus (an appropriate device in a film whose plot is driven by deception of one sort or another) and reveal herself, fleetingly, to an astonished Astaire. She then mingles with the chorus (showing a remarkable grasp of their fast-moving routine) while Astaire frantically searches for her, finally unmasking each of the lookalikes in turn until he comes upon her – now no longer holding a mask to her face.[6]

There is only a minute to go, and at last our impatience to see the pair dance together is rewarded by an exquisite but tantalisingly short duet of reconciliation. We are given a mere forty-five seconds in which to savour the grace with which Rogers, in her simple but stylish black chorus-dancer's dress (not unlike the beautiful black gown she wears for 'Smoke Gets in Your Eyes' in *Roberta*), headdress and long black gloves, swings round Astaire and then drops to her knee in one of the most elegant of all her poses (**5.5**). She repeats the move, giving us a welcome second chance to appreciate its elegance, but even so the duet is over almost before it has begun. Perfect though it is while it lasts, its unfair brevity, at this climactic moment, and after the unwelcome length of what has gone before, is more than a little frustrating.

5.5 Rogers, the picture of elegance in a hastily donned chorus-dancer's outfit, partners Astaire in an unfairly brief dance of reconciliation, the title number at the end of *Shall We Dance*.

6

THE PLAYFUL DUETS

The predominantly fast and humorous or lighthearted duets that may be classified as playful are a splendidly diverse group, ranging from the pure comedy of 'I'm Putting All My Eggs in One Basket', the joyful frolics of 'I'll Be Hard to Handle' and the exuberant high spirits of 'I Won't Dance' and 'Let Yourself Go', to the charming flirtation of 'Isn't This a Lovely Day', the mischievous display of hitherto-unsuspected dancing prowess of 'Pick Yourself Up' and 'They All Laughed', and the merry romp of 'The Yam'. Each of the films in the series contains at least one playful duet (in a fairly broad definition that includes the 'Table Dance' from *The Gay Divorcee*), and *Roberta* is particularly well supplied, with two of the finest. The second of the two in *Shall We Dance*, 'Let's Call the Whole Thing Off', is the only disappointment in the group, and indeed the series, the novelty of a dance on roller skates failing to compensate for its limitations in other respects.

Whether the playful duets are, as John Mueller declares, 'the greatest single achievement in the Astaire–Rogers series',[1] is a matter for debate, but their claim is certainly a strong one. Rick Altman, who categorises most of the numbers in this group as 'challenge dances' – 'the dance that grows out of a difference, out of quarreling, even out of mutual insults' – regards them as the Astaire–Rogers trademark (more so than the romantic dance, which became a staple of the musical), and argues that it 'has never again been used with the same effectiveness'.[2] Certainly at least six of the ten duets in this group do grow out of some sort of difference, if not of actual quarrelling, and in four of them the resolution of that difference is the whole point of the dance, and an essential element of the plot.

There is no difference of any sort involved in the brief 'Table Dance' that concludes *The Gay Divorcee* (to the music of 'The Continental'), following on immediately from the unmasking of Rogers' husband as a philanderer and Astaire's announcement to the assembled gathering that she is to be his wife. This joyful celebration of their union, the first such event in the series, is not a truly playful duet, for there is no element of play as such, or any really humorous content; but it is full of high spirits and undoubtedly more akin to the playful than to the romantic in style and mood. Set in Rogers' hotel suite, now vacated of the supporting characters who participated in the denouement, the number is prefaced by a charming little episode involving four bellboys. Smartly lined up by the entrance with the couple's luggage (they are clearly about to go off on their honeymoon – formalities are swiftly concluded in the world of Fred and Ginger), the boys one by one, in time to the upward-swooping music, take up their allotted suitcases in their right hands then, as Astaire enters (a carnation in his lapel, and his hat and coat under his arm), take off their top hats, into each of which he casually tosses a coin. (And he injects variety and a degree of mischief into even this simple action, keeping the last boy waiting as he makes to pocket the coin before sending it the way of the others.) Then Rogers appears from inside the suite, dressed for the occasion in a smart, pale-coloured suit with contrasting hat and scarf – the most formal of all her dancing costumes in the series. Tossing aside his own coat and hat, Astaire joins her for their celebratory waltz around the room – not the usual secluded or purpose-made dancing area, or extravagant art deco set, but a modestly furnished affair, with sofas, tables and chairs. Undaunted by these obstacles, the pair happily and effortlessly dance their way round, on and over them, the music again swooping upward at appropriate points in their progress. Finally, their acrobatics over, the tempo slows and they conclude with a jaunty coda by the entrance – the watching bellboys still in attendance – before leaving the scene arm in arm, Astaire casually helping himself to one of the boys' top hats in the process.

The 'Table Dance', borrowed from the stage version of *The Gay Divorcee*, where it caused a sensation, is a delightful number, and if it appears less than sensational now it is because we view it in full knowledge of what Astaire and Rogers were later to achieve. The 'Table Dance' is simply a taster of the incomparably more exciting playful duets to come – and the one that concludes their very next film offers the clearest demonstration of their prodigious development.

'I Won't Dance', from *Roberta*, occupies exactly the same position, and fulfils exactly the same purpose, as the 'Table Dance': a celebration of the pair's union in the closing moments of the film. But while the earlier duet was merely enjoyable, this one is electrifying – a glorious, ecstatic frolic, overflowing with youthful energy and high spirits, and imbued too (in keeping with the general character of their relationship in *Roberta*) with a sense of fun. It bursts onto the screen only moments after their slow, beautiful dance to 'Smoke Gets in Your Eyes' at the end of the fashion show that Astaire has been compering, the brief intervening dialogue backstage serving to settle the marriage question in typically unsentimental style. We are kept waiting just a few more moments while Irene Dunne and Randolph Scott sort out their own relationship, and as if to underline the impatience of all concerned to proceed with the real business of the film, the opening bars of the music are heard as Scott delivers his trademark 'Gee that's swell'. Here come Astaire and Rogers, without another moment's delay, to give a superbly uninhibited and apparently spontaneous display of mutual joy. Rogers, who like Astaire (who is in tails) has of course had no time to change out of her costume for 'Smoke Gets in Your Eyes' – a gorgeous black sleeveless ballgown with an exceptionally full skirt, in which she created a picture of the utmost grace and elegance (**7.1**, p. 195) – now exploits it brilliantly, hoisting the skirt to her knees and flinging it about to exhilarating effect. Her performance in the 'Table Dance', in her smart suit and hat, seems restrained by comparison; and though 'I Won't Dance' is only two-thirds the length of its predecessor (it lasts a mere fifty seconds), and involves no acrobatics, its pace is much faster and its impact far more vivid. The dance ends as the pair bolt up a short flight of steps to meet at the top in a gleeful embrace, bringing the film to its most uplifting, and satisfying, conclusion.

'I Won't Dance' demonstrates that Astaire and Rogers scampering about a bare stage are truly sensational, and it was a mistake for them to resort to gimmick later in the series. As suggested above, 'Let's Call the Whole Thing Off', from *Shall We Dance*, is the one disappointment in the playful group – a disappointment that is all the keener because the film contains only one other full-scale duet. Dancing on roller skates was certainly an original idea, but it was to prove more of an impediment than an inspiration.

Astaire and Rogers, their skates on their feet and dressed in their everyday clothes (a light suit for Astaire, a casually smart dress and jacket for

Rogers, and both wearing trilby-style hats), are sitting on a stone bench in a secluded corner of New York's Central Park, where they have fled to escape the reporters besieging their hotel. They have concluded their disagreement over pronunciation in what Altman calls a 'challenge song',[3] and the challenge extends to some competitive tapping as, still seated, and with the music issuing an irresistible invitation, they 'clack out their disagreement, haughtily spinning the wheels in the air for emphasis', as Arlene Croce aptly puts it.[4] But the challenge evaporates as they rise, as of one mind, to begin the dance, and it proceeds around the circular paved area at their disposal without either dramatic or emotional interest (**6.1**). Astaire and Rogers dance on roller skates as skilfully and as apparently effortlessly as we might expect, but the gimmick severely limits the choreographic range of the dance, which remains not much more than a curiosity among their work. Performed by another dance team it would

6.1 'Let's Call the Whole Thing Off': Astaire and Rogers don roller skates for a bit of harmless fun in New York's Central Park. On screen, both partners wear trilby-style hats for this number.

probably count as a sensation (like the acrobatics in the 'Table Dance' in the stage version of *The Gay Divorcee*), but in comparison with the superbly expressive pieces to which we are accustomed from this partnership it falls rather flat. Not as flat, however, as Astaire and Rogers themselves fall, quite literally, as their experiment comes to an undignified conclusion on a grassy bank – the one truly humorous episode in the number, resulting in a conspicuous dent in Rogers' hat.[5]

Follow the Fleet contains the only other duet in the series that has no dramatic or emotional significance, but 'I'm Putting All My Eggs in One Basket', rich in humour from start to finish, is altogether more successful than the roller-skating experiment. Not so much a dance as a comedy act, its whole purpose is to amuse, and, remarkably, the jokes don't grow stale with repeated viewing. The number reverses the pattern of 'Let's Call the Whole Thing Off', where a 'challenge' song led to a challenge-free dance; here a song warmly expressive of mutual affection leads to a dance that sees Astaire and Rogers continually at odds with each other, though in the most lighthearted and playful of spirits.[6]

The dance concludes the 'rehearsal' sequence on board the *Connie Martin*, in which the pair run through their routine for the forthcoming benefit show. As Rogers, sitting on a wooden trestle, sings her final phrase, Astaire pulls her up by the hand and without more ado the dance begins. Both are in casual rehearsal clothes (Astaire retaining his white sailor's hat), with Rogers at her most unglamorous in a pair of loose-fitting slacks (seen in **3.8**, p. 129); and she gives an equally unglamorous performance, initiating the comedy by continually frustrating Astaire's attempts to perform a duet with her. Only a few seconds into the dance she takes such a liking to a low, kicking step that she repeats it several times more than she is supposed to, before eventually getting back into line with Astaire; and this blithe disregard for what her partner is doing sets the pattern for what follows. In the course of an action-packed three minutes she bumps into him, sending him flying (twice), before suffering the same fate herself; she engages in fisticuffs as he tries to control her; then, having given him a very hard time, causes him to walk off in despair as she reverts to the step that started it all off, grinning impishly in her tenacious self-absorption.

In the final stages of the duet both partners are thwarted by unexpected changes of tempo from the on-board band. As Astaire sits reading a newspaper the music abruptly shifts to a waltz; Rogers duly starts waltzing on her own, positioning her arms as if holding a partner, and Astaire quickly steps in to fill the gap – the first time in this duet that they hold each other in *dance*, as opposed to the punch-ups and other bits of mischief that have gone before. But after only a few moments the tempo speeds up jazzily, taking them both by surprise; again it slows and speeds up, and this time Astaire flings Rogers around rather too enthusiastically, causing her to topple into what Mueller describes as 'a stupendous fall – twisting, full out, pell mell, terminal – one of her most glorious moments'.[7] It is indeed a wonderful move, so utterly spontaneous in effect that it is even harder than usual to believe that it was rehearsed. While Rogers sits glowering on the floor Astaire, quite unconcerned, has his moment of fun in a fast-moving solo routine, until, the music apparently approaching its end, Rogers hurriedly gets up to join him for an applause-seeking finale. But again the band deceives them, thwarting their attempts to synchronise their moves to the music, until, after a series of uncoordinated stops and starts, they finally get it right.

This protracted and seemingly chaotic ending, in which Astaire and Rogers appear most convincingly out of step not only with the music but with each other, is another triumph of spontaneity. But the whole performance is a delight, and while both partners share the credit it is Rogers' mischievous sense of fun that sets the whole thing going and sustains the greater part of the comedy.

Earlier in the series, about half an hour into *Roberta*, comes another playful demonstration of Rogers' capacity to make life difficult for Astaire, but this time the dance emerges spontaneously, a casual extension of some lighthearted banter between the pair, and comedy is enriched by the expression of a warm mutual affection. 'I'll Be Hard to Handle', the first of what Altman calls 'challenge dances', and the first truly playful duet of the series, is, according to Arlene Croce, 'the big event of the film, the number in which "Fred and Ginger" became fixed screen deities'. As she rightly observes, the dance sustains 'a magical rapport . . . through three minutes of what looks like sheerest improvisation'.[8] Nowhere in the series is the illusion of spontaneity more successfully maintained – and nowhere in the group of playful duets does a dance reflect more precisely the spirit and tenor of the dialogue that precedes it.

Astaire and Rogers are in the Café Russe, where Rogers, in Polish mode, has given her characterful, no-holds-barred performance of Jerome Kern's song (in rehearsal) to an appreciative audience of one – Astaire, lounging in casual dress on the central staircase while his band accompanies her. Her performance over, she joins him (the camera showing her in full figure for the first time as she leaves the stage, revealing that she is wearing a pair of very floppy black trousers to complement her smart white blouse) and, in their first scene together since the pure tease of their initial meeting, they reminisce about the happy days of their past friendship (**2.7**, p. 71). With the band playing softly in the background, they each admit to having been in love with the other – Rogers in reflective mood, Astaire responding in his usual teasing style (with a frisky little tap phrase for good measure), but both clearly full of affection. Astaire continues the tease as Rogers recalls the beauty contest she won, thanks to him, revealing (with another frisky tap phrase) that he rigged some of the votes for her by using a picture of Lillian Russell. 'What was the matter with *my* picture?' asks Rogers indignantly, getting up to confront him. 'Well, if you must know, we got a lot of votes from the farmers with a picture of a prize heifer,' says Astaire. 'Oh, you!' responds Rogers affectionately, making to punch him. He wards her off, catching hold of her wrists; they smile happily – and the next moment they are dancing.

The affection, the teasing, the indignation, the mock violence, the happy smiles – all are reflected in this wonderfully playful duet, which also features some friendly rivalry, some deliciously natural laughter from Rogers and a rare whoop from Astaire, both partners revelling in the sheer joyous fun of dancing together (**6.2**).[9] The duet begins in very relaxed fashion with some casual tapping, but gradually gathers momentum and builds up to an infectiously energetic climax, with several stops and starts for some comic business on the way. In one episode the band falls silent as the pair try to outdo each other with alternate bursts of tap, in a sort of wordless dispute; as the dispute grows more heated Rogers stamps her feet in mock anger, slaps Astaire's face, and then stamps on *his* foot, looking mightily pleased with herself as he staggers about the floor. Eventually they resume friendly relations and, with the band now in full swing again, give themselves exuberantly over to dance, finally winding down, with the music, and dropping breathlessly onto two chairs. Though they have danced purely for their own

6.2 'I'll Be Hard to Handle': This image of the first truly playful duet of the series conveys beautifully the warm affection between Astaire and Rogers and their joyous fun in dancing together.

enjoyment their performance is now enthusiastically applauded by an audience of two bartenders and a cleaner; the pair duly acknowledge the applause and then bow to each other – a charming and beautifully uncontrived conclusion to the event.

'I'll Be Hard to Handle' is the first duet of the series with a comic element, and Rogers, who in *The Gay Divorcee* had little occasion to show how mischievous she could be, here seizes the opportunity with glee. But comedy is not the most memorable feature of this duet; the abiding impression it leaves is of the joy of dancing together shared by two old friends, reinforcing the emotional bond between them. In their dialogue throughout *Roberta* Astaire and Rogers do little more than tease each other; it is exclusively through dance that the true depth of their mutual affection is expressed.

The two old friends (and former dancing partners) meet in another playful duet at a similar stage in *Follow the Fleet*, just moments after their affectionate reunion backstage in the Paradise Ballroom. By this stage in the series, however, Astaire and (especially) Rogers had achieved enormous advances technically, and 'Let Yourself Go' is considerably more complex and more demanding in technical terms than 'I'll Be Hard to Handle'. We do not seriously imagine that they are making it up as they go along, and yet it is just as successful as that earlier duet in maintaining the illusion of exuberant spontaneity – with sensational results.

The number is quite explicitly a 'challenge' dance, the challenge being issued in the dialogue that immediately precedes it. On the floor of the ballroom a contest is announced, and couples start dancing to the song that Rogers had performed a short time before. She and Astaire (both wearing sailors' costumes – his authentic, hers a more glamorous version) enter from backstage and, unaware of the contest, try out a few 'neat' manoeuvres in between purely social dancing. Astaire, chewing gum as he talks, confidently announces his expectation that Rogers will ask him to marry her when his enlistment is up, and she responds with light sarcasm. They carry on dancing, affectionately, until, the adjudicator tapping Astaire on the shoulder to signify that they are out of the contest, Rogers realises what is going on. She is not supposed to take part, she tells Astaire, but he has other ideas. 'Maybe you're right – you probably couldn't keep up with me any more, anyway,' he says, to which Rogers, casually adjusting her costume, replies 'Oh, you think

not? Well, I'm not so sure *you* could keep up with *me*.' Astaire grins,
spins her around a couple of turns, and the dance is on.

By this time all but two other couples have been eliminated from the
contest, and in the first stages of the duet shots of Astaire and Rogers
performing fast and fancy manoeuvres are alternated with shots of their
competitors (whom they eye up warily), and of the enthusiastic audience of sailors. The initial challenge between Astaire and Rogers quickly
evaporates in the face of the more pressing challenge to defeat the competition, and they present a united front as they get into their stride
and become more and more adventurous. After their brief moment of
glory the other two couples, not surprisingly, disappear from the scene;
Astaire and Rogers have no difficulty in keeping up with each other,
but they are in a spectacularly different league from their rivals – even
before the tempo speeds up.

More than usually energetic and inventive leg movements – forward
kicks, backward kicks, wiggly jumps, hopping pirouettes (to mention but a few), all performed at a cracking pace – are the most striking choreographic feature of this ebulliently humorous duet, and their
visual impact owes a great deal to the floppy trousers that both partners
are wearing (**6.3**). For the greater part of the number they dance separately, and symmetrically, holding each other only for the occasional
brief sequence, but they join together in the final stretch for a sustained,
dizzyingly fast burst of tapping. Their performance over, they hold their
arms aloft in triumph, acknowledging the enthusiastic applause; in a
nice comic touch Astaire (still chewing) brings his jubilant partner back
to earth by unceremoniously pulling down her arm, which she seems
disposed to keep aloft indefinitely.

In all the duets considered so far, Astaire and Rogers begin on equal
terms: whether or not an element of challenge is involved, they enter
into the dance together in response to a shared impulse. In the four
remaining duets in this group one of the partners takes the lead, and has
to overcome a certain resistance on the part of the other for the dance
to proceed – a challenge of a different sort. It is, of course, Astaire who
persuades Rogers in the majority of cases; only once (in 'The Yam') does
Rogers take the lead and initiate a duet with Astaire.

The three duets that feature Astaire inducing a reluctant Rogers to
join him in dance, and winning her over completely in the process, are

6.3 'Let Yourself Go': Having seen off the competition on the floor of the Paradise Ballroom, Astaire and Rogers demonstrate just how unbeatable they are. This image shows the pair about to leap into the air for one of the wiggly jumps that are part of this duet's unusually inventive repertoire of leg movements – all enhanced by those floppy trousers.

essential to the development of the plot. To the elements of humour and emotional richness that distinguish the best of their other playful dances are added those of drama and romance – a uniquely potent and attractive mix.

The first of the three, 'Isn't This a Lovely Day', from *Top Hat*, follows on immediately from the song with which Astaire begins his wooing of Rogers as she takes shelter from a thunderstorm in a deserted band-stand in the park. She has been out horse-riding, the morning after their first meeting (her masculine-style riding habit will prove an important feature of the choreography), and, having been tricked by Astaire into journeying to the stables in a hansom cab driven by him, initially resists his friendly advances. She is quickly captivated when he turns to song (as she makes plain to the viewer), but, the song over, she feigns indif-ference, allowing him to get up from the bench on which they have been sitting and stroll about the bandstand alone.

Casually he whistles a part of the tune; she signals her complicity by whistling the next part, then gets up in her turn, putting her left hand in her trouser pocket in imitation of him, and slyly mimicking his step. Moments later she follows suit as he puts his right hand in his other pocket, all the while imitating his casual stride. Astaire now breaks the parallel pattern with a brief venture into tap; again Rogers imitates his move, and then surprises him by rapping out a frisky little step of her own. The introductory manoeuvres over, they dance in tandem for a while, side by side, then, as the tempo speeds up, face each other for the first time.

The outcome of the event has been a foregone conclusion from the moment Rogers rose to her feet, but a nice degree of suspense is maintained by the device of separation, whereby the dancers resist the temptation to hold each other until three-quarters of the way into the duet. Instead they continue their delightful, knowing game of imita-tion, whether side by side or facing each other, simultaneously or in sequence – a game that progresses in style and mood from challenge to cooperation (**6.4**). As Mueller points out, in his detailed and highly illuminating analysis of the twin devices of separation and imitation, 'The imitations that opened the dance were performed challengingly and mockingly, Rogers doing hers behind Astaire's back', whereas later 'the steps are done *for* the other dancer: as one does the step, the other stands back and admires'. Thus 'a single choreographic idea is

6.4 Challenge progresses to cooperation in 'Isn't This a Lovely Day (To Be Caught in the Rain)'. Rogers' masculine outfit is integral to both the setting and the choreography of the duet.

developed to suggest an emotional progression'.[10] And Rogers' outfit of jodhpurs and tweed jacket, as masculine as Astaire's suit, is integral to this choreographic idea, which depends for its effect on similarity of dress. Her outfit also precisely reflects the context of the number – an aborted horse-ride, for which any other dress would be inappropriate. There is no other instance in the series of such a close, organic relationship between context, costume and choreography.

Separation and imitation finally give way to true partnership as, after a thunderclap and a burst of rain, followed by a tantalising transitional sequence, the tempo speeds up again and Rogers crooks her left arm in a gesture that explicitly calls for Astaire to join her. In a joyful climax they whirl around the bandstand in each other's arms; at the very end they separate again and, leaping down from the stage, discover that it is still raining, whereupon they leap back up, sit down and shake hands with a smile of mutual congratulation.

'Isn't This a Lovely Day' makes its enchanting impact with remarkable economy of means, exploiting with great skill the humorous and dramatic potential of basically simple choreographic ideas. In 'Pick Yourself Up', the climax of the dancing-lesson sequence from *Swing Time*, Astaire and Rogers move into a different gear, to perform one of the most stunning of all their routines.

Astaire, immaculately attired in his morning suit, has seen his little ruse backfire: having successfully contrived to receive a lesson from Rogers at Gordon's Dancing Academy, and overcome her initial hostility through song, he has inadvertently caused her to lose her job. He protests when Mr Gordon (Eric Blore), after overhearing Rogers advise her hopelessly clumsy pupil to save his money, abruptly informs her that she is fired, but Blore, misunderstanding the situation, doesn't give him a chance to explain. Astaire seizes the opportunity a few moments later (by which time the irascible Blore has also fired Helen Broderick for her ungracious treatment of Victor Moore), and, taking Blore by the arm, tells him that Rogers was just trying to flatter him by saying she couldn't teach him anything. 'She's the most wonderful little teacher I've ever heard of,' he declares, as Rogers reappears on the scene, a small case in her hand, on her way out. 'I want to show Mr Gordon how much you've just taught me,' says Astaire, giving her case to Blore, and ignoring her protests as he leads her swiftly onto the dance floor. 'I'm very anxious for Mr Gordon to see this because I think it's a most interesting experiment. Now, how did you say that last step went? Er, oh yes' – whereupon he executes a nifty little tap salvo, forcing Blore to move hurriedly out of his way. The music strikes up, and a close-up shot of Rogers' face shows her expression of amazed delight. 'Shall we try it right through?' continues Astaire blithely. 'Won't you sit down, Mr Gordon?'

As Blore takes his place (off screen) the dance begins, modestly enough, with the simple 'three steps to the left, three steps to the right' that Rogers was attempting to teach her pupil, but it rapidly develops into something altogether more spectacular. 'Pick Yourself Up', crowning a sequence of matchless appeal on all fronts, is a duet unsurpassed before or since in its combination of technical brilliance, humour, dramatic and romantic interest, and the expression of unbounded joy.

At first Rogers, in her simple black dancing instructor's dress, dances in spite of herself, transfixed by Astaire's transformation from novice to expert in the space of a few moments, and her expression of astonished disbelief, yielding gradually to delight as she allows herself to be swept around the floor, is wonderful to watch. Soon she proves herself to be more than a match for her astounding partner, fully equalling him in intricacy of step and ease of execution (an ease that becomes positively impudent), and contributing her own special flavour of mischievous glee to their dazzling routine. Astaire, having initiated the performance ostensibly to impress Blore, glances towards him frequently, especially in the early stages of the dance, with an expression of justifiable self-satisfaction (**6.5**), and two brief cuts to Blore show him looking suitably amazed. Rogers seems less concerned with impressing Blore (although, once she has got over her shock, she clearly relishes this aspect of her performance) and more absorbed in the sheer joy of dancing with Astaire – which she conveys quite brilliantly. For Mueller, the number 'constitutes Ginger Rogers' most glorious two minutes', and though one might quibble about exactly which of her performances is the *most* glorious, 'Pick Yourself Up' is certainly 'a superb example of how much she contributed to their duets – not so much steps as flavor and point'.[11]

The pair make their exit in unforgettable style, first swinging each other exhilaratingly over the dance-floor railing and back again, then hurtling out with a hair-raising leap at full speed on the opposite side, and, miraculously, leaving the screen half a second later at a

6.5 Astaire and Rogers, glancing towards an off-screen Eric Blore, relish equally their joyous display of dancing prowess in 'Pick Yourself Up'.

casual walking pace. Blore, exclaiming 'Sheer heaven, my dears, sheer heaven!', rushes after them, and having rapidly reinstated Rogers in her post, arranges a try-out for them at a prestigious nightclub. Meanwhile Moore sets out to emulate his friend's success, but his clumsy attempt at partnering Broderick ends in an ignominious crash through the railing that Astaire and Rogers had negotiated with such spectacular ease.

Though Rogers gets her job back we never see her working again in Gordon's Dancing Academy; and some considerable time, both on and off screen, will elapse before she and Astaire get the chance to perform the try-out that Blore has arranged. Both these outcomes are secondary to the real point of 'Pick Yourself Up' – the transformation in the relationship between the pair, begun with the song and now complete, that will see them henceforth united as partners not only in dance but in romance.

'They All Laughed', a number that in many ways parallels 'Pick Yourself Up', and the last of the three in this group in which Astaire induces a reluctant Rogers to join him in dance, is the one duet from *Shall We Dance* that does not fall short of the new standards of excellence set in *Swing Time*. The number is indeed a worthy successor to 'Pick Yourself Up', with which it shares a broadly common structure and mood, though the two duets are of course quite different in choreographic terms.

Rogers, the star guest in the rooftop nightclub of her New York hotel, has completed her attractive rendition of George Gershwin's song for the benefit of the assembled crowd, unaware that her manager has been plotting with the bandleader behind her back to reunite her with Astaire – currently the object of her anger for supposedly spreading the rumour that they are married. As she acknowledges the applause, the bandleader takes her by the hand and prevents her from leaving the stage. Announcing that she has graciously consented to dance for them, he compounds her dismay by introducing her 'famous partner', Petrov. Astaire, equally taken by surprise but, unlike Rogers, delighted at the turn of events, slowly rises from his table in the midst of a fresh burst of applause, then swoops onto the stage and around Rogers in extravagantly balletic style, matching the bombastic, pretentious gestures of the introductory music. (He is, of course, not dressed for ballet, and in his rather more congenial tails he cannot fail to appear graceful despite the deliberately overblown nature of the choreography.) Rogers, who is wearing a very conspicuous, rather gaudily patterned dress, stands there motionless, at a loss; despite the fact that her relationship with Astaire is already well advanced, she has never danced with him, and is as ignorant of his true credentials as she was at the start of the 'Pick Yourself Up' sequence. Finally her so-called partner comes to a halt, and as he bows graciously to her, taking her left hand in his, she asks quietly 'What am *I* supposed to do?' 'Tweest,' he replies, in a mischievous echo of their first meeting, and she duly performs some graceful turns. He has not yet finished his balletic exhibition, however, and Rogers retreats instinctively as he swoops some more, placing such a distance between them that the camera can no longer contain them both in one shot. But she is not to be outdone, and having now recovered from her initial embarrassment she decides to turn the tables with a teasing little tap routine, clicking her fingers decisively on the last step. To her astonishment he responds in kind, first with deliberate restraint and then (after yet another bit of balletic swooping), emphatically, with a burst of noise that, like his salvo at the start of 'Pick Yourself Up', leaves no doubt as to his ability to tap. There is a brief pause of activity, during which the pair exchange pointed glances while the orchestra plays a soft arrangement of the opening bars of the song – then as the verse begins, the dance is on.

It starts cautiously, in contrast to the humorously flamboyant prologue. Astaire and Rogers are sizing each other up, still exchanging pointed glances as they tap side by side with studied casualness. Soon it gathers momentum, and the remaining vestiges of Rogers' resistance melt as she yields, once again, to the joy of partnering Astaire (**6.6**). The dance develops into perhaps the most rhythmically satisfying and infectious of their duets; its most memorable sequence sees Astaire tapping energetically and continuously, while with his right hand he guides Rogers, an expression of mischievous self-satisfaction on her face, in a series of graceful turns around the floor. The pace quickens for the duet's finale, an inspired sequence during which two strategically placed grand pianos provide the opportunity for some effortless, impeccably timed acrobatics. Guided by Astaire, Rogers springs onto each of the pianos in turn: the first time he pulls her back down for some more energetic partnering on the dance floor; the second time he leaps up to join her, just as the final chord is played, and they sit beaming with delight as the audience, quite rightly, applauds thunderously.

'Never was a fight so rhythmical, so varied, and so beautiful to

6.6 'They All Laughed': After having been tricked into dancing with Astaire against her will, Rogers (in an untypically gaudy dress) yields once again to the joy of partnering him.

watch,' declares Altman,[12] and though the fight is really over before the dance proper begins, there is no disputing his assessment of the quality of this number. Like 'Pick Yourself Up', 'They All Laughed' marks a transformation in Astaire's relationship with Rogers, but this time the effects are short lived, frustrated by the further, misguided machinations of Rogers' manager. The duet is, however, not only an essential element of the plot but the major event of the film in every respect.

Having been very publicly trapped into dancing with Astaire against her will in *Shall We Dance*, Rogers gets her own back in *Carefree*, in keeping with the role reversal that is so characteristic of this film. In 'The Yam', the final duet of this endlessly inventive playful group, and equally as essential to the plot as the three more typical duets discussed above, she takes the lead for the one and only time in the series, engineering an opportunity to dance for real with the man she has fallen in love with, and who has so far only danced with her in her dreams.

She is in mischievous mood as she enters the Medwick Country Club to dine with Astaire in the company of her aunt, her fiancé and their friend the judge, and when her attempt to engage him in social dancing (under threat of causing trouble if he refuses) is cut short she resorts to song in order to persuade the bandleader to play another dance number. The song, the only one in this group that is actually about a dance step, is well chosen, and having demonstrated the step in great style as she sings, Rogers is certainly not going to be deprived of the pleasure of performing it with Astaire at her side. She approaches his table and gaily motions to him to dance with her; he shakes his head, whereupon she takes a dish laden with food and weighs it up in her hand with ominous intent. At this he speedily gets to his feet, and 'The Yam' begins.

The role reversal extends into the first few moments of the dance, when Rogers teaches Astaire the basic 'Yam' step; as described by Mueller, 'every time a held note occurs in the music, the dancers are required to fling their hands limply out to the side, palms up, and then waddle forward while rapping out a pert tap phrase'.[13] Astaire, immediately entering into the spirit of the thing, proves a quick learner, and the dance is soon in full swing. After about a minute of fun-filled partnering, the pair separate and draw in members of their delighted audience to join them – not forgetting to come together for the Yam step each time the music calls for it. As Mueller notes, the forward waddle makes

the Yam a travelling step, and as more and more couples take to the
floor Astaire and Rogers yam their way out of the dining area, leading
their onlookers in a merry dance around the various other rooms and
passages of the country club.

Clearly, such a number could not be filmed in the one, two or three
shots that suffice for the great majority of the Astaire–Rogers duets. As
well as involving numerous changes of location 'The Yam' is unusually fragmented in structure, with pauses for the crowd to perform, for
Astaire and Rogers to show off for each other's benefit, and for Rogers
to resume singing halfway through the proceedings (with an entertaining little coda to the main song that affirms her commitment to the
Yam rather than a variety of other colourful-sounding dance steps). Not
surprisingly it is also by far the longest of the Astaire–Rogers duets, at
fully four minutes. But despite the fact that it was, astonishingly, filmed
in a hundred takes over two days, 'The Yam' never loses its momentum;
it has the character of a joyful romp, in which everybody has a great
deal of boisterous fun – and none more so than Rogers, who is bounced
off the furniture and runs around the place with infectious high spirits and energy, brimming over with gaiety and mischief. She is at her
most attractive in this dance (as indeed she is in the rest of *Carefree*),
with her hair in the flatteringly loose, shoulder-length style she adopts
throughout the film, and wearing an exceptionally stylish, rather fasci-
nating two-tone dress (best seen in **3.7**, p. 125), nicely complementing
Astaire's dark lounge suit.[14] She evidently enjoys wearing it, and generally seems to be having the time of her life, revelling in every moment
of what was all her idea in the first place.

Romp it may be, but 'The Yam' is no child's play, and for much of the
time the crowd can only gape as the manoeuvres performed by Astaire
and Rogers become more and more intricate. Eventually the pair re-
enter the main hall, where it all began, for the duet's sensational finale.
Here, making the most of the now deserted tables lining the dance floor,
Astaire props his leg on each of them in turn (there are eight in all) and
swings an ecstatic Rogers up and over, to the increasingly wild cheers
of the crowd (**6.7**). Three or four times would have been exciting; eight
creates a thrilling momentum, and an unforgettable conclusion to this
astonishing series of playful duets.

'The Yam' is unique in almost every respect, but perhaps its most
extraordinary feature is that it does not prompt any perceptible change

6.7 The thrilling conclusion to 'The Yam': an ecstatic Rogers swings over Astaire's outstretched leg for the eighth and final time, completing their sensational circuit of the dining tables in the Medwick Country Club.

in Astaire's feelings towards Rogers. While sharing fully in her exuberant joy throughout the duet, he remains afterwards immune to her charms and unaware that she is helplessly in love with him. The role reversal therefore proves only partially successful, though it does provoke Rogers' fiancé into admitting, quite understandably, that he was jealous of the way they danced together – an admission that, prompting Rogers to confess the truth to him, triggers all the subsequent twists and turns of the plot.

THE ROMANTIC DUETS

Set to some of the finest music in the series, supremely expressive and a visual feast, the romantic duets have at least as much claim as the playful duets to be counted the greatest achievement of the Astaire–Rogers partnership. They are certainly just as rich in choreographic invention, in emotional content and in dramatic and romantic interest; and their essential seriousness, taking Astaire and Rogers to realms of expression that they rarely touch in dialogue, or even in song, gives them a very special place in their work.

With the exception of *Shall We Dance*, where the omission is all too keenly felt, each of the seven films in the series contains one romantic duet, from 'Night and Day', the couple's first dance in *The Gay Divorcee*, to 'Change Partners', their last in *Carefree*. These six duets, while highly individual in choreographic terms, form a relatively homogeneous group, all predominantly serious in mood and (at least initially) slow in tempo. In addition, *Swing Time* and *Carefree* each contain a second romantic duet, rather different in style from the other six. The 'Waltz in Swing Time', though unquestionably romantic rather than playful in mood, is ebullient and fast-moving throughout, with extensive use of tap; and 'I Used to Be Color Blind' is unique in its fantasy setting and its use of slow motion.

Unlike the playful group, there is not a single disappointment among the romantic duets; on the contrary, seven of the eight are of consistently superlative quality, and while 'I Used to Be Color Blind' is not in the same class it serves its purpose admirably well and is genuinely innovative in more than one respect.

The 'Waltz in Swing Time' is a purely instrumental number, but the remaining duets are all based on song (usually following on immediately from that song), and these songs include many of the most outstanding of the series – not only 'Night and Day' and 'Change Partners' but also 'Smoke Gets in Your Eyes', 'Cheek to Cheek' and 'Let's Face the Music and Dance'. 'The Way You Look Tonight' also features prominently, at the start of 'Never Gonna Dance' (itself one of the less memorable songs of the series). These classic songs are given orchestral arrangements to match, and the result is a musical feast in its own right, complementing the visual feast that is the spectacle of Astaire and Rogers dancing together in romantic mood.

The musical soundtrack of the playful duets is not intrinsically memorable to quite the same degree, partly because the songs themselves are not in quite the same league as the romantic classics, and partly because the purely musical elements of the soundtrack are to a large extent inseparable from the sound and rhythm of tapping, on which much of the impact of the duets depends. Similarly, visual beauty is not necessarily an important aspect of the playful duets, whose appeal derives substantially from their humour, and where both partners often appear in casual or everyday dress. But in the romantic duets the sheer beauty of the image that Astaire and Rogers present is as compelling as any other aspect of their performance – and in this, as in every other respect, Rogers' contribution is quite crucial.

Gene Kelly is reputed to have once remarked that 'When Ginger Rogers danced with Astaire, it was the only time in the movies when you looked at the man, not the woman.' One can only assume that he was speaking in jest, for his statement does not bear a moment's rational scrutiny on any front. As I have already argued, the Astaire–Rogers partnership *as it appears on screen* was one of equals, and in terms of purely visual appeal Rogers' contribution, especially in the series of romantic duets, can hardly be overstated.

In the two less typical numbers, the 'Waltz in Swing Time' and 'I Used to Be Color Blind', Astaire deviates a little from his usual dress, but throughout the rest of the series his appearance is identical. In his trademark black suit with tails, white shirt and tie (a costume he did not enjoy wearing but which he appears born to wear[1]), he is unfailingly elegant and immaculate – so immaculate that we forget he was not handsome; a joy to watch, beautiful in his grace and strength, profoundly moving in his restrained expression. He is most usually in a position of control: often initiating the dance and willing a reluctant

Rogers to join him; always guiding her, supporting her; and even, in 'Change Partners', hypnotising her to follow his every direction. He is the constant, the perfect foil for the exquisitely variable Rogers, and it is to her that our eyes are drawn for the greater part of their performances together.

The only constant about Rogers' appearance is her sensuously slim figure – what Arlene Croce has called 'one of the most elegant dancer's bodies imaginable'[2] and another commentator, William Park (writing in 1970), 'one of the greatest figures of all time'.[3] Rogers' dress and hairstyle are different on each occasion, and our image of each dance is indelibly shaped by the way she looks. Her dresses, especially, form an integral part of the choreography; they are not merely beautiful in their own right but reflect, and to some extent even determine, the character of each dance – for they are often actively used by Rogers rather than merely worn by her. As we have seen, her costumes are also an important element of some of the playful duets (two notable examples are 'Isn't This a Lovely Day' and 'Let Yourself Go'); generally she does not draw attention to them, but just how vividly her imaginative use of costume can contribute to the style and mood of a dance is demonstrated by 'Smoke Gets in Your Eyes' and 'I Won't Dance', performed in quick succession in the closing stages of *Roberta*. Here, uniquely in the series, a single dress serves for two dramatically different dances, the one serenely romantic, the other exuberantly playful; and in Rogers' hands the dress changes character equally dramatically, from unruffled elegance to an uninhibited partner in play.

It is one of the most beautiful costumes she wears in the series – a sleeveless, low-cut gown of heavy black satin, with a simple bodice (adorned by 'a wonderful piece of faux jewelry'[4]) flowing into a luxuriantly full skirt, which, in 'Smoke Gets in Your Eyes', Rogers allows to fall around her (holding it, very unobstrusively, only at the very end) in shapes that at least partly define the contours of the dance. The mutual warmth and affection between the pair, the loving closeness of their relationship in this duet, is reflected in the complementary black-and-whiteness of their appearance, and a perfect symmetry is achieved in one particularly memorable, quite breathtakingly lovely pose: their two heads, cradled together, forming the apex of an exquisite double triangle, defined by the gently sloping lines of their limbs and filled by the voluptuous sweep of Rogers' full skirt (**7.1**).

Her costume for 'Let's Face the Music and Dance' could not be more different. The heavy beaded gown clings to her closely, coils and uncoils as she moves, clothes her protectively with its long sleeves and fur collar (it is the only dress that allows neither her arms nor her shoulders to be exposed), and precisely reflects the glamour and aloofness that are the distinguishing features of this duet – the only occasion in their entire partnership when Astaire and Rogers dance as strangers (**7.6**, p. 208).

Rogers reveals that the coiling and uncoiling of her gown was an unplanned effect and achieved with some difficulty: 'Every time I whirled, the weight of the skirt would flare out and slap me, throw-

7.1 'Smoke Gets in Your Eyes': A pose of perfect symmetry and complementarity, reflecting the loving closeness of the relationship between Astaire and Rogers in this duet (compare both Rogers' gown and the pose in **7.6**). This still, which was used on the cover of the original press book for *Roberta*, is probably the most widely reproduced of all images of Astaire and Rogers. On screen, where the orchestra can be seen in the background, Rogers does not actually hold her gown at this point, while Astaire cradles her head in his left hand, lending even greater intimacy to the moment.

ing me off balance. I had to learn to steel myself against the onslaught of the "third person" in our dance, my dress.'[5] However, this costume has become famous because of the (much less interesting) problems it created for Astaire – the heavy sleeves hitting him in the face early on in the first take. For similar reasons the ostrich-feathered dress Rogers wears for 'Cheek to Cheek' (seen in **7.4**, p. 204) is equally renowned: a large number of the feathers flew off in Astaire's direction when filming began and had to be sewn in place before it could proceed. Somewhat surprisingly, given their crucial role in the duets, Astaire was not involved in any way in the design of Rogers' costumes. Rogers herself, however, took the keenest interest in all her costumes and how they would work in a dance; as she remarks when describing her dress for the 'Waltz in Swing Time' (**7.10**, p. 219), 'When I put it on, I wanted to turn and whirl in it. Dresses always affected me that way. I can never emphasize enough how important clothing was to me. Fred could wear white tie and tails over and over, but I had to have different dresses and they had to be made for dancing.'[6] Rogers and her designers – chief of whom was Bernard Newman, who was responsible for the costumes in four of the seven films – therefore deserve the credit for creating in each case a dress which is unerringly appropriate to the style and mood of the dance, and which, as it moves with her, or as she holds it and twirls it and flings it about, creates shapes that are as beautiful and as important to the impact of the dance as are the steps themselves.

'Never Gonna Dance' is an outstanding example of Rogers' active use of costume in the romantic duets, her simple, low-cut white gown with diaphanous folds becoming an unforgettable feature of the choreography. At first, as the pair glide into the dance from a slow, hesitant walk, the dress simply enhances the beauty of Rogers' body, and delicately emphasises her vulnerability; throughout the subdued opening sequence she does little more than let it fall naturally about her. As they come to a halt and she begins to walk slowly away from Astaire, she holds a fold of the skirt unobtrusively in her left hand; when he catches hold of her right hand and abruptly pulls her round, the dress swirls round with her, held in a white arc from floor to waist. From that moment on, as the dance gains momentum and then explodes into action, she exploits the dress brilliantly, twirling and flinging it around her in stunning contrast to the formal lines of Astaire's black suit (**7.7**, p. 211). As they separate to ascend a wide double staircase Rogers holds the skirt in both hands, forming a great swirling semicircle of white which rotates as she rotates; then, in the last, impassioned moments of the dance, when she spins rapidly and repeatedly, propelled by Astaire, the dress spins with her, waist high, before falling slowly to its full length as she comes to a rest, briefly, in his arms. Finally, tearing herself away from him and fleeing from his sight, Rogers holds a fold of the dress across her body in a gesture of despair, while he stands back alone, broken and helpless. It is a powerful image, completing a powerfully moving dance and an exceptionally vivid visual experience.

Rogers uses her costume to equally memorable effect in the 'Waltz in Swing Time' (as we shall see later), but in the other duets in this group, as in 'Smoke Gets in Your Eyes' and 'Let's Face the Music and Dance', she simply lets it work for her – moving as she moves, shaping our image of the dance, and enhancing the beauty of the performance as a whole. In 'Change Partners', notably, Rogers is oblivious of what she is wearing; she moves, hypnotised, wholly at the command and under the control of Astaire (even the raising and lowering of her arms is directed by him), and her dress twirls and untwirls about her, quite independently, as she performs his bidding.

The visual beauty – the purely aesthetic appeal – of the romantic duets is of course complemented, and enhanced, by their expressive qualities and their dramatic and romantic interest. With the sole exception of 'Let's Face the Music and Dance' they mark an important stage in the development of the relationship between Fred and Ginger; in the case of 'Smoke Gets in Your Eyes' and the 'Waltz in Swing Time' they simply express the depth of the emotional bond between the pair at the height of their romantic attachment, while the remaining five duets move that relationship forward in a sequence that is essential to the plot. And though 'Let's Face the Music and Dance' is extraneous to the main action of the film, featuring Astaire and Rogers as strangers in a contrived setting, it is as rich in emotional, dramatic and romantic interest as any of the other duets in this group.

It is also, like all but one of the other duets, essentially serious in mood ('I Used to Be Color Blind', different in so many ways, is much lighter in tone). Whereas the playful duets delight and amuse, the romantic duets, with an expressive range from ecstatic joy ('Waltz in Swing Time') to deep despair ('Never Gonna Dance'), have the power to move – a power that never seems to diminish with repeated viewing. Indeed, it is *only* with repeated viewing that the full power, and beauty, of these superb duets can be properly appreciated.

The first of the group of six predominantly serious and slow duets, and indeed the first Astaire–Rogers dance of the series, 'Night and Day', suffers from some very distracting direction and editing, which imposes numerous cuts in the early stages and obliges us to view the dancers momentarily through a venetian blind and then from under a table. But the performance triumphs over the clumsy production, and, as Croce justly observes, 'no more thrilling or more musical dance had ever been presented on the screen'.[7]

Astaire and Rogers (who is of course dressed for dancing, in a sleeveless white ballgown with a full, frilly skirt) have spotted each other by chance in the seaside hotel where she and her co-respondent are to have their assignation. Rogers, embarrassed by the affair, has tried unsuccessfully to escape Astaire (who knows nothing of her predicament), and, against the romantic backdrop of the sea at night, has listened with mixed feelings – walking away from him more than once – as he sings of his longing for her in Cole Porter's passionate song. At its close, and as the orchestra takes over the theme, she walks off again, very deliberately, but he stands in her way. Three times she tries to escape and three times he thwarts her, but the fourth time he takes hold of her hand and does what Mueller (in his detailed and masterly analysis of this number) describes as 'a little supplicating "mating" dance' for her.[8] She ignores it and again moves away – but now Astaire finally succeeds in drawing her into the dance, in a sudden, unusually abrupt transition: all at once she is pulled into his arms, despite herself, her resistance overcome.

For a while she partners him closely, then – uniquely in this series of romantic duets – becomes absorbed in her own private world (her demeanour is unusually dreamy and abstracted throughout this dance), and almost seems to forget that he is there as she dances for and by herself. Astaire, by contrast, never takes his eyes off her, and eventually she meets his gaze and allows him to partner her again. When he repeats his little supplicating dance she responds by doing a little dance for him in her turn, but then, quite unexpectedly, has a change of heart, abruptly breaking off and walking away from him for the fifth time. Her resistance reaches its peak when she 'strikes' him across the face, sending him reeling away from her, but when he recovers his balance he finds her waiting for him. She joins him without protest for the final sequence of the dance, and this time, when Astaire again repeats his supplicating dance and she responds, they are holding hands. Thereafter they separate only briefly; as Mueller points out, 'as if to symbolize their new relationship, Astaire for the first time in the dance turns his back on her, confident at last that she won't try to run away'.[9] Finally he brings her gently to rest on a low, circular seat, from where she gazes up at him, entranced (**7.2**); after a brief pause he offers her a cigarette, which she refuses without changing her expression.

'Night and Day' is remarkable for the way in which Rogers' changing moods and attempts to repulse Astaire are incorporated into a seamlessly flowing choreography; every gesture and movement, including the 'blow' to the face with which she sends him reeling, is accomplished within the idiom of the dance, and with unfailing grace. Even more remarkable is that this extraordinarily eloquent performance was the first Astaire–Rogers pairing since 'The Carioca', for the two dances are simply worlds apart – in style, in mood, in richness of choreographic invention and, above all, in expressive power. Astaire had danced like this before, in the stage version of *The Gay Divorcee*, but it was a new experience for Rogers, and she responds to the challenge brilliantly. She would become technically freer and more assured as the series progressed, but already she demonstrates a faultless grasp of the dramatic and emotional import of the dance, and makes a more than equal contribution to its visual appeal. The final moments are particularly rich in beautiful images, as Rogers performs some delicate spins and twists in Astaire's arms, the elegant movements of her body enhanced by the graceful shapes of her full white dress.

Astaire certainly deserves his conquest; in no other duet does he have to work quite so hard to win Rogers over, and though his offer of a cigarette brings the scene back down to earth it is certainly not his fault that the mood of rapture in which the dance ends is rudely shattered by the misunderstandings of the ensuing dialogue.

There are no such problems in their next romantic duet, where drama gives way to the serene expression of the warmest mutual affection. Finally abandoning the playful teasing that has characterised their relationship throughout *Roberta*, Astaire and Rogers come together for two minutes of pure tenderness in 'Smoke Gets in Your Eyes'. The lengthy musical fashion show at the Café Russe has closed with Rogers' entrance, and Astaire, his role as conductor and compere completed, has begun

7.2 The ending of 'Night and Day', Astaire and Rogers' first romantic dance duet. Rogers, her earlier resistance having completely crumbled in the course of the dance, gazes rapturously up at her seducer. In a moment he will casually brush his hands together and offer her a cigarette.

to serenade her, admiringly, in 'Lovely to Look At'. Jerome Kern's lyrical song sets the mood of romantic togetherness that the dance will
sustain, and Rogers' reaction, and her own brief contribution, establish
beyond any doubt that she reciprocates Astaire's sentiments. They walk
slowly, arm in arm, away from the orchestra, and the dance gently slides
into being as, the final, unspoken word of the song merging seamlessly
into the theme of Kern's classic ballad, they descend the four steps to
the dance floor.

'Smoke Gets in Your Eyes' is the slowest of all the Astaire–Rogers
duets, though the leisurely walking pace at which it is performed gives
way briefly to a burst of energy in the middle section of the song, where
the dancers match the grand, dramatic gestures of the orchestra. But
whatever the tempo their performance is intensely intimate throughout;
though it supposedly has been rehearsed and is given for the benefit
of their audience (the first such duet in the series), Astaire and Rogers
dance purely for each other, exchanging looks of the greatest tenderness.
Their intimacy is conspicuous even when they dance separately, but the
closeness of their relationship is never more memorably, or more touchingly, expressed than when Astaire lovingly cradles his partner's head in
his arm, in the sequence that sees them united in the stunning 'double
triangle' pose described earlier (**7.1**, p. 195).

The predominantly slow tempo and the basic simplicity of the
choreography allow us to savour to the full the sumptuous visual spectacle of this duet, and especially of Rogers in her low-cut, voluptuously
full-skirted gown of heavy black satin, which moves beautifully throughout the dance and lends a seductive grace to her every step. It creates
one ravishing effect after another: as she simply sways gently from side
to side; as she crosses one leg unhurriedly over the other; or, in one of
the most memorable moments of the dance, as she spins rapidly round
in Astaire's outstretched arms, arching her back ever further away from
him and rising again in one superbly controlled and supple movement.
Later, at the climax of the impassioned middle section of the dance, her
dress sweeps the floor as she sinks even deeper, supported by Astaire's
arm encircling her waist, in a sensuous pose that was to feature in more
than one subsequent duet (**7.3**).

The dance is presented, gloriously uncluttered, in one continuous
shot until a few bars before the end, when there is an unobtrusive cut
to a different angle which allows us to watch from the most advanta-

geous viewpoint as the pair make their exquisite exit. After a flawlessly controlled backward leap up three steps,[10] and a casual spin or two by Rogers, they leave the stage arm in arm at an ultra-slow walk, eyes glowingly fixed on each other, lost in their own private world.

Backstage, Rogers (in the absence of the expected lead from Astaire) brings matters to their inevitable conclusion in a brief, lighthearted and typically unsentimental scene (at the start of which, uniquely, they comment favourably on their performance), and, their mood now one of exuberant joy, the newly engaged pair bound back onto the dance floor for the film's triumphant finale.

Astaire returns to the role of seducer for 'Cheek to Cheek', the second of the three duets in *Top Hat*. A far more elaborate dance than 'Smoke

7.3 The climax of an impassioned sequence in 'Smoke Gets in Your Eyes', Rogers' dress sweeping the floor as she falls into a deep backbend in Astaire's arm. This sensuous pose will be seen again, though in quite different contexts, in 'Cheek to Cheek' (**7.5**) and 'Change Partners'.

Gets in Your Eyes', performed at a much faster pace and virtuosic in parts, it is a direct successor to 'Night and Day' in its overall pattern and dramatic function. But in *Top Hat* Astaire has already successfully seduced Rogers (in 'Isn't This a Lovely Day'), and he has a much easier time on this second occasion, in both song and dance, than he had in 'Night and Day'.

Astaire has arrived in Venice in pursuit of Rogers (now wearing her famous white feathered dress[11]), and, encouraged by Helen Broderick, they have engaged in a little social dancing. Rogers' misgivings at the idea of dancing with the man she believes to be married to her friend crumble as Astaire starts to sing Irving Berlin's exquisite song, and she offers no further resistance to the end of the number. Thus, the song over, and without a pause in their dancing, he is able to lead her away from the crowded floor where the sequence began (the music building dramatically as he does so), and across a bridge to a secluded ballroom area where he will complete his seduction. It is an extravagant set, and in the initial moments of the duet the dancers, shown in unusually long shot from behind some pillars supporting a large canopy, are dwarfed by it, until a welcome cut brings them into closer view.

Although, in contrast to the drama of 'Night and Day', Rogers is unresistant for the whole of 'Cheek to Cheek', the choreography (as Mueller points out[12]) clearly traces a process of seduction. In what is its single most memorable feature, this justly famous dance exploits, to ravishing effect, Rogers' deep, supple backbend, a pose which was briefly, incidentally, seen in 'Smoke Gets in Your Eyes', and which here takes on a much more significant role. Astaire, never merely repeating a choreographic idea from one dance to another, transforms this most sensuous of poses from something that was largely decorative into the most important motif of the duet, using it to trace Rogers' ever-increasing surrender, and reserving its final, most sensational manifestation for the dramatic climax of the dance.

Thus when, in the first few moments, Rogers falls back and swings round voluptuously in Astaire's arms, it is a rapid, fleeting movement, suggesting but not dwelling on the sensuality of her experience (**7.4**). The movement is repeated twice, first almost immediately and again some way into the dance, when she hesitates very slightly before pulling herself out of it. At this stage Rogers is still in full control of herself. There follows some delicate tapping to the first few bars of the jaunty

7.4 An early moment from 'Cheek to Cheek', when Rogers, wearing her famous feathered dress, sinks fleetingly into the first of her sequence of backbends in Astaire's arms.

middle section of the song; the musical sequence is then repeated exactly, but, in a breathtakingly effective move, the dancers abandon their tapping to float gracefully across the floor, coming to a rest as Rogers, almost as if in slow motion, sinks back dreamily in Astaire's arms. Gently he pulls her up, and they repeat the sequence, but this time Rogers, with exquisite lightness of movement, sinks back even more deeply and dreamily than before. She is weakening, but rouses herself to join Astaire in a burst of impassioned activity (with a distracting cut showing them, again, from behind the pillared canopy), which is followed by a resumption of the quiet, flowing mood in which the dance had begun. Finally, the music builds to a grand climax, and the dancers traverse the length and breadth of the floor in a series of bold, dramatic manoeuvres, culminating in three swirling lifts, during which Rogers' feathered dress creates dazzling spirals of white. She falls out of the last lift directly into the last and deepest of the supported backbends – a stunning movement, accomplished with flawless timing exactly as the music comes to a resounding halt (7.5). Rogers, her surrender complete, makes no attempt to rouse herself from this ravishing pose, and both dancers remain motionless in the telling silence before the music softly resumes. Now Astaire tenderly lifts his partner up and they conclude the dance in loving warmth and closeness, a few gentle, rocking steps and graceful turns bringing them to rest by a low wall at the rear of the stage, where they gaze at each other wordlessly.

There are obvious similarities between this ending and that of 'Night and Day', but while Astaire's manner is here more tender and less matter-of-fact (he waits silently, watching Rogers solicitously), she, for the first time since the sequence began, seems troubled; after a pregnant pause she looks aside uneasily and then walks slowly away from him, as if brought back to earth and reminded that their relationship is doomed to disaster. Soon the blissful mood established by the dance will (as in 'Night and Day') be rudely shattered, but this silent, unhurried transition to the ensuing dialogue allows the spell to be sustained for a gratifying few moments.

While Mueller is unequivocally impressed by 'this ravishing duet',[13] Croce is extraordinarily unenthusiastic, damning it with faint, casual praise ('It's a good number . . . and there are several dreamy backbends for Rogers') and criticising it as 'a bit ritzy, a bit too consciously "poised"'.[14] It is true that 'Cheek to Cheek' appears at times slightly less

7.5 The stunning climax of 'Cheek to Cheek', the deepest of Rogers' backbends reflecting her total surrender to Astaire's seduction.

spontaneous than the great majority of the Astaire–Rogers duets, but it certainly does not fall short in choreographic richness or brilliance of execution, and it contains some of the most stunning visual images of the entire series. Concluding her brief assessment with a dismissive 'the dramatic action – the grand seduction – has already occurred', Croce (untypically) misses the point of the 'several dreamy backbends' and the emotional progression they trace.

No grand seduction occurs in *Follow the Fleet* until the closing number, and nothing in the film prepares the viewer for the magnificent spectacle of 'Let's Face the Music and Dance'. For once, the principle of dramatic relevance is jettisoned, and we can only be grateful for the fabrication of a benefit show that allows Astaire to change out of his sailor's bell-bottoms into his dress suit and to woo the aloof, heartbroken Rogers into this sublimely beautiful dance.

In an glamorous set overlooking the sea at night, Astaire, on the point of suicide after losing all his money at the gambling table, has saved Rogers, equally in despair, from throwing herself into the sea. Instead of shooting himself he sings to her (in one of Berlin's greatest inspirations) – of moonlight, and music, and love; and by the time he reaches the end of his song her despair has given way to a muted, sombre readiness to join him in dance.

The dance (presented without a single cut) begins slowly, as Rogers, weighed down with gloom (her heavy beaded gown precisely reflecting her mood) and seemingly hardly aware of what she is doing, sways wearily from side to side, while Astaire circles her, coaxing her into movement. Gradually she comes to life, and, in a symbolic gesture, flings aside the scarf she has been clutching, to join Astaire as a willing partner. She maintains her glamorous aloofness, however, scarcely looking at Astaire for the greater part of the dance, which remains intensely serious in mood almost to the end. There are no smiles, no exchange of loving glances, though Astaire's expression is tender and solicitous; they begin as strangers and dance purely for the sake of dancing. It could have been a cold, passionless performance, but it is quite the reverse, for although the familiar rapport and mutual warmth that distinguishes their other duets is missing, the dignity and absorption with which Astaire and Rogers perform is profoundly moving (**7.6**). Only at the very end do they acknowledge the presence of an audience, and by this time it is clear that they have become partners in more than dance.

Dance and music, equally glorious, are triumphantly worthy of each other in this duet. But while the music pursues its sumptuous course at an even, untroubled tempo, the dance weaves ever-changing patterns and, from its slow, hesitant beginnings, punctuated by languid pauses, builds up a rapid momentum. The second half of the dance is remarkably fast-moving, while never straying from its dreamy, abstracted mood, or losing any of its exceptional grace and nobility. In perhaps the most beautiful sequence of all, Rogers circles Astaire, and the stage, in a series of tiny repeated steps, her body arching slightly backwards and her arms uplifted, weaving delicately in and out of Astaire's. Arm

7.6 'Let's Face the Music and Dance': In this magnificent closing number from *Follow the Fleet* Astaire and Rogers dance, uniquely in their partnership, as total strangers. The dignity and absorption of their performance, and Rogers' glamorous aloofness in her protective beaded gown, are well captured in this still.

movements are an important feature of the choreography throughout, and the heavy, bell-shaped sleeves of Rogers' gown (best seen in **1**, p. 5) are exploited to striking effect. In the closing moments of the dance, as the music reaches a climax, she simply stands, arms outstretched first to her left and then on either side, as Astaire circles her in a grand, impassioned manner; such a static pose is unusual in their dances, and its elegance derives in no small part from those heavy, pendulous sleeves.

Seconds before, Rogers had finally abandoned her demeanour of dreamy abstraction as, swept up in the ecstasy of the dance's climactic moments, she allowed a joyous smile to break across her face. Thus signalling a new phase in her relationship with Astaire, she joins him uninhibitedly for their spectacular finale. In a dazzlingly swift, seamless manoeuvre, Rogers spins into Astaire's arms and drops with him to one knee. Here, at last, as they pause, clasped closely together, she looks him fully, knowingly, in the face; then they rise, walk a few steps swiftly backwards while the music, in its closing fanfare, swirls furiously around them, then walk slowly and deliberately towards the wings and leave the stage in a sudden, extraordinary gesture of defiance, arching deeply backward, with one leg raised high, their faces turned towards the audience for the first and last time. The manner of their exit suggests that their relationship, though it began with the dance, will not end with it, and that their shared experience has banished any thought of the suicide that threatened at the beginning of the scene.

Of the duets considered so far, 'Night and Day', 'Smoke Gets in Your Eyes' and 'Cheek to Cheek' explore essentially happy themes, albeit in a serious emotional key. 'Let's Face the Music and Dance' is darker in mood but ends triumphantly, and, being in any case one step removed from the main action of the film, does not disturb the carefree tone of the series. In their next film, however, Astaire and Rogers enter new territory, and 'Never Gonna Dance', the last of the three great duets from *Swing Time*, begins and ends in despair. It is a powerfully moving and dramatic work, expressive of the most profound emotion, and magnificently performed. Conceived on a grand scale, it covers an exceptionally large area, comprising not only the usual deserted ballroom floor but also a sweeping double staircase, leading to an upper landing where the dance is concluded. It is a fragmented dance, broken into several disparate pieces, but unified by an emotional coherence and dramatic force that are utterly compelling. This 'dance of dances'[15] has every claim to be considered the very greatest of all the Astaire–Rogers duets.

No other dance progresses through so many different moods, or covers such a wide choreographic range. In under three minutes it moves from quiet, reflective sorrow, through a wild, unrestrained exuberance, to abject despair, recapitulating key moments in the film as it proceeds.

Astaire and Rogers are in dejected mood, each reluctantly committed to another relationship, and each equally helpless to alter the unhappy turn of events. They are on the point of parting for ever, and Astaire has sombrely proclaimed, first in dialogue and then in Jerome Kern's strange, yearning song, that he's 'never gonna dance' again. To a beautiful orchestral reprise of 'The Way You Look Tonight', which he had sung to Rogers in much happier circumstances earlier in the film, he takes her by the hand and they walk slowly about the stage, stopping and starting as he turns to look at her in despair. Rogers, as reluctant to leave him as he is to leave her, maintains a sad, wistful expression as she quietly follows his lead. Their slow walk merges into dance with the utmost grace, and for a few moments they partner each other in a sequence of exquisite beauty and simplicity. But they both know it cannot last, and as the music of 'The Way You Look Tonight' gives way to the 'Never Gonna Dance' theme the dance peters out; Rogers walks with sad determination away from Astaire while he stands, bowed and dejected, where she has left him. Then he rouses himself, grasps her right hand and pulls her round, almost violently, to face him. (We have already seen how, from this moment on, Rogers' low-cut, diaphanous white gown becomes an integral and unforgettable feature of the choreography.) She gazes at him in astonishment, motionless; he pleads with expressive gestures of his whole body and draws her, as if mesmerised, into a transitional, tension-building sequence, to the accompaniment of an insistently repeated phrase in the orchestra. The dance then explodes into activity as, the tension released, the orchestra launches into a resounding version of 'Never Gonna Dance'. Both dancers sweep the stage in a gloriously uninhibited, virtuosic display (**7.7**); Rogers especially is sensational, justifying that famous cartoon by performing in high heels the same hair-raising, acrobatic leaps and turns as her partner. This dazzling sequence ends as the music modulates to the 'Waltz in Swing Time', performed earlier in the film at the height of their happiness; in the brief modulating phrase the dancers spin round

7.7 To the resounding theme of 'Never Gonna Dance', Astaire and Rogers sweep the stage in a virtuosic display, Rogers creating a swirling white arc with the folds of her diaphanous dress.

slowly, deliberately, before sweeping together into a reprise of the most ecstatically exuberant portion of that joyful duet. But the joy this time is short lived. After only a few seconds they drift apart, and as the music of the 'Waltz' continues (now, ironically, reprising the closing sequence of blissful togetherness) they spin their way separately up the curved double staircase leading to the upper landing. Here, for the last time, they come together again, and the music changes to a climactic rendering of 'Never Gonna Dance'. In a thrilling finale Rogers, propelled by Astaire, spins furiously around the floor: twice he catches her and spins her again; the third time she comes to a sudden, dramatic stop in his arms, but then tears herself away and, with desperate determination, rushes out of his sight. The picture fades on a heart-rending image of Astaire, bowed with the helpless misery of losing her.

'Never Gonna Dance' towers among the other five duets in this group, unmatched by any in its dramatic and emotional power. It is not altogether surprising that *Shall We Dance* found itself unable to produce a successor to such a masterwork, and omitted altogether the romantic duet that had been the highlight of every preceding film, resorting to gimmick in its search for fresh ideas. Fortunately gimmick gave way to truly creative innovation in *Carefree*, and the final duet in this film is in every respect a worthy conclusion to the series.

'Change Partners' is the shortest duet of this group of six, and one of the shortest of the entire series, but it is a masterpiece of concentration, flawlessly conceived and performed. One simple, inspired idea motivates the choreography from beginning to end: that Astaire hypnotises Rogers into dancing with him, controlling both her mind and her body. He has hypnotised her before in the film, with primarily comic effect, but here the purpose is intensely serious: to remove the disastrously unfavourable thoughts about him that he himself has implanted in her, and restore her genuine love towards him.[16]

Astaire, ignoring the judge's prohibition on seeing or even speaking to Rogers again, has tried to persuade her, first in speech and then in Berlin's classic song, to 'change partners' and dance with him, but has been met only with hostility. When her fiancé, true to the lyric of the song, is called away to take a (fictitious) phone call, Rogers goes outside, to the pavilion of the Medwick Country Club, to wait for him. Astaire now takes his chance and, following her out, asks 'Amanda, may I speak to you please?' She refuses; he entreats 'But please, Amanda' – only to abandon any attempt at speech in the next instant. Rogers (looking especially beautiful in a black, slightly shimmering gown,[17] her hair in a delicate snood) succumbs instantly to the magnetism of his hands, coaxing her to dance with him to the music that only moments before had failed to win her over.

Astaire is supremely eloquent in this duet, and our attention is focused on him to a greater degree than usual as we watch, transfixed, the strong, expressive gestures of his hands, bending the compliant Rogers to his will (**7.8**). The choreography is extraordinarily simple, for Astaire establishes his power over Rogers with the utmost economy of means, causing her to raise or lower her arms, twirl around and then stop, while he moves little but his hands. His control and her submission are absolute: in one particularly memorable moment he passes his hand over her eyes to close them, and allows her to fall backward, as if insensible, before supporting her so that she sinks gracefully into the deep backbend which is familiar (in quite different contexts) from earlier duets.

7.8 'Change Partners': Rogers, hypnotised by Astaire into dancing with her, submits absolutely to his control, expressed by the eloquent gestures of his hands.

There is a touch of arrogance in Astaire's manipulation of his entranced partner, but it is coupled with a great tenderness which reflects the warm, caressing tones of the music. And Rogers responds to him not only with a touching obedience but with increasing feeling and awareness. While at the beginning she clearly has no will of her own, and wears a blank expression, as the dance progresses she demonstrates a greater independence of movement and a conscious, loving warmth towards Astaire which suggests that he has tapped her deepest feelings for him. As the tempo of the music changes for the middle section of the dance, she partners him on equal terms in a beautiful, swirling waltz, which ends as she spins away from him and comes to rest a few feet in front of him, her back to the camera. Now Astaire draws her slowly towards him again, his hands and whole body expressing the intensity of his yearning for her. The camera cuts, for the first and only time, to a closer shot, showing the dancers in a rapt embrace, which they sustain for a few, lingering moments as they glide slowly across the floor, lost in each other. The music has almost reached its end before they separate briefly for the dance's extraordinary conclusion, which sees Astaire, in a sudden, deliberate movement, lift Rogers right off her feet and spin her round, supine, like a lifesize doll, before bringing her gently to her feet again and placing her with tender care on a low seat. She is still under his spell, but this is abruptly broken by the arrival of her fiancé, and Astaire's expression of despair as she comes out of her trance and embraces his rival is poignant to watch.

In its concentration of dramatic purpose combined with its extreme economy of choreography 'Change Partners' is unique among the Astaire–Rogers duets. Modest in scope but daring in innovation and intensely moving and vivid in impact, it demonstrates that the Astaire–Rogers dancing partnership was as compelling at the end of the series as it had ever been.

The two duets that remain to be considered stand at opposite ends of the spectrum, the one a relatively minor work, the other a masterpiece of such stature that it rivals 'Never Gonna Dance' in its claim to be counted the very greatest of all the Astaire–Rogers duets. Both stand apart from the other duets in the romantic group, 'I Used to Be Color Blind' for its lighter tone, its dream context and use of slow motion, the 'Waltz in Swing Time' for its speed, its exuberant mood and its extensive use of tap. In both numbers, too, Astaire sheds his white tie and tails, wearing a morning outfit of dark jacket, light grey trousers and spats in Rogers' dream, and a dark suit with a floppy bow-tie in the 'Waltz' – costumes that reflect the different character and mood of the respective duets.

True to the general spirit of *Carefree*, 'I Used to Be Color Blind' is initiated by Rogers – in this case quite literally dreamed up after her dinner of dream-provoking foods prescribed by Astaire, her psychiatrist who has so far shown only a professional interest in her. To the accompaniment of some vague, transitional music involving an off-screen chorus, the shot of a smiling Rogers stretched out asleep on her bed slowly dissolves into the fantasy setting. The romantic couple, led onto the scene by Rogers, are initially somewhat dwarfed by the giant, unreal vegetation and the fairy-tale castle in the background (seen in **3.6**, p. 118) – all framed by appropriately blurred edges; but the camera soon brings them into closer view, as Rogers settles herself happily on a bank to listen to Astaire serenade her. She gets up as he launches into the first verse, and they move about the dream landscape as he sings, until, on the last line (extolling the blue in her eyes) she offers her hands to him and the dance begins. After a very few moments there is a gradual shift to slow motion (achieved without a cut), and the remainder of the dance is shown in slow motion while the music continues at normal speed; as Mueller notes, 'enormous care had to be taken to fit the dance to the music'.[18] The dance area itself takes the form of two giant, adjacent water-lily leaves, and the dancers leap slowly across the water from one to the other in the course of the sequence.

Rogers has a wonderful time in this dance, enjoying a series of twirls and leaps and lifts that float dreamily across the screen, and her ecstatic delight in the experience is most unmistakably conveyed. She looks enchanting, in a white, diaphanous gown, with a bow in her hair and a long, gossamer-like scarf in her left hand; another such delicate piece of fabric is attached to the right shoulder of her dress, and both float up and around her as she moves – with an exquisite lightness of touch, hardly seeming to touch ground as she alights from Astaire's sweeping lifts. The dance culminates, against the backdrop of a rainbow, in a dreamy, very low backbend in Astaire's arms and a rapturous, satisfyingly long kiss; but unfortunately for Rogers the rapture ends with that kiss, and she has a long way to go before the reality of her relationship with Astaire lives up to the stuff of her dreams.

While 'I Used to Be Color Blind' is by no means the most remarkable of the Astaire–Rogers duets in purely choreographical terms – dance as such being subordinate to the manner of presentation and the dramatic implications of the piece – it is a delightful number and its use of slow motion is not only innovative but wholly appropriate for the purpose. It is a pity that the sequence could not have been filmed in colour, as originally planned and as demanded by the lyric of the song, but though the picture is monochrome the mood is sunny throughout.[19]

Finally we come to the 'Waltz in Swing Time', a magnificent creation that is pure dance, the most virtuosic and choreographically complex of all the Astaire–Rogers duets. Thinly disguised as an audition for a night-club engagement, it has no significant dramatic purpose; it is, as Astaire casually remarks to his nervous partner shortly before they are due to go on stage, 'only a dance'. But what a dance! This rapturous expression of youthful, exuberant love, uniting the effervescent high spirits of 'I Won't Dance' with the serene contentment of 'Smoke Gets in Your Eyes', represents a level of choreographic invention and technical accomplishment that could not even have been imagined at the time of *Roberta*. It is a dance of quite dazzling beauty and virtuosity, performed at a remarkably fast pace and without so much as a pause for breath (at over two and a half minutes it is also one of the longer duets of the series), and it is necessary to view it at least a dozen times before we can even *begin* to grasp the wealth of detail with which it abounds. But as one thrilling sequence flows into the next, the abiding impression we are left with is not the complexity of the choreography, or even the technical brilliance of the performance, but rather the sheer beauty of the spectacle and the expression of pure joy with which every moment is imbued – especially on Rogers' part, for in this duet more than in any other she simply radiates joy in her partnership with Astaire.

The 'Waltz', the only duet in the series to be based on purely instrumental music, is performed at the height of the pair's romantic partnership, shortly after their tender reconciliation in 'The Way You Look Tonight' and immediately (in screen time) before Rogers receives the devastating news of Astaire's engagement in the 'Fine Romance' sequence. It is, ostensibly, the audition secured for them by Eric Blore after their dazzling display of a different sort in 'Pick Yourself Up', but as a result of some plot complications they end up performing the dance at the wrong nightclub, in the absence of the man who was supposed to be auditioning them. This, of course, doesn't matter in the slightest to anyone; any vestiges of dramatic significance are swept away the moment they take to the floor.

'The lovely "Waltz in Swing Time"' is announced by Astaire to the nightclub audience as the newest composition of bandleader Georges Metaxa, Rogers' would-be suitor, who has hitherto refused to play for the pair but now finds himself trapped into doing so. Astaire raises the startled Metaxa's baton for him and the orchestra strikes up; Rogers makes her entrance, he removes her cape, and the dance begins (**7.9**).

The 'Waltz' (which is shown in one continuous shot) is not only brilliantly virtuosic but raptly intimate, reflecting the contrasting moods and styles of the music – both quietly lyrical and exhilaratingly upbeat, rhythmically complex but with an irresistible swing. Croce comments that the dance flows through 'so many intricacies and surprises, so many acts of mutual gallantry and faith that they can't possibly be cited, much less described'.[20] Mueller, admirably, does both, but really no description can hope to do justice to such a piece. One astonishing sequence among the so many: when Rogers, facing Astaire, joyfully curves her body for him to vault over it, twice, and a third time presents her slightly inclined back for him to repeat this most intimate manoeuvre – just before they both rush headlong, in each other's arms, into the final stage of the dance. Another: when the partners, separate but close, trace a diagonal line backwards across the floor in a series of tiny repeated steps – Rogers, rejoicing in the moment, holding the skirt of her dress up before her in a delicious frothy curve. The dress, pure white and modestly cut (it could be her wedding dress), with an unusually high neckline in the front, short, extravagantly frilly sleeves and a full skirt with layer upon layer of the same frills, is truly a third partner, making a hugely important contribution to the shape of the dance and its stunning visual impact. Rogers exploits it superbly; she has said that when she put it on she 'wanted to turn and whirl in it',[21] and she does just that, creating glorious waves of white as she swirls it around her (**7.10**).

7.9 Astaire and Rogers, at the height of their romantic partnership in *Swing Time*, take to the stage for the 'Waltz in Swing Time', while bandleader Georges Metaxa glowers in the background. This posed still has no counterpart on screen, where the pair launch into the duet without pause after Astaire removes Rogers' cape, but it reflects precisely the mood of the dance.

After the breathtakingly fast and ever-changing sequences of the first two minutes of the duet, culminating in a climactic burst from the orchestra and an onward rush of partnered waltzing, the music quietens, and for the last half-minute the pair, tapping gently and continuously, simply circle the floor in each other's arms, blissfully, as if entranced. Finally, on a closing fanfare, they sweep each other off the stage, disappearing in a whirl of white behind a venetian blind. White is the colour of this dance, and it is incandescent, blazing a trail of incomparable brilliance, and leaving the warmest of glows in its wake.

7.10 Astaire, Rogers and the 'third partner' in the 'Waltz in Swing Time': Rogers' extravagantly frilly dress, which she swirls around her in waves of white.

EPILOGUE

Fortunately we do not have to decide whether the 'Waltz in Swing Time' is a greater piece of work than 'Never Gonna Dance', or whether the romantic duets are a greater achievement than the playful duets. We can simply rejoice that all have been preserved on film (and, moreover, are available on video or DVD), and many viewers may well reach the conclusion that the greatest Astaire–Rogers duet is the one they happen to be watching at the time. For it is a measure of the quality of these dances that, with very few exceptions, none is diminished by comparison with other, more spectacular examples. The brilliance of the 'Waltz' does not eclipse the beauty of 'Smoke Gets in Your Eyes', any more than the power of 'Never Gonna Dance' overshadows the quiet drama of 'Change Partners'. And however much we are seduced by the brilliance, beauty, power and drama of these romantic masterpieces, when we watch a playful duet as superlative as 'Pick Yourself Up' we can readily concede that it's the best of the lot.

Astaire and Rogers could never have imagined that, decades after they first appeared on screen, their dances would be endlessly viewed, re-viewed and analysed, their every step subjected to the most exhaustive examination. The original audiences of the 1930s had the priceless pleasure and privilege of experiencing the Astaire–Rogers dancing partnership as it was born and reached its peak; but viewers in the twenty-first century have the equally priceless advantage of being able to watch the dances at will, in their own homes, as many times as they wish – and even in slow motion. There is, of course, a danger in such exhaustive familiarity: perhaps hitherto unnoticed flaws will become obvious, or the dances will gradually lose their original appeal. On the contrary, however: they emerge triumphant after even hundreds of viewings, after the most searching scrutiny of their every detail; their appeal undiminished and the perfection of their construction and execution inspiring only ever-increasing admiration.

The Astaire–Rogers dancing partnership is, of course, just one facet of the phenomenon of Fred and Ginger, and if the pair had never danced a step together in the seven films of the series (admittedly a somewhat absurd hypothesis, as dance is the films' *raison d'être*) they would probably still be remembered with affection today as one of the most appealing and entertaining screen partnerships that Hollywood produced. But it is in those fifty minutes of dance that they really made their mark and attained legendary status, and it is those fifty minutes that will ensure their immortality, as successive generations fall under the spell of the most electrifying dancing partnership in cinema history.

After the heyday of that partnership came to an end in 1939, Astaire, despite an uncertain start as he sought new partners, went on to make several very successful and enjoyable musical films (as well as a few failures) without Rogers. Later, as the golden age of the Hollywood musical declined in the mid-1950s, he moved, equally successfully, into a varied career on television and in non-musical films. Though he was never again involved in a partnership that captured the public imagination as Fred and Ginger had done, he suffered no diminution in his dancing prowess or his inventiveness, and long before he finally retired from dancing after his last television special in 1968, at the age of sixty-eight, his reputation as one of the greatest dancers and choreographers of the twentieth (or any other) century was secure.

Rogers, by contrast, saw her career decline from the mid-1940s. Having made some highly engaging and successful non-musical comedies in the late 1930s (*Stage Door*, with Katharine Hepburn, in 1937, and *Bachelor Mother*, with David Niven, in 1939, are two outstanding examples) and won an Oscar for her performance in the romantic drama *Kitty Foyle* in 1940, she was for a time one of Hollywood's highest-paid stars. But her films of the 1940s, in which she played a variety of non-musical roles in a series of increasingly improbable and unflattering hairstyles, are a very mixed bag indeed. Even *Kitty Foyle* seems too sentimental today, and few of the rest bear repeated viewing. After mistakes such as the pretentious *Lady in the Dark* (1944), Rogers' brief return to musical comedy, and her partnership with Astaire, in *The Barkleys of Broadway* is a welcome reminder (the Sarah Bernhardt scene apart) of how much more effective she – like her character in the film – was when she didn't take herself too seriously. She made several more (largely forgettable) films in the 1950s and one or two in the 1960s, as well as some television specials, and eventually returned, not very successfully, to stage musicals. Despite her Oscar, and some very commendable solo performances, she will always be chiefly remembered for the films she made with Fred Astaire.

The Astaire–Rogers partnership, born of the chance pairing of two very different and not obviously well-matched performers, was one of the happiest miracles of the twentieth century. In a radio interview following the UK release in late 2003 of a DVD set of four Fred and Ginger films, Astaire's daughter was asked why they don't make them like that any more. 'Because there has never been another Fred Astaire or another Ginger Rogers,' she replied. It is unlikely that there ever will be.

NOTES

Introduction

1 Croce, p. 6. All references to Croce are to *The Fred Astaire and Ginger Rogers Book* unless otherwise indicated.

2 Croce, p. 33.

3 Croce, p. 17.

4 The song was nominated for an Oscar in 1934 (John Funnell, *Best Songs of the Movies*, p. 7).

5 Interviewed in *The RKO Story, Episode 2*.

6 Astaire, *Steps in Time*, pp. 238, 238–9.

7 Stanley Green, in *Starring Fred Astaire*, gives a detailed analysis of the differences between the film and the factual details of the Castles' lives (Green and Goldblatt, pp. 193, 196, 198–9).

8 The duet can be viewed unobscured by the opening titles in MGM's compilation film *That's Entertainment! III* (1994).

9 Croce takes a different view, judging that Astaire and Rogers are 'miraculously on top of the old form' and that the number is 'the best thing in the movie' (pp. 172, 173).

10 Mueller, p. 292.

11 Again Croce differs, finding the performance 'too aggressively professional' (p. 176).

12 Mueller, p. 296.

1   The Fred and Ginger films

1 The title of the stage show, *Gay Divorce*, was modified to *The Gay Divorcee* in the USA on the grounds that it was improper to describe a divorce as 'gay' (in the original sense of lighthearted or carefree). However, prints of the film released in Britain bear the original title.

2 Mueller, p. 54n.

3 For all the advantages of video and DVD, the experience of viewing the films, and especially the dances, on the big screen, and in a packed theatre (as the original audiences of the 1930s viewed them), is not to be missed.

4 Among the unreal characteristics that Green identifies as typical of what he calls 'Astairogersland' (from which he excludes *Roberta* and

Carefree as not representing the best of Astaire and Rogers) are the settings – 'All hotels were dazzling white . . . Nightclubs were huge and amply chandeliered, and usually high in the sky. Private homes were surrounded by grounds so vast they could easily accommodate outdoor dance floors' – and the laws relating to marriage, which were 'so liberal that it was never any problem to find someone to perform the ceremony at a moment's notice' (Green and Goldblatt, pp. 5, 7).

5   Green gives a detailed listing of the films' many similarities (Green and Goldblatt, p. 98).

6   One of the script's many pleasures is the nice symmetry of these two lines, spoken twenty minutes apart:
     Astaire (puzzling over why has Rogers slapped his face): 'If I ever forgot myself with that girl I'd remember it.'
     Rogers (plotting her revenge): 'I'll make him remember me in a manner he'll never forget.'

7   Mueller, p. 65.

8   A rare error of judgement on the part of Stanley Green; he does, however, exclude the 'buoyant Astaire–Rogers routines' from this damning assessment (Green and Goldblatt, p. 88). Arlene Croce, writing at around the same time, recognises *Roberta* as 'a key film', observing that 'it widens their range and establishes them unshakeably as a team' (p. 46).

9   Mueller, p. 101.

10   In her autobiography, *Ginger: My Story*, Rogers, who singles out *Swing Time* as her 'favorite child' of the films she made with Astaire, is warmly appreciative of Stevens' direction: 'He had an incredible sensitivity to an *actress* playing a scene. He looked for nuances and was always delighted when I added something new' (p. 146). She found Mark Sandrich much less sympathetic: he worshipped Astaire but 'I was dismissed as a little bubblehead' (p. 133).

11   Croce, p. 101.

12   Croce, p. 103.

13   Mueller, p. 117.

14   Edward Gallafent, in *Astaire and Rogers*, explores nine ways in which *Shall We Dance* is innovative in relation to the rest of the series, including the rather dubious distinction of its being the only film to make references to pregnancy and children (pp. 62–5).

15   *Shall We Dance* made a profit of $413,000 – half that of *Swing Time* and less than a third of the $1,325,000 made by *Top Hat*. *Carefree* was the only film of the series not to make a profit for RKO; it had a deficit of $68,000 (Mueller, p. 410).

16   It was in the interval between *Shall We Dance* and *Carefree* that Astaire

made his only film without Rogers in the course of the series, *A Damsel in Distress*, with Joan Fontaine (1937).

17   Mueller, p. 139.

18   The supporting cast also features Hattie McDaniel, in two brief but memorable appearances as Rogers' maid, just a year before she gained stardom (and an Oscar) for her portrayal of Mammy in *Gone With The Wind*.

19   Green and Goldblatt, p. 174. The film is still undervalued in some quarters even today; a review in 2003 declared that 'This rather silly comedy musical is one of the weakest of the Astaire/Rogers features' (*Radio Times*, 20–26 September 2003).

2   The Astaire–Rogers acting partnership

1   In *The Runaway Bride: Hollywood Romantic Comedy of the 1930s*, Elizabeth Kendall points out that Astaire's persona in *The Gay Divorcee* was essentially established in the stage version, whereas Rogers brought to her role qualities that her stage counterpart, Claire Luce, wholly lacked – a 'natural sincerity . . . a lovely unguardedness' (p. 95).

2   Croce, p. 59.

3   See note 5.

4   Actually whipped cream, which, as Rogers reveals in her autobiography, was the only substance that created the desired effect without running down her face, as did the various soaps, the shaving cream and the beaten egg white that were previously tried (pp. 144–5).

5   Mueller, p. 144. Astaire himself cites only the first two of these reasons in his autobiography, *Steps in Time*: 'It was my idea to refrain from mushy love scenes, partly because I hated doing them and also because it was somewhat novel not to have sticky clinches in a movie' (p. 233).

6   Astaire, p. 233.

7   Mueller, p. 144.

8   Mueller, p. 111. He adds in a footnote that 'In the various scripts for *Swing Time* the dialogue for this scene got briefer – and better – with each revision.'

3   The musical numbers

1   The only numbers not discussed in this chapter are the vaudeville-type 'organ' number at the beginning of *Roberta* (a minor and very untypical piece) and two dance fragments – the opening sequence of *Swing Time* and Rogers' first appearance in *Shall We Dance* (see also note 24).

2   Mueller, p. 58.

3   'Night and Day' was ineligible for nomination because the Academy rules excluded songs that had not been specifically composed for the films in which they appeared (Funnell, pp. 2–3).

4   The song, the only one newly composed for the film, lost out (along with Berlin's 'Cheek to Cheek' from *Top Hat*) to Harry Warren and Al Dubin's 'Lullaby of Broadway' from *Gold Diggers of 1935* (Funnell, pp. 15, 20).

5   Mueller, p. 91.

6   Mueller, p. 107.

7   Mueller, p. 142.

8   Stanley Green reports that 'Although the final footage [of the whole number] showed sixteen actual swings, Astaire had to slam out almost a thousand tee and iron shots during his ten-day, eight-hour-a-day rehearsal period. It then took two and a half days to film the sequence, which lasted less than three minutes on the screen' (Green and Goldblatt, p. 177).

9   Quoted in Larry Billman, *Fred Astaire: A Bio-Bibliography*, p. 89.

10   Quoted in Mueller, p. 21.

11   Altman, pp. 136–8. Philip Furia, in his *Irving Berlin: A Life in Song*, reinforces the point, noting that film recording techniques (the use of microphones and pre-recording) allowed the composer to disregard the old 'singability' rules that applied to stage performance (long notes and open vowels). 'In Hollywood, Berlin could concentrate on Astaire's ability to enunciate syllables and follow the trickiest of rhythms. Using shorter vowels and clipped consonants, Fred Astaire's singing could now sound more like Astaire talking' (p. 174).

12   Mueller notes that the number 'makes some people uncomfortable today' (p. 108), but that it could be seen as a homage to Robinson, although Astaire had much greater admiration for another black dancer, John Bubbles, and his costume suggests the character Sportin' Life, from Gershwin's *Porgy and Bess*, which Bubbles had created on stage the year before (pp. 108–9).

13   Mueller, p. 120.

14   Hermes Pan, Astaire's dance director, recalls that the number was inspired by the rhythm of a cement mixer on the RKO lot (*Fred Astaire: Puttin' On His Top Hat*).

15   There is a case for including an eleventh song, 'Lovely to Look At' (from *Roberta*), in this group, but as Rogers makes a brief contribution to it, it strictly belongs with the duets.

16   As Berlin himself remarked: 'The melody line keeps going up and up, he *crept* up there. It didn't make a damned bit of difference. He made it' (quoted in Mueller, p. 83n.).

17   Mueller, p. 106.

18   The reference to the Major would have been less puzzling at the time of the film's release: he was the impresario of the 1930s radio talent-spotting show *Major Bowes' Original Amateur Hour*. Among the hopefuls who appeared in it was the twelve-year-old Maria Callas, singing 'Un bel dì' ('One Fine Day') from Puccini's *Madama Butterfly* (a brief audio clip of her performance featured in the documentary *Queens of Heartache*, shown on BBC 1 on 27 July 2006).

19   Astonishingly, the song failed to win the Oscar in 1937, losing out to Harry Owens' 'turgid and dreary' 'Sweet Leilani' from *Waikiki Wedding* (Funnell, p. 39).

20   Mueller, p. 123.

21   'To this day,' says Rogers in her autobiography, 'it drives me up a wall when I see what was done to "They Can't Take That Away from Me"' (pp. 159–60). Furia reports that Gershwin himself was upset that the song 'was not given the full-scale dance treatment' (p. 186).

22   According to Mueller (p. 143) the colour plan was abandoned because of financial constraints. Croce (p. 150) and Furia (p. 187) state that the idea was shelved because the colour tests were disappointing. Furia also gives an interesting insight into how Berlin improved his lyric: the original version read 'I never could see the green in the grass, the gold in the moon, the blue in the sky' (p. 187).

23   Green and Goldblatt, p. 180. The song was one of ten Oscar nominees in 1938, including another Berlin song, 'Now It Can Be Told', from *Alexander's Ragtime Band*. The winner was 'Thanks for the Memory', by Ralph Rainger and Leo Robin, from *The Big Broadcast of 1938* (Funnell, pp. 42, 51).

24   In *Shall We Dance* Rogers is briefly seen dancing on stage with a male partner in her role as a musical comedy star (and throwing him unceremoniously into a pool after he gets fresh with her). This is the only other occasion in the series in which she dances (other than socially) without Astaire.

25   Croce notes that the fanfare, 'Bugle Call Rag', was 'an old hoofers' cue' (p. 83); it is heard on two other occasions in this film as well as in *The Gay Divorcee* (at the start of Astaire's first solo dance) and in *Roberta*, where it twice interrupts the dance duet 'I'll Be Hard to Handle'.

26   Mueller, p. 121.

27   The published lyric is 'For ho ho ho'; Rogers' 'But' makes much less sense.

28   She was in fact looking at her friend Cary Grant, who had dropped by on the set during the filming of this number, and made an excellent audience: 'Now I had someone for whom to perform, and Cary reacted beautifully' (Rogers, p. 163).

29   In the documentary *Astaire and Rogers: Partners in Rhythm* (2006) the
      film director Robert Scheerer, a friend of Astaire's, reveals that the song
      was given to Rogers because Astaire refused to sing it, thinking it silly.

30   It is actually a two-piano arrangement, the second part being played off
      screen by Hal Borne, Astaire's rehearsal pianist (Mueller, p. 71).

31   The others being 'Beginner's Luck' and 'They Can't Take That Away
      From Me' (*Shall We Dance*), and 'A Fine Romance' (*Swing Time*). Of
      these, the first two, while not featuring as Astaire–Rogers dance duets,
      serve respectively as a brief Astaire solo and his ill-conceived duet with
      Harriet Hoctor.

32   Croce, p. 107.

4   The dance duets: Introduction

1   As she says in her autobiography, 'I had more fun rehearsing than in
      actually performing. Inspiration comes during the preparation as you
      seek a better turn, step, or jump. In performance, you do it once and
      that's it! The time for improving is over' (Rogers, p. 121).

2   Quoted in Mueller, p. 15n.

3   Rogers, pp. 124, 133, 181–2, 182.

4   Rogers, p. 121. In a television documentary she recalls that the shoes
      were never ready in time: 'I always danced in shoes that had just been
      dyed and were still wet from the dyers. That is not very much fun' (*Fred
      Astaire: Puttin' On His Top Hat*).

5   In the same documentary Pan calls the floors 'our nemesis', as they
      became scuffed after every take, and teams of men would have to rub
      out the marks and polish the floor again each time.

6   Croce, p. 90.

7   Mueller, p. 20n.

8   Mueller (p. 30), who also quotes Astaire's famous dictum on the subject:
      'Either the camera will dance or I will' (p. 26).

9   Quoted in Mueller, p. 28.

10   Mueller, p. 29.

11   Mueller, pp. 87, 79.

12   Billman, p. 101.

13   Quoted in Mueller, p. 23.

14   Mueller, p. 18.

15   Quoted in Mueller, p. 18.

16   *The RKO Story, Episode 2.*

17   Astaire, p. 7.

18   *The RKO Story, Episode 2.* This documentary also reveals that although
      Astaire was given a percentage of the profits of each film, Rogers was

not; and that she was insured by the studio for only half the one million dollars that he was insured for.

19   Delameter, p. 56.

20   *The RKO Story, Episode 2.* In *The Barkleys of Broadway*, where the pair play a husband-and-wife musical-comedy team, Astaire explicitly claims to have made Rogers what she is, declaring 'There isn't a gesture you do that I didn't teach you . . . I molded you, like Svengali did Trilby.' She responds by throwing something at him.

21   Rogers names the creator of this cartoon, in a Los Angeles newspaper, as Bob Thaves, and notes that countless other people have claimed credit for it since (pp. 121–2). The line is unpardonably misquoted and assigned to Rogers herself in Sheridan Morley's *Shall We Dance: The Life of Ginger Rogers*, where 'Everything Fred did, I did backwards and in high heels' appears as the title of the first chapter, no less.

22   As *Life* magazine put it in the early 1940s, 'She is not uncomfortably beautiful. She is just beautiful enough' (quoted in Jocelyn Faris, *Ginger Rogers: A Bio-Bibliography*, p. 1).

23   Mueller, p. 8.

24   Bruce Babington and Peter William Evans, *Blue Skies and Silver Linings: Aspects of the Hollywood Musical*, p. 93.

25   Interviewed in *Fred Astaire: Puttin' On His Top Hat.*

26   Croce, p. 6.

27   Croce, in *Afterimages*, p. 436.

28   Quoted in Tim Satchell, *Astaire: The Biography*, p. 127.

29   Astaire made his final musical film, *Finian's Rainbow*, eleven years later, in 1968. In it he plays a grizzled old Irishman and, apart from some brief duetting (of sorts) with Petula Clark, playing his daughter, does not have a female dancing partner.

30   Gallafent, p. 154.

31   For example: '[Vera-Ellen] looks to be the best partner he's ever had' (*Variety*, quoted in Billman, p. 128); 'there could be no doubt that [Rita Hayworth] was the best partner he had ever had' (*Time*, quoted in Green and Goldblatt, p. 227); '[Cyd Charisse] is the best dancing partner Astaire has had' (*New York Journal*, quoted in Billman, p. 146).

32   Charisse had earlier made a brief appearance with Astaire, also as a ballerina, in *Ziegfeld Follies* (1946).

33   Astaire, p. 219.

5   The production numbers

1   Quoted by Mueller (p. 62), who gives a detailed analysis of the various steps.

2   Mueller, p. 63.
3   In his biography of Irving Berlin, Philip Furia claims that 'The Piccolino'
     was conceived as a deliberate parody of Berkeley-type finales – 'a spoof
     of such numbers that would be so overblown, so elaborate, that it would
     refreshingly send up all musical finales' (p. 178). This assessment seems
     at odds with the rather moderate proportions of the number.
4   Mueller, p. 87.
5   Croce, p. 122.
6   Edward Gallafent stretches credulity by suggesting that the creators of
     Shall We Dance had the statue scene of Shakespeare's *The Winter's Tale* in
     mind when devising this sequence (pp. 72–4).

6   The playful duets

1   Mueller, p. 69.
2   Altman, pp. 163, 164. Arlene Croce had earlier used the term 'challenge
     dance' in her discussion of 'Isn't This a Lovely Day' (p. 61).
3   Altman, p. 164.
4   Croce, p. 121.
5   In the documentary *Astaire and Rogers: Partners in Rhythm* Rogers'
     personal assistant, Roberta Olden, reveals that the bank was not
     cushioned at all, and that the pair's grimaces of discomfort as they
     recovered themselves were not entirely feigned.
6   Jerome Delameter, convinced of his Svengali–Trilby thesis (see p. 145),
     and ignoring the evidence of the song, absurdly misinterprets the spirit
     of this duet: 'Rogers, still annoyed that Astaire has lost her a job and
     ruined her audition . . . seems to be acting out her hostility for his
     interference with her life; she purposely does not cooperate in order to
     show that he doesn't have the control over her that he thinks he has' (p.
     54).
7   Mueller, p. 96.
8   Croce, p. 47.
9   Rogers confirms that the laughter was truly spontaneous, not added
     later, and the taps too were 'just as we did them, with no additions'. (In
     later films Astaire and Hermes Pan would dub the taps.) This was made
     possible by the real wood floor, 'which caused each tap to come out
     distinctly from each dancer' (p. 121), unlike the slippery Bakelite floors
     used in their subsequent films.
10   Mueller, pp. 81, 80.
11   Mueller, p. 105.
12   Altman, p. 164.
13   Mueller, p. 145.

14   As Rogers describes it, 'the dress was chiffon panels of red flame and
      steel gray, and it looked scalloped at the bottom because each panel was
      cut in a semicircle and accordion-pleated in half-inch pleats . . . It was
      a special thrill to pick up the skirt as we danced and see it flutter like a
      silken kite' (p. 181).

7   The romantic duets

1   'At the risk of disillusionment,' writes Astaire in his autobiography, 'I
      must admit that I don't like top hats, white ties and tails' (p. 8).
2   Croce adds that Rogers was 'physically incapable of ugliness' (p. 88).
3   Quoted in Mueller, p. 46.
4   Rogers, p. 120. She adds that 'Men always commented on that gown;
      indeed, I never met a man who didn't like that dress.'
5   Rogers, p. 134. The richly made silver-grey dress can be seen in close-up
      colour in the 2004 French television documentary *L'Art de Fred Astaire*.
6   Rogers, p. 144. Her taste and sense of style in dress let her down only
      once in the entire series of duets, with her rather gaudy costume for
      'They All Laughed'.
7   Croce, p. 35.
8   Mueller, p. 58.
9   Mueller, p. 60.
10   It was no doubt this move that Rogers had in mind when she referred,
      with pardonable hyperbole, to the difficulty of appearing graceful while
      thinking 'whether you're near enough to the steps to leap up six of them
      backward without looking' (see p. 142). In her autobiography she recalls
      that she nearly lost her balance when filming this manoeuvre, having
      rehearsed the dance only in low heels (p. 121).
11   Though it appears pure white on screen the dress, made of 'form-fitting
      satin' with 'myriads of ostrich feathers', and cut 'low in the back and
      high in the front', was in fact pale blue (Rogers, p. 124).
12   Mueller, p. 84.
13   Mueller, p. 86.
14   Croce, p. 66.
15   Croce, p. 108.
16   Mueller's comment that the dance is 'wonderfully and absurdly comic
      in conception' seems wide of the mark, though he does add that it is
      'performed with an intense seriousness' (p. 146).
17   'For this number, Howard Greer created a beautiful black marquisette
      gown, with a picoted bodice with silver threads, which caused a slight
      glimmer of reflected light as I danced around the floor' (Rogers, p.
      182).

18   Mueller, p. 144.
19   In general the black-and-whiteness of the films does not detract in the slightest from their impact and appeal (it is, indeed, a part of their charm), although just occasionally the urge to see Astaire and Rogers dance in colour is very strong – as, for instance, in 'The Yam', where monochrome does not do justice to Rogers' costume. The documentary *L'Art de Fred Astaire* includes some tantalising colourised sequences of Rogers and her costumes in *The Gay Divorcee*, though as these are described as 'imagined' they do not necessarily reflect the actual colours. It is unfortunate that the experience of finally seeing the pair dance in colour in *The Barkleys of Broadway* is, for the most part, so unsatisfactory in other respects.
20   Croce, p. 105.
21   Rogers, p. 144. Revealing that this 'dream' dress was actually not white, she writes that 'The pink organza panels had a one-inch ruffle falling from the center like rose leaves forming a rosette. The top of the dress was very tailored, with thirty self-covered buttons.'

APPENDIX

THE MUSICAL NUMBERS

This appendix lists the principal musical numbers in the Fred and Ginger films in order of performance, using the abbreviations listed below.

	Song	Dance
Astaire solo	A	**A**
Rogers solo	R	**R**
Chorus	C	**C**
Astaire with chorus	AC	**AC**
Rogers with chorus	RC	
Astaire solo to Rogers	A/R	
Rogers solo to Astaire	R/A	
Astaire–Rogers duet	AR	**AR**
Other performers	O	**O**
Astaire with other performers	AO	**AO**
Instrumental = I		

Notes

a   Simultaneous song and dance is indicated as follows: A + **A**.

b   Song leading to dance (or vice versa) without a break is indicated as follows: A/R → **AR**.

c   Numbers that appear in more than one guise are listed in the order of their first main appearance, as follows: R/A, **AR**. Where a number is later reprised in some form outside its main appearance(s) this is indicated by a note.

The Gay Divorcee
1, 3   Music by Harry Revel, lyrics by Mack Gordon
2, 5   Music by Con Conrad, lyrics by Herb Magidson
4   Music and lyrics by Cole Porter

1	Don't Let It Bother You	O, **A**
2	A Needle in a Haystack	A → **A**
3	Let's K-nock K-neez	O + **O**
4	Night and Day	A/R → **AR**
5	The Continental	R/A, **AR** → **C** → O + **C**[1] → **AR**
6	Table Dance	**AR**[2]

Roberta
Music by Jerome Kern. Lyrics: Various

Let's Begin	AO → **AO**
Russian Song	O
I'll Be Hard to Handle	R/A, **AR**
Yesterdays	O
I Won't Dance	AI, AR → **A, AR**
Smoke Gets in Your Eyes	O, **AR**
Lovely to Look At	I, O, **AR**[3]

Top Hat
Music and lyrics by Irving Berlin

No Strings	A → **A**
Isn't This a Lovely Day (To Be Caught in the Rain)	A/R → **AR**
Top Hat, White Tie and Tails	A → **AC**
Cheek to Cheek	A/R → **AR**
The Piccolino	**C** → R/A → **C** + **C** → **AR**[4]

Follow the Fleet
Music and lyrics by Irving Berlin

We Saw the Sea	**AC**[5]
Let Yourself Go	RC, **AR, R**
Get Thee Behind Me, Satan	O
I'd Rather Lead a Band	A → **AC**
But Where Are You?	O
I'm Putting All My Eggs in One Basket	AI, AR → **AR**
Let's Face the Music and Dance	A/R → **AR**

Swing Time
Music by Jerome Kern, lyrics by Dorothy Fields

Pick Yourself Up	AR, **AR**
The Way You Look Tonight	A/R[6]
Waltz in Swing Time	**AR**[7]
A Fine Romance	R/A, A/R[8]
Bojangles of Harlem	C + **C** → AC → A
Never Gonna Dance	A/R → **AR**

Shall We Dance
Music by George Gershwin, lyrics by Ira Gershwin

Beginner's Luck	**A**, A/R
Slap That Bass	O → AC → **A**
Walking the Dog	I, I
They All Laughed	R, **AR**[9]
Let's Call the Whole Thing Off	AR → **AR**
They Can't Take That Away From Me	A/R, **AO**
Shall We Dance	**AC** → **OC** → A + **C** →
	A → **AC** → **AR** → AR + **C**[10]

Carefree
Music and lyrics by Irving Berlin

Golf Solo (Since They Turned 'Loch Lomond' into Swing)	AI/R → **A**
I Used to Be Color Blind	A/R → **AR**
The Yam	R → **AR** → R/A → **AR**[11]
Change Partners	A/R, **AR**

Notes

1   This stage of the number, involving two separate renditions of the song, is intercut with various bits of non-musical business.

2   This dance is performed to the music of 'The Continental'.

3   The duet leads directly to the dance duet 'Smoke Gets in Your Eyes'.

4   In addition to the main duet the film ends with a brief dance tag to the same music.

5   Though this number does not include any dance, it does feature movement, as the chorus of sailors briefly toss Astaire around.

6   This music is later reprised at the start of the 'Never Gonna Dance' dance duet, and also in the brief vocal duet that ends the film, in counterpoint with 'A Fine Romance'.

7   Though the Waltz is strictly an instrumental number it does feature briefly in vocal form above the opening credits, sung by a chorus. It is also reprised in the course of the 'Never Gonna Dance' dance duet.

8   The song, loosely classed as a duet in chapter 3, is reprised (with a different lyric) in counterpoint with 'The Way You Look Tonight' in the duet that ends the film.

9   The song is also briefly reprised by Astaire and Rogers at the end of the film, concluding the 'Shall We Dance' production number.

10   This analysis is a slight simplification of a uniquely complicated and fragmented number, and it relates only to the sequence that begins at the point when the 'Shall We Dance' music is first heard. The production number as a whole begins to other, indeterminate, music, and this opening sequence features a female corps de ballet; Harriet Hoctor performing solo, with the corps and with Astaire; and finally a Hoctor–Astaire duet to the music of 'They Can't Take That Away From Me'. Hoctor and the corps reappear during the 'Shall We Dance' sequence (again to indeterminate music), which otherwise features a chorus of Rogers lookalikes; and both the corps and the lookalikes are on stage at the end, when Astaire and Rogers sing a brief duet to 'They All Laughed'. The number is also intercut with Rogers' arrival in the audience and other non-musical business.

11   Astaire and Rogers are joined by their onlookers for part of the duet, both before and after Rogers resumes singing halfway through it. Astaire completes the final section of the song in a rhythmical non-singing voice.

SELECT BIBLIOGRAPHY

Books

Altman, Rick, *The American Film Musical* (Bloomington and Indianapolis: Indiana University Press, and London: British Film Institute, 1989)
A valuable historical and analytical commentary, this is an academic text intended as 'a reasoned introduction to the problem of film genre study'. There are chapters on the structure and style of the American film musical (which the author describes as 'the most complex art form ever devised') and extensive comment on Astaire and Rogers, especially in the chapter 'The fairy tale musical', which discusses the Astaire–Rogers films under the heading 'Sex as battle'.

Astaire, Fred, *Steps in Time: An Autobiography*. With a Foreword by Ginger Rogers (1981) and a new Introduction by Jennifer Dunning (New York: Cooper Square Press, 2000; first published New York: Harper and Row, 1959, and London: Heinemann, 1960)
An engaging read, but the chapters covering the period of Astaire's film career are disappointingly unrevealing and unilluminating, with very little detail about the films or the musical numbers, and a gentlemanly reticence about his relationship with Rogers and his other partners.

Babington, Bruce, and Evans, Peter William, *Blue Skies and Silver Linings: Aspects of the Hollywood Musical* (Manchester: Manchester University Press, 1985)
Written for both the general reader and students and teachers of film studies 'looking for incisive analysis of a critically neglected field', this book analyses ten musicals from the 1930s to the late 1970s. The chapter on *Swing Time* and the Astaire–Rogers musical includes useful introductory comment on the partnership, and analysis of the characters and their relationship.

Billman, Larry, *Fred Astaire: A Bio-Bibliography*. Bio-Bibliographies in the Performing Arts, No. 76 (Westport, Connecticut, and London: Greenwood Press, 1997)
Clearly a labour of love, this is an invaluable volume, with a wealth of detailed information and comment about all aspects of Astaire's life and work. Includes the following sections: Biography; Chronology; Stage; Filmography; Radio; Television; Videography; Discography; Musical Compositions; Collectibles; Awards, Honors, and Tributes; Projects Announced for Astaire; and Bibliography.

Croce, Arlene, *The Fred Astaire and Ginger Rogers Book* (New York: Outerbridge and Lazard/E. P. Dutton, and London: W. H. Allen, 1972, reprinted E. P. Dutton, 1987). All references to Croce in the text are to this book unless otherwise indicated.
A chronological survey of all ten Astaire–Rogers films, generously illustrated, with useful information on the background and production of the films and perceptive and entertaining comment on all aspects of the Astaire–Rogers partnership. Coverage of the musical numbers is uneven (in length rather than quality), but nevertheless a splendid introduction to Astaire and Rogers.

Croce, Arlene, 'Dance in film', in *Afterimages* (New York: Alfred A. Knopf, 1977, and London, A & C Black, 1978)
Written in 1971, this essay is a valuable history of dance in film from the early twentieth century to the 1960s.

Delameter, Jerome, *Dance in the Hollywood Musical.* Studies in Photography and Cinematography No. 4 (Ann Arbor, Michigan: UMI Research Press, 1981)
A detailed and comprehensive study, ranging from dance in film before 1930 to the decline of the musical in the late 1950s. Chapters include 'Astaire and Rogers at RKO', 'Dance in film (1930–1945)' and 'The integrated dance musical'.

Dickens, Homer, *The Films of Ginger Rogers* (Secaucus, New Jersey: Citadel Press, 1975)
A useful chronological survey of all Rogers' films, with an introduction on her life and career. Generously illustrated.

Faris, Jocelyn, *Ginger Rogers: A Bio-Bibliography.* Bio-Bibliographies in the Performing Arts, No. 49 (Westport, Connecticut, and London: Greenwood Publishing Group, 1994)
Similar format to Billman's volume on Astaire, but less packed with supplementary information and comment.

Funnell, John, *Best Songs of the Movies: Academy Award Nominees and Winners, 1934–1958* (Jefferson, North Carolina: McFarland, 2005)
A comprehensive and very readable survey all the Oscar-nominated songs of the period, including those from the Astaire–Rogers films.

Furia, Philip, *Irving Berlin: A Life in Song* (New York: Schirmer Books, 1998)
A biography that includes useful comment and information relating to the songs Berlin contributed to the Fred and Ginger series.

Gallafent, Edward, *Astaire and Rogers* (Moffat, Dumfriesshire: Cameron and Hollis, 2000, and New York: Columbia University Press, 2002)
A serious, thoughtful and substantial study, which covers not only the Astaire–Rogers films but all the films the pair made separately in the period from 1933 (*Flying Down to Rio*) to 1949 (*The Barkleys of Broadway*). It takes a very different approach from other books by focusing primarily on the non-musical content of the Astaire–Rogers films – any discussion of the musical numbers is restricted to their non-musical significance – and the partnership itself often takes a back seat (a considerable part of the section on *Roberta*, for example, is devoted to the minor character of Randolph Scott's girlfriend). A welcome addition to the bibliography; but a book that devotes space to discussing *Follow the Fleet* in terms of 'how [the film] invokes the power structures of the navy and entertainment business, and points to the connections between them', and that draws parallels between *Shall We Dance* and Shakespeare, perhaps takes its subject a little *too* seriously. Well illustrated, with a detailed filmography.

Green, Stanley, and Goldblatt, Burt, *Starring Fred Astaire* (New York: Dodd, Meads and Co., 1973, and London: W.H. Allen, 1974)
An entertaining and very thorough chronological survey of all Astaire's films to 1969, lavishly illustrated (in black and white). An amusing introduction analyses the happy world of 'Astairogersland'. Chapters on the films include detailed plot description, with snippets of dialogue, as well as much background information and extracts from contemporary reviews.

Kendall, Elizabeth, *The Runaway Bride: Hollywood Romantic Comedy of the 1930s* (New York: Cooper Square Press, 2002; first published New York: Knopf, 1990)
A study focusing on the women who starred in the romantic comedies of the 1930s and their directors. The chapter on George Stevens, Rogers and *Swing Time* includes interesting comment on Rogers' (and Astaire's) roles in this and earlier films, and illuminates her crucial contribution to the series.

Morley, Sheridan, *Shall We Dance: The Life of Ginger Rogers* (London: Weidenfeld and Nicolson, and New York: St Martin's Press, 1995)
Published shortly after Rogers' death in 1995, this is a 'celebration' rather than a serious biography. But lavishly illustrated (in colour and black and white), and the only book of its kind on Rogers.

Mueller, John, *Astaire Dancing: The Musical Films* (New York: Alfred A. Knopf, 1985, and London: Hamish Hamilton, 1986)
A monumental study of all Astaire's musical films. An extensive introduction

on Astaire's career, his partnership with Rogers, working methods, etc., is followed by a chapter on each of the films, in chronological order. All the musical numbers, and especially the dances, are analysed in considerable, sometimes quite technical, detail, and the text is illustrated by over two thousand frame enlargements, as well as other photographs. Essential reading for the serious Astaire–Rogers enthusiast.

Nochimson, Martha P., *Screen Couple Chemistry: The Power of 2* (Austin: University of Texas Press, 2002)
An academic text examining four 'synergistic' screen couples – 'the most dangerous, fascinatingly powerful type of couple in commercial, mass media film'. The substantial chapter on Astaire and Rogers focuses on two 'major' films (*Top Hat* and *Swing Time*), two 'transitional' films (*Shall We Dance* and *Carefree*) and two 'entopic' films (*The Story of Vernon and Irene Castle* and *The Barkleys of Broadway*). An appendix examines the personal and professional relationship between Astaire and Rogers at RKO.

Rogers, Ginger, *Ginger: My Story* (New York: HarperCollins, and London: Headline, 1991)
Long overdue, this lively autobiography by the eighty-year-old Rogers is considerably more informative and illuminating than Astaire's about their work together.

Satchell, Tim, *Astaire: The Biography* (London: Hutchinson, 1987, reprinted Arrow Books, 1988)
A comprehensive biography of Astaire, first published in the year of his death. A useful appendix includes detailed listings of Astaire's shows, films, television appearances and audio recordings.

Sennett, Ted, *Hollywood Musicals* (New York: Harry N. Abrams, 1981)
This large-format book, lavishly illustrated in both colour and black and white, is an excellent, detailed survey of the Hollywood musical from 1927 to 1980. Astaire and Rogers, 'The peerless pair', are given a chapter to themselves.

Thomas, Bob, *Astaire: The Man, The Dancer* (New York: St Martin's Press, 1984, and London: Weidenfeld and Nicolson, 1985)
An enjoyable biography, with an emphasis on Astaire's performing career and extensive comments from the man himself. Generously illustrated.

Thomas, Tony, *That's Dancing!* (New York: Harry N. Abrams, 1984)
Published to accompany the film of the same title (see below), this profusely illustrated book is a much more detailed and comprehensive survey of the

genre. After a useful general introduction it devotes a chapter to each of nine outstanding dancers (beginning with Astaire) and to director Busby Berkeley.

Thomas, Tony, and Terry, Jim, with Busby Berkeley, *The Busby Berkeley Book*. With a Foreword by Ruby Keeler (New York: New York Graphic Society, 1973)
A comprehensive survey of Berkeley's life and career, with a substantial biographical introduction and chronological coverage of each of Berkeley's fifty-three films. Lavishly illustrated (in black and white).

Video material

L'Art de Fred Astaire (Arte France, 2004, 73 minutes)
A French television documentary, directed by Catherine Dupuis, mainly covering Astaire's RKO partnership with Rogers. Includes 1974 interviews with Astaire, dance director Hermes Pan, rehearsal pianist and arranger Hal Borne and other personnel involved in the films, as well as a substantial contribution from one of Astaire's later partners, Leslie Caron. Notable for 'imagined' colourised sequences from *Flying Down to Rio* and *The Gay Divorcee*.

Astaire and Rogers: Partners in Rhythm (Warner Home Video, 2006, 76 minutes)
A DVD documentary included in the *Complete Film Collection* box set (see below), covering the ten Astaire–Rogers films and the before-and-after careers of the stars. Includes archival interview footage (largely taken from *The RKO Story*) and new contributions from John Mueller, Ava Astaire McKenzie (Astaire's daughter), and friends or associates of Astaire and Rogers.

Fred Astaire: Puttin' On His Top Hat (Educational Broadcasting Corporation, 1980, 60 minutes)
The first of a two-part television documentary about Astaire, covering the period of his early life and his partnership with Rogers at RKO. Features clips from all the films, and interviews with Rogers, Hermes Pan, Hal Borne and producer Pandro S. Berman, as well as Astaire himself; and comments from Adele Astaire, Gene Kelly and Rudolf Nureyev.

Fred Astaire: Change Partners and Dance (Educational Broadcasting Corporation, 1980, 60 minutes)
The second part of the above documentary, covering Astaire's later career.

The RKO Story: Tales from Hollywood. Episode 1: Birth of a Titan; Episode 2: Let's Face the Music and Dance; Episode 3: A Woman's Lot (A BBC Television Production in association with RKO Pictures, 1987, 60 minutes each)

The first three parts of an informative and illuminating six-part history of RKO, presented by Edward Asner, including film clips and interviews with the stars and other personnel involved. Episode 1 covers the period from the birth of RKO in the late 1920s to *Flying Down to Rio* in 1933; Episode 2 (broadcast just a few days after Astaire's death) covers the Astaire–Rogers years; Episode 3 focuses on the careers of RKO's two pre-eminent women stars of the 1930s and early 1940s, Ginger Rogers and Katharine Hepburn, and also features comments from Lucille Ball. The series, retitled *Hollywood: The Golden Years*, was later shown on American television.

That's Dancing! (MGM, 1985, 105 minutes)
A valuable overview of dance in musical film, from the silent era to contemporary times. Includes, from the 1930s, footage of Busby Berkeley numbers, Eleanor Powell, Shirley Temple and Bill 'Bojangles' Robinson, as well as Astaire and Rogers.

That's Entertainment! (MGM, 1974, 132 minutes); *That's Entertainment! II* (MGM, 1976, 129 minutes); *That's Entertainment! III* (MGM in association with Turner Entertainment, 1994, 113 minutes)
These three lengthy compilations of choice musical numbers from MGM films include a great many dance sequences not featured in *That's Dancing!* Astaire and his various partners are extensively represented, as are Gene Kelly and a host of other performers. The complete collection is available as a Warner Home Video DVD box set in both Region 1 (US and Canada) and Region 2 (Europe) formats.

The Astaire–Rogers films

All the films except *Roberta* are available in VHS and/or Region 2 (Europe) DVD formats. *Fred and Ginger: The Collection* is a DVD box set of eight films (excluding *Roberta* and *The Barkleys of Broadway*), released by Universal Studios in 2006; the collection is also available in two separate sets of four films each.

All ten films are available as a Region 2 (US and Canada) DVD box set, *Astaire and Rogers: The Complete Film Collection*, released by Warner Home Video in 2006. The set includes a bonus DVD, the documentary *Astaire and Rogers: Partners in Rhythm*, coupled with a CD of ten songs from the original soundtracks, as well as reproductions of original press books for *Roberta* and *Shall We Dance* and behind-the-scenes stills. Special features on the DVDs include theatrical trailers, and excellent full-length commentaries on *Top Hat* (by Larry Billman and Ava Astaire McKenzie) and *Swing Time* (by John Mueller). The ten films, but not the bonus DVD, are also available separately and in two sets of five.

INDEX

Page numbers in **bold** denote main or substantial discussion of the subject. Page numbers in *italics* denote illustrations. Page and note numbers in square brackets indicate that the author referred to is cited in the text but named only in the endnote.